The Yellow Snow
MELTDOWN

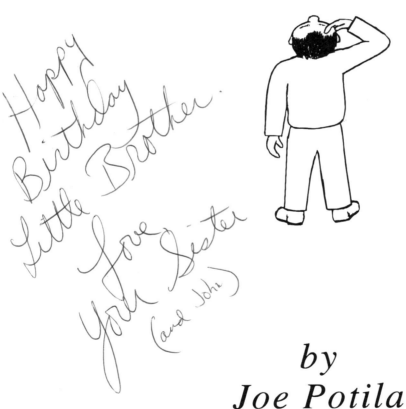

Happy Birthday
Little Brother.
Love
Your Sister
(and John)

by
Joe Potila

Shields Publishing Company

We would like to thank our children
for their love and support
throughout the years.

We love you dearly.

Kristi   Ryan   Evan   Tyler

The Yellow Snow Meltdown
Copyright © 1997 by Joe Potila

For information contact:
Shields Publishing Company
1050 Cooper Lake Road
Ishpeming, MI 49849
(906) 485-5998
e-mail: ysgzt@aol.com
http://members.aol.com/ysgzt/ysg.htm

ISBN 0-9661724-0-X

The Yellow Snow Gazette is published 5 times a year. For subscription information contact Shields Publishing Company.

Publisher's Note:
Yellow Snow, Michigan is a fictitious town and the features in this publication are works of fiction. The contents are fictitious and not intended to represent specific places, persons, or events.

A note from the Author

Ever since I was six years old and too shy to talk I was destined to write. At that young age I was afflicted with a slight speech impediment which has since been corrected. But it did, at an early age, make me reluctant to speak, and at six years old, I was so shy that most people thought I was incapable of speech. It was only natural that I would be drawn to other methods of communication. Early in my life I became interested in drawing, writing, and later in music. Because of my interest in music, I spent nearly thirty years of my life as a working musician. Nineteen of those years were spent with the Joe Arkansas Band, which evolved into the comedy group *Da Yoopers* in the mid '80's. Those who knew of my shyness were puzzled by my willingness to get up on stage before large crowds of people and sing. The reason why I could do it was simple. The lyrics I sang were first written. More important, they were written by someone else. So I was not revealing anything of myself beyond my ability to vocalize. The hardest thing I ever did in my musical career was to sing lyrics that I had written myself. It became easier over the years, especially after some success in writing, notably the Culture Shock album, which was well received by the public. During my time with *Da Yoopers* I co-wrote six comedy albums. Some of the characters we immortalized in song were completely fictional. Others were composites of people we had known. To me, the most challenging part of the whole process was the creation of believable, if somewhat bizarre stories and characters. That challenge is what eventually led me to this book. The Yellow Snow Meltdown is a journalistic if not literary extension of the kind of humor presented in the songs. This is not a group effort as those six albums were. Working in partnership with my wife Rhonda in our own publishing company gives me a greater sense of individual creative freedom. Her layout design and editorial guidance are instrumental in giving meaning to my bizarre ramblings. The result of this collaboration is our newest offspring, the Yellow Snow Meltdown.

A Note of Thanks

To the people who accepted my contributions to the creative process in the past and inspired me to continue my exploration of the written word, I offer my eternal gratitude. To the fans who paid their hard earned money to buy the tapes and to come and see me sing the songs, I say *t'anks, you guys.* It is because of people like you that I write. I hope you get a few laughs out of this book.

Joe Potila

Foreword

Deep in the backwoods of Michigan's Upper Peninsula, far from the neurotic convolutions of big city life, lies the town of Yellow Snow, Michigan. Its people are a simple lot, honest in thought and deed, direct in demeanor, if somewhat twisted by generations of questionable breeding. But in its isolation the town flourishes, and its people industriously go on about their daily lives. Until recently, few outsiders were even aware of the existence of the town of Yellow Snow. But in 1995, in a slick deal involving some cash, a truckload of potatoes, and a lot of arguing and screaming, Shields Publishing Company acquired the right to reprint the town's newspaper, The Yellow Snow Gazette. The Yellow Snow Meltdown is a compilation of stories, editorials, essays, cartoons, jokes, and assorted what-nots from two years of YSG issues.

The Yellow Snow Gazette

June 1, 1995 | MELTDOWN | Yellow Snow, Michigan

Summer Comes to Yooperland!

Meteorologists Amazed

The U.S. Weather Bureau predicted today that summer will be coming to the U.P. in 1995. The surprise announcement of this rare occurrence has caused great excitement and anticipation among area residents as well as among the Yooperland scientific community. U.P. scientists, skeptical of the report, conducted their own research and were forced to concur with Weather Bureau findings, especially in light of the fact that Eino Aho's gout condition clearly indicates warm and dry weather ahead. Professor Aho heads up the Yooperland Meteorology Research Team at National Mine University. His team has for years attempted to successfully predict Yooperland weather. The team accurately forecasted the last recorded summer in the U.P., which was on a Tuesday in 1983. It was the appearance of the sun on that day in 1983 that made national headlines when thousands of members of an obscure Yooperland religious cult who worship Heikki Lunta, the Yooper god of snow, believing that they had done something to anger their god, marched through the streets of Marquette, beating themselves with cedar boughs and chanting, "Holy wha! What da heck did we do wrong?"

Local retailers are gearing up for the anticipated run on summer items, such as bathing suits, garden tools and mosquito repellent. "Most people have long since thrown away all their summer items in disgust," says the proprietor of one local sports shop.

One favorite children's game in July is to hop from bare spot to bare spot, the object being to see who can go the farthest without having to step in snow.

Yooperland tourism organizations are mounting a comprehensive promotional campaign urging tourists to take advantage of this opportunity to experience the rare phenomenon of summer in the U.P. in all its splendor and glory.

The Yellow Snow Gazette

The YSG editors and staff would like to thank our loyal subscribers who have risked permanent brain damage by reading the Gazette. We salute those courageous readers without whose continued support this book would not have been possible. Thanks for reading the Gazette, and thanks for your encouraging letters and calls. If you have a question or comment, you can write to any member of the YSG staff in care of Shields Publishing Co.

YSG staff and contributors

Rhonda Potila * Managing Editor/Layout Design
Joe Potila * Writer/Artist/Stamp-licker
Martha Maki * Summer Kitchen
Gravel Gertie * Husband Training Tips
Professor Eino Aho * Science Department
Werner Warpula * Editorials
Madame Brewsky * News that ain't happened yet
Joe & Tyler Potila * Hairold Cartoons
Kristi, Ryan & Evan Potila * Words of Whizdom

Special Features:

Jessica Kerkela * Da Case of Da Missing Case/ Top 10 reasons why U.P. men are good catches/Yooper yard test
Gary Massey * King of the Jokers
Margaret Roberts * Cartoon Caption Winner
Ed McKelvie * What I did on my Vacation
Reprinted by permission : The secret room/The Night before Christmas/Yooper Dictionary/Rusty Chevrolet/Second Week of Deer Camp— Joe Potila /Jim DeCaire
Special thanks to Mike Marsden for the title "Meltdown."

Weather... or Not!

I sit out on the deck with my first cup of the day, basking in the quiet of the morning, contemplating the meaning of life and the price of potatoes. I enjoy sitting out here in the mornings at this time of year, watching for those telltale signs that winter is really gone for good and that summer is really on the way. The best indicator of the changing of the seasons is the actions of the wildlife. Animals are acutely aware of the subtle, subliminal signs of nature that elude our dulled senses. They seem to know something we don't. Well, usually they do. But it's possible that the wildlife in some areas are perhaps not as bright, or maybe the seasonal changes in some areas are just tougher to get a handle on. Whether it is one or the other or both, such is the case in this part of Yooperland. For instance, it's really encouraging to see robins in my back yard, but it's a little disheartening to see them standing there on the snow shivering, their little beaks chattering like tiny Teletype machines. One female robin chirps loudly at the dejected male standing beside her. Now, I'm not too swift on robinese, but I can pretty well imagine the gist of the one-sided conversation. *"...there we were, basking in the sun, drinking Singapore slings, not a worry in the world and then you get this stupid idea hey, honey, let's go back up north! It's springtime in Yooperland! My mother was right when she said.." (yak, yak,* ☞

etc., etc.) The male just stands there shivering and never makes a peep. As a married man myself, my heart goes out to him. Poor little guy. As I sit and try to imagine what might be going through his tiny mind, a flash of color catches the corner of my eye. Hopping across the lawn from Old Lady Keskinen's yard comes a young robin wearing a little pink sweater and a tiny knitted cap complete with ear flaps, and singing a happy little song. I immediately go back in the house and check my coffee can for foreign substances. You never know what those Columbians are up to these days. It checks out okay, so I pour myself another cup and go back outside. The little robin is still there, chirping cheerfully. That Old Lady Keskinen would knit a sweater for a beer fart if she could. I think it's an addiction. So I'm taking this all in and beginning to feel a little depressed about it all, when I hear a sound that instantly lifts my sagging spirits. Geese! Now there's a sure sign of the end of winter. Geese have an uncanny sixth sense, an unerring instinct for seasonal changes. If the geese are coming back, you can bet your last beer that summer is on the way. I search the horizon. Yup, there they are, a big flock, coming over the hills to the south, honking like a Detroit traffic jam. I can tell by the tone of their honking that they are excited about the prospect of a summer of frolic in the waterways of Yooperland. They're making pretty good time, too, until suddenly the lead goose spikes the brakes. Must have hit a real cold spot. I can almost hear the screech of webbed feet against icy arctic air. I've never seen a 30-goose pileup before, and I hope I never see one again. I haven't heard such squawking since my gerbil got loose at Aunt Alma's Tupperware party. It was horrible. About a dozen geese go down in the swamp behind Helsten's farm. Their wings must have iced up. The survivors break formation and make a quick U-turn, heading back south as fast as their wings can flap. I'm thinking about taking a walk over the hill and picking up a fat goose for supper when suddenly the sun goes behind a cloud and an icy wind kicks up. One of the robins keels over and lies still on the snow, and the rest walk, stiff-legged, over to where the clothes dryer vent comes out of the basement window. They huddle around it, rubbing their little wings together and stamping their tiny frozen feet. I go inside to pour myself another cup and stoke up the fireplace. Spring? Nope. Not today.

How to keep 'em Whipped!

Gravel Gertie's
Husband Training Tips

Dear Gertie,
My husband thinks he's such a stud. Whenever we go to a local tavern where there are young and pretty women, he makes such a fool of himself. He struts around like he's God's gift to women, flirting and drooling over them like a teenager with a hormone problem. I can't take it any more. What should I do?
Desperate

Dear Desperate,
When will they ever learn? My Eugene used to have the same problem. Here's how I solved it. I took a No. 8 fish hook and stuck it through the little piece of flesh between his nostrils. Then I tied a piece of fishing line to the hook. I tied the other end of the line to the zipper on his trousers, leaving the line just long enough so he could keep his head up straight. Every time he zips his fly down at the urinal, he's forced to look down and see how truly inadequate he really is. It sure takes the wind out of his sail.
Gertie

Dear Gertie,
I would like to say a few words for husbands, of which I am one. My wife is an overbearing, tyrannical ruler of our household. I haven't been fishing or hunting in years. I work hard every day, and when I sit down on the weekend to watch the ball game on TV, she gripes and nags about how lazy I am. She makes me do the dishes every night, and I have to do all the laundry, house-cleaning, and baby-sitting while she's off at her daily coffee clutch with her cronies. I feel like a slave in my own home.
Oppressed Husband

Dear Wimp,
So what's the problem?
Gertie

Dear Gertie,
Every weekend my husband has his buddies over to play cards. They consume vast quantities of beer and fill my home with stinky cigar smoke and beer farts. They tell stupid jokes and then laugh so loud that I can't hear my TV. I feel like my home is being invaded. What can I do?
Almost Homeless

Dear A.H.
What a coincidence! I had that very same problem with my Eugene. This one's too easy. Here's what I did. I invited all my friends over for a sanitary napkin party, which is like a Tupperware party, only more fun. We sat in the next room loudly talking about our menstrual cycles and the symptoms that accompany them, like cramps and retaining water. We described in great detail our trips to gynecologists, including the stirrups, pap smears, and related topics. We moved on from there to graphic descriptions of what childbirth feels like. By the time we got to our water breaking and labor pains, it was quiet in the other room. The poker game had broken up, and now Eugene can't get any of his friends to come over anymore. Another victory for our side.
Gertie

✳✳✳✳✳✳✳✳✳✳✳✳✳✳✳✳✳
Words of Whizdom:
*Yellow snow
ain't lemon flavored.*
✳✳✳✳✳✳✳✳✳✳✳✳✳✳✳✳✳

One day God finally got fed up with it all, and he threw in the keys and quit. He decided to spend his retirement in human form, seeking peace on earth, mostly through fishing, golfing, and sitting in the outhouse with an Outdoor Life magazine. His fame tends to interfere with his privacy, however, especially after his appearance on the Letterman show. No matter where he goes, some poor soul recognizes him and wants something from him. God, being a really nice guy, can't refuse.

Sneak preview
An excerpt from

The Big Guy

The upcoming brain-damaged book from the diseased mind of Joe Potila.

God sat in a booth in the back of the Nighthawk Cafe, sipping on a cup of coffee and working on a crossword puzzle in the Gazette. It was quiet in the place, except for the occasional clank of pots and pans in the kitchen and the clink of a spoon in a coffee cup. God was groping through his mind for a nine-letter word meaning *"a type of puzzle in which intersecting words, indicated by clues, have to be inserted into a diagram"* when his concentration was broken by a shadow that loomed over the table. God looked up. A big, bearded man in a red flannel shirt, blue jeans, and a green tossle cap stood with a newspaper in his hand. Behind his beard he wore a forlorn expression. The man shuffled his feet, shifted the newspaper in his grasp, and cleared his throat.

"You God?" he asked.

God folded up his Gazette and took off his John Lennon specs.

"Yes, I am," he said. "Don't tell me--you saw me on Letterman."

"Yup." the bearded one said. He glanced around the room. "Can I talk to you?" he asked.

"Sure," God said. "Have a seat."

The man slid into the booth across from God.

"I have thith probwem," he said.

"Oh?" God said, raising an eyebrow.

"Yeth. I've had it all my wife. Boy am I gwad I ran into you."

God, being all-knowing and supremely percep-tive, was able to pinpoint the problem immediately.

"Ah," he said, "The old S&L deficiency. I'm familiar with it."

The bearded one looked relieved.

"You can't imagine how it wath to be a kid, growing up with a probwem wike thith," he said.

"No, I can't imagine," God said, shaking his head.

"Now I know you're retired and everything, but do you thuppothe you could do jutht one widow favor for me? I've been good, and I prayed to you a wot, but you probabwy had a wot on your mind. War and pethtiwenthe and thtuff, you know."

"True," God said. "I was pretty busy."

"I'd give anything to be able to thay 'awuminum' and 'winoweum' and 'thithter' and wordth like that

without getting teathed and waughed at."

"Say no more," God said. "I can fix it for you."

The man's eyes lit up. "Reawy?"

"Yeth--I mean yes," God said. "Stick out your tongue and say 'Ah'."

The bearded one stuck out his tongue. "Ah."

God touched the tip of the man's tongue with the point of his red pencil. There was a faint sizzling sound.

"Okay," God said. "Say 'linoleum'."

"Linoleum."

"Now say 'aluminum'."

"Aluminum."

"Now say, 'six slimy snakes slithered slowly southward'."

The man repeated it perfectly.

"Okay," God said,   "Now say, 'rubber baby bubby--rubber bubby bagy--rubby bugger----'never mind. You're cured."

The bearded one jumped up from the table. "Holy wha!" he cried.

"Dis is great! I kin talk perfect! It's a miracle! I can't wait ta tell da wife en da kits. Dis is da greatest ting dat ever happened. Hey, tanks, eh!" and he rushed out the door, leaving God sitting in the booth mumbling softly to himself.

"Rubby bubby bugger--rubber bubber--rubber baby bummy..."

Hairold

"You tell him to hurry up!"

Watch for the continuing adventures of God in the up coming book, The Big Guy, by Joe Potila.

At the tender age of one year old, while on a family picnic near the Escanaba river in the heart of Yooperland, little Toivo Maki wandered off in pursuit of a pretty butterfly. His father, a professional unemployed guy, was busy with his fly rod on the river bank. His mother, a volunteer beer taster at the Paradise Bar, was engrossed in her blueberry picking. All the other little Makis, a dozen or so of them, frolicked in a shallow stretch of river like a pack of albino water monkeys. Since even mom and dad Maki weren't sure of how many little Makis there were, no one missed little Toivo.

The life and times of Toivo Maki known by evil-doers and bad guys as... **YOOPERMAN**

Consequently, when they headed home that evening, they were not aware that they were one Maki short. Although they both had vague feelings that something was amiss, neither one could nail down exactly what it was. They had counted heads once they herded the tribe into the back seat of their '49 Chevy, and had come up with the usual numbers--he counted an even dozen and she came up with thirteen or fourteen. The usual argument followed, him saying that a dozen was the correct number, ma insisting that she distinctly remembered being in labor thirteen times, or maybe fourteen. Of course, there was always the possibility that one of the little monsters was a neighbor kid, slipped in on them somewhere along the way when they weren't looking. At any rate, never having been sure of the exact number of their brood, they finally agreed that, whatever the proper amount, they had them all. So they bounced along the two ruts toward home, leaving little Toivo lost and alone in the wilderness with nothing but a baby blanket and the diaper on his butt. The little guy wandered aimlessly for days, and was eventually found unconscious in a hollow stump by a family of muskrats, who took him in, nursed him back to health, and raised him as one of their own. He learned to speak muskrat, to eat bugs and frogs and stuff, and learned to skitter along through the underbrush without being seen. Because of his slightly superior intellect and strength, he advanced rapidly in muskrat society and by the time he reached his eighteenth birthday had come to be known by the denizens of the forest as "Toivo, King of the Muskrats". At about this time Mama Muskrat realized that the large and still growing adopted son had an appetite to match. It took a tremendous amount of bugs and frogs to keep him satisfied, and he was eating them out of house and home. It was time for her to tell him the truth, that he wasn't really a muskrat after all, that he was a human from a race called "Yoopers", and that it was time

Hairold

"Of course I remembered to pack spare underwear...Why do you ask?"

for him to haul his lazy butt out and get a job. So she pulled out his diaper and baby blanket and dressed him so he wouldn't look out of place in Yooper society. Then with a tearful goodbye and a big sigh of relief she sent him off to civilization.

Toivo Maki walked down the main drag of National Mine, confidently standing straight upright like a human, determined to blend in with society. The citizens of National Mine were a pretty laid back bunch and were willing to accept people of different cultural backgrounds with open minds, but the sight of the King of the Muskrats strutting down the road clad only in a stained diaper and a ratty old baby blanket was too much for them. Someone started to snicker, then someone else chuckled, and before Toivo knew what was happening, the whole town was in stitches, nudging each other and pointing and doubling over in laughter, sending Toivo running for the Ely swamp in shame and embarrassment.

Toivo wandered aimlessly through the wilderness, eventually ending up back at his muskrat home. The muskrat burrow was empty and silent. Mama Muskrat had apparently moved away and left no forwarding address. Toivo wandered through the Yooperland wilderness, living on bugs and frogs, a man without a home, without a place in the world. His depression was so deep that, try as he might, he could find no reason to go on living. He stood at the top of a high bluff, contemplating the rocks far below. He knew he didn't have the nerve to jump, but he figured maybe he could climb down, take one of those rocks and beat himself to death with it. He was about to start down when a strange disembodied voice that seemed to come from everywhere called his name.

"Toivo."

He looked around. No one in sight. He shook his head and slapped himself in the ear, then listened intently.

"Toivo," the voice boomed again.

"Who's dat?" Toivo said.

"Guess," the voice answered.

Toivo thought really hard for a moment, and his brain started to hurt. Then he took a stab at it.

"Is this the Lord?" he asked.

"Nice try," the voice said. "Never mind. You'd never guess in a million years. Look up."

Toivo looked up. A huge saucer shaped object hovered a few feet above his head. Instantly a bright beam of blue light shot out of the bottom of the saucer, and Toivo found himself standing in a round room. Around him stood a group of strange beings about three feet tall with big eyes

"But what if they're lost too?

8. The ability to see through really dirty windows.
9. The ability to write your name in the snow without using your hands.
10. An assortment of unlabeled super powers we found in our warehouse. No one knows what they are, but we threw them in as a bonus.

Sincerely,
The Little Blue Guys

P.S. You must never reveal your true identity to anyone, not even to impress your date, should you ever have one. This paper will self-destruct in 0.001 seconds.

Suddenly the paper burst into flames. As Toivo jumped to his feet, his heel caught a rock, sending him careening over the edge of the bluff. His whole life flashed before his eyes in color and without commercial interruption as he plummeted toward the rocks below...

Will Toivo survive to embark on his superhero career? Will he ever get a date? Will the little blue guys form a rock group? And what about Alicia?

For the answers to these and other burning questions, turn to page 17 for the next exciting episode of **YOOPERMAN!**

and blue skin.

"What do you guys want?" Toivo blurted out. "Are you here to invade earth?"

One of the little blue guys stepped forward and gave Toivo a slap on the side of the head. "Don't be such an idiot!" the blue guy said. "We're little blue men. We're here for the good of mankind. It's the little green men that invade. Just remember, blue, good, green, bad."

"Blue good, green bad," Toivo repeated.

"Now listen up," the alien said. "You are here because it is your destiny. You are the one chosen to be the champion of your race. We will give you certain special powers that you will use to aid and protect the weak, to uphold law and order, and to kick bad guys' butts." The alien pointed a glass tube at Toivo and everything went black. He woke up on the ground. He checked the sky for foreign objects, but there was nothing in sight.

"Holyowha!" he said. "I musta been dreaming!" He sat up and noticed a manila envelope lying on the ground next to him. He picked it up and took a closer look. The words SUPERHERO STARTER KIT were printed on it.

"So it was real!' he exclaimed, and tore the envelope open. Inside he found a superhero certificate, a list of superpowers, and a pack of gum with a little note taped to it that said, *Do something about your breath!*" He popped a stick into his mouth and began to read:

Here is a list of the special powers you have been given. Due to a shortage on the superpowers market, this is all we had in stock. Use them wisely.

1. The ability to change clothes really fast.
2. The ability to drink 32 beers without puking.
3. The ability to talk to winged insects. (They won't understand you, but you can talk to them anyway)
4. The ability to burp and fart at the same time without your chest caving in.
5. The ability to endure an attack by 50,000 mosquitoes without scratching, slapping or swearing.
6. The ability to sneak around in the bushes.
7. The ability to run faster than anybody except guys who can run *really* fast.

Rintala's

Believe It or Shut Up!

Yoopers have a keen instinct for survival.

On June 18, 1968, while serving in the infantry in Vietnam, PFC Arvid Heikkinenenen from Suomi was stationed at a remote firebase near the Cambodian border. During the night, the firebase was overrun by the VC. PFC Heikkinenenen was the sole survivor, overlooked by the enemy because he was unconscious...

Under a pile of beer cans!

Gold Panning

A beginner's crash course on how to catch gold fever

The first recorded discovery of gold in Yooperland was made by Douglass Houghton in 1845 near the present site of Negaunee. Since then, gold has been discovered and mined in virtually every county in the western half of Yooperland. Special thanks to my brother, Ron (Sonny) Potila, explorer/discoverer extraordinaire, for his assistance in researching this article and for his efforts in helping to keep the explorer spirit alive in a shrinking modern world.

So you're on your favorite trout stream in Yooperland, beating the water with your fly line or cursing the loss of still another expensive lure, and still no fish to be found. Or maybe your arms are tired from reeling in your limit of lunkers and you just need a break. The day is young, and there are dozens of household chores waiting at home. What to do? You have a choice. Either go home for a ho-hum afternoon of lawn mowing and garage cleaning, or break out your gold panning kit and embark on an adventurous afternoon of gold seeking in the time-honored tradition of the grizzled old prospector.

What you need

Assembling your own gold panning kit is easy and inexpensive. Basically, all you really need to get started is a pan, a stream, and a touch of gold fever. The pan can be any size that you can comfortably carry and handle. It is the shape of the pan that is most important. It should be fairly deep with a flat bottom and angled, not rounded, where the side meets the bottom at about a 45 degree angle. It is in the little corner where the side and bottom meet that the gold settles during panning. The pan should look something like this:

How to use your pan

Gold panning technique is very easy to learn and takes little practice. Once you've found a likely spot in a stream or river, just scoop up a panful of gravel and water. Any large rocks in the pan can be picked out and thrown away. If any of the large pieces are breakable, you can smash them and return the remains to the pan. Give the pan a few vigorous shakes from side to side and from front to back to get the larger pieces to come top of the

gravel. Repeat this procedure and keep on picking out the larger pieces until you have reduced the contents to coarse gravel. At this point, alternate the shaking motion with swirling motion, tilting the pan to allow the lighter sand and gravel to wash over the side. The shaking allows the heavier residue to sink to the bottom. The swirling motion washes the lighter surface material out. Keep adding water and washing the light material over the side. Don't be discouraged if you haven't seen any gold yet. So far you've only invested a minute or two of actual panning time. Now you should be getting down to an inch or two of coarse sand in the bottom of your pan. Keep shaking, tipping, and swirling to work the heavy minerals to the bottom and wash out the lighter material. Once you have worked the contents of your pan down to heavy black sand, you're approaching gold country. The black sand in the bottom of your pan is made up of various minerals, the most common of which are hematite and magnetite. These minerals are the gold-bearing ones, since they tend to settle out by weight where the gold does. It is in this black sand in the bottom of your pan that you'll most likely find gold, if any is to be found. Once you have reduced the sand down to a single layer on the bottom, wash it up onto the flat side of the pan and you'll see the gold gleaming in the sun.

If you would like to refine your technique before you actually go out to the stream, try panning lead shavings for practice. Just take a sharp knife and shave some tiny pieces from a lead sinker. Chop them up as small as you can and mix them in with some sand and gravel, preferably of a light color, so the lead will be easier to see. Just

add water and practice your panning technique. Once you have successfully panned your make-believe gold you might want to practice leaping into the air, excitedly yelling, "Gold! I've struck it rich!"

Where to look

Gold is where you find it. Just as in fishing, there is no sure-fire method for finding the best spot. Though there is no way to guarantee that you'll find gold in a certain location, there are ways to determine where it might most likely be found. Just below fast waters is a good starting place. Heavy gold carried along by the current would be deposited in the calmer waters below. Try bends in the stream on the inside of the curve. The faster water on the outside tends to carry the gold right on through. The best chance is to find water running over bedrock, especially a tilted slab where the rough edge is sticking up. The heaviest material, gold included, gets caught in the cracks, so you may want to include one of those little rock hammers in your gold panning kit to dig the goodies out for panning. If you begin to find color in your pan, try moving upstream until the color peters out. Then go back and start up any side streams to determine where the gold is coming from. You can also try panning material from gravel banks along the stream, or on hillsides where seasonal run-off feeds the stream. It is not necessary that the material you are panning be found actually in the water. You can scoop dry material into your pan, add water and use the regular panning technique.

Regulations and Permits

Here's my rule of thumb when it comes to panning. If I can legally fish a stream or river, I figure it's fair game for recreational gold panning. In theory, one could pursue the elusive thread of obscure and unenforceable regulations and restrictions that wind through a dozen different bureaucratic commissions, divisions, and departments. In reality I find it much easier to say, if anyone asks what I'm doing, "Oh, I'm just rinsing out my camp cooking gear." I'm such a rebel. ∎

Professor Eino Aho

Science Department

Lost in the Ozone

A brilliant comprehensive report on a little known but potentially catastrophic danger to the world we live in, prepared by Prof. Eino Aho, distinguished head of the National Mine University Environmental Research Department.

I recently read a research paper by one of my students on the effect of fluorocarbons and other chemical substances on our ozone layer. I was surprised to find that one significant source of ozone-eating chemicals was the gas released into the atmosphere by cows. Having grown up in an area where cows were quite numerous, this fact caused me great concern. As a small boy I had found cow farts to be a great source of entertainment, since we were a poor family and couldn't afford a television set. My concern over the possibility of cow farts being a danger to our environment dictated that I conduct immediate research on the subject. The research paper I had read posed a hypothetical in which the gas from cow farts, which are lighter than air, would rise up into the jet stream and be carried around the world to seriously damage the ozone layer worldwide. As head of the Environmental Research Department at National Mine University, I immediately formed a research group called the **O**zone and **J**etstream Defense Team. This **O.J.** Defense Team was made up of some of the finest minds at NMU. We chose a sample group of cows, which I called the cow fart control group, otherwise known as Helsten's herd. I asked Mr. Helsten, who lives not far from the Institute, if he would permit my research team to monitor cow farts in his pasture. He was quite helpful and agreed to let us count farts in his pasture for a small fee per fart per cow. The **O.J.** Defense Team immediately applied for and was awarded an unlimited grant to cover this cost. Our team went immediately to work. Our cow fart control group consisted of 50 cows. During the course of one day, we recorded a total of 632 audible

farts. We estimated that there were at least as many SBD's, for a total of 1,260 cow farts. This averages out

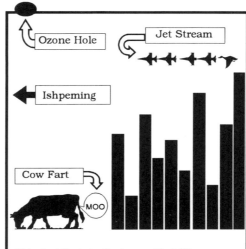

This chart illustrates the danger. The tall bars mean big numbers. The short bars mean little numbers.

to 25.2 farts per day per cow. This number we called the flatulence frequency. Based on the flatulence frequency, we calculated that the average cow will let about 9,198 farts fly each year. We multiplied that number by the number of cows in the United States, which is 98,896,000. So the number of cow farts per year in the U.S. alone is an astonishing **909,646,408,000!** This statistic has come under criticism by some fanatic fringe groups, who leveled charges of sloppiness in the cow fart collection procedure. There have even been accusations of cow fart tampering. In these unfounded accusations, one anti-environmental spokesman claimed that he actually saw an acquaintance of someone whose third cousin's uncle once shook Vice President Al Gore's hand lurking near the grassy knoll on the south end of the pasture with a tire pump in his hand. National Mine University categorically denies all

such charges and stands by the statistics quoted here. Using these statistics as our database, we determined that in a cow fart, the average cow releases enough gas to fill a two pint pickle jar, with some left over. So a conservative estimate of the amount of gas released in cow farts annually in the U.S. alone computes to a whopping **1,520,017,476,767.8** cubic feet! Now if my calculations are correct that comes to... hmm... let's see... (scribble, scribble)... okay... (scribble, scribble)...carry the 3-- (scribble, scribble)...it comes to--hmmm! Just a little over one cubic mile. Doesn't sound like so much when you look at it that way. Oh, well...never mind.

Dr. Eino Aho is one of the leading research scientists in his field, as well as in Helsten's field. He almost even won a prize once.

How twisted are you?
Take this simple test and find out.
Answers & psychiatric profile on page 12

Twisted Trivia Questions
(Hint: Think *really* stupid!)

1. Why?
2. Who is Bob?
3. Name 3 guys who were never president.
4. What things are purple?
5. What's the difference between a chicken?
6. Name three things.
7. If a tree fell on you, would it hurt?
8. How does a Yooper spell relief?
9. Who are you?
10. How many fish are there in Lake Superior?

Martha's Summer Kitchen

First of all, I would like to thank these wonderful people at the Yellow Snow Gazette for giving me the opportunity to write this column. I must admit I'm a little nervous, because this is my first job. My editor was so sweet that she even offered to pay me, but I just don't have the heart to take money for something that I really enjoy. There I go, rambling on. Well, I'll get right down to work now. For my recipe in the first issue, I chose one of my favorites, my pasty recipe. The pasty was originally a Cornish meal, but it has been altered by most cooks in our area. The Cornish pasty uses turnips, but our family has always used rutabagas, which are easy to find here in the U.P., but depending on the time of year, sometimes hard to find in other areas. I don't care for parsley so I never use it in my recipes. I've seen pasties served in several different ways. My husband likes a little gravy over the top, and the grandkids, well folks, by the time they get through with the ketchup, you can't see the pasty anymore. I like mine plain and still piping hot from the oven.

Pasties
Makes 2 Pasties

CRUST:
1 1/3 C. flour, sifted together with 1/2 tsp. salt cut in 1/2 C. lard until the size of a small peas. Add approximately 1/3 C. cold water. Mix with pastry blender until dough is well blended. Divide into two equal parts. Roll into 9-inch circles.

FILLING:
1/2 C. each— turnips (or rutabaga), potatoes, carrots(cubed)
                1 medium onion (diced)
2 tbsp minced parsley, fresh or dried
1 Lb Pasty meat, or boneless beef (cubed)
1/2 tsp. salt
1/4 tsp. pepper
1 tbsp. butter

Mix Filling Ingredients: Equally divide onto rolled crust, top with butter. Lift and fold top half of crust over filling. Seal, folding and crimping into rope edge along top of pasty. Slit each pasty about 1/2 inch in several places. Place on cookie sheet several inches apart and bake at 375 degrees for 1 hour.

Recycling tips: For those who really can't cook, (like my sister) an overcooked, dried out, rock hard pasty can be very useful as a doorstop, a paperweight, or a hockey puck.

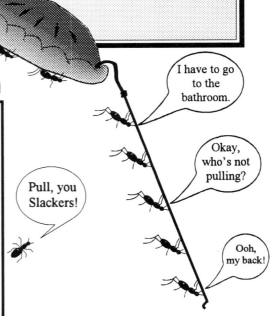

I have to go to the bathroom.

Okay, who's not pulling?

Pull, you Slackers!

Ooh, my back!

Answers to Twisted Trivia

1. Because.
2. Bob.
3. If you named any 3 guys who were never President you're right.
4. Purple things.
5. One leg is the same.
6. Okay, we'll give you this one- it's too easy.
7. Yes.
8. r-e-l-i-e-f.
9. If you missed this one, get help.
10. Lots.

See below your score and evaluation

0-Correct
Don't worry, you're fine.
1-3 Correct
With practice you could appear to be normal.
4-6 Correct
You really must get out more.
7-9 Correct
Be very careful around real humans.

ALL 10 CORRECT
Welcome to Gumbyland!

NMU Professor Invents Revolutionary New Engine

Last week, members of the local news media were invited to a press conference at Moose Crossing, where National Mine University Professor Eino Aho staged a demonstration of his latest invention, a music-powered engine. Professor Aho has been working on the concept of converting the harmonics contained in music into electrical energy for the last five years. At the press conference he unveiled the prototype, a 1959 GMC pickup truck body housing the new engine. As a power source he used his wife's old upright piano, which he bolted down to the tailgate. A microphone attached to the soundboard of the piano carried the sound to an audio-electrical converter which converted the music to electrical energy to drive the engine. Prof. Aho's wife, Olga, an accomplished pianist and church organist, assisted in the demonstration. After explaining the theory of the music powered engine to members of the press, Prof. Aho and his wife took their places for the demonstration. He got behind the wheel and she took her place at the piano. At his signal, Olga began to play The *Blue Danube Waltz*. It took a few measures to build up power, but soon, to the amazement of all, the truck began to move. The crowd cheered as the old GMC bounced down the two-rut road toward Beaver Whiz Creek, Prof. Aho at the wheel and Olga proudly banging away on the keys. Prof. Aho signaled again and Olga went into *Chopsticks* without missing a beat. The truck began to pick up speed. Members of the press ran alongside, cheering them on. The demonstration appeared to have been a resounding success. Then, as they rounded a bend in the road, the unexpected happened. Apparently attracted by the sound of music, a big bull moose stepped out of the swamp. Its already romantic mood apparently heightened by the sound of Olga's piano, it began to trot along behind the truck, cooing softly, a lovesick look in its eye. The crowd scattered and climbed whatever trees happened to be nearest at hand. Prof. Aho, assessing the situation via his rear-view mirror, shouted out the window, "More power, Olga!"

Mrs. Aho, also aware of the potential danger, started into a lively rendition of The *Pennsylvania Polka*. The truck picked up speed, but the moose, its excitement intensified by the increased tempo of the music, picked up the pace and stayed with it. Prof. Aho, seeing that the moose had definite designs on the truck and its occupants, yelled again, "Play, Olga, Play!" To this Olga replied, "Drive, Eino, Drive!" Then she kicked into *The Twelfth Street Rag*. The truck was now flying down the road, Prof. Aho at the wheel, Olga banging away on the keys, and the moose in a full gallop behind, making a sound that caused one to imagine a ruptured walrus molesting the horn section of the Tapiola fifth grade band. Prof. Aho hollered, "Play, Olga! Play like the wind!" Olga's fingers flew across the keys as she finished *The Twelfth Street Rag* and started into an accelerated version of *The William Tell Overture*. "Play, Olga, play like you never played before!" Prof. Aho wailed as he saw the moose gaining in the rear view mirror. "Shut up and drive!" Olga screamed back. Suddenly black smoke began to billow from under the truck. Apparently the audio electric converter overheated and caught fire. The cab of the truck filled with smoke and Prof. Aho, unable to see the road, missed the hairpin turn ☞

Believe It or Shut Up!

Some Yoopers are more active than others.

Waino Millimaki, an unemployed miner from Tapiola, sat on his couch unmoving with remote in hand for 13 days before his wife finally realized that he was **dead!**

Said Mrs. Millimaki, "Well, he didn't **act** or smell any different."

★★★★★★★★★★★★★★★★★★★
★ **Words of Whizdom:** ★
★ If it came from the ★
★ back end of a cow, ★
★ it's probably not bean dip. ★
★★★★★★★★★★★★★★★★★★★

near the bottom of the hill. The truck, with the moose close behind, was bearing down on a huge oak tree when Prof. Aho abandoned ship, hollering as he leaped from the truck, "Jump, Olga, Jump!" Olga bailed out just moments before the truck slammed into the tree and burst into flames. The moose, unable to put on the brakes in time, also smacked into the tree, bounced back and sat down suddenly. It sat there looking surprised and dazed for a minute, then it snorted, shook its head, stood up and wobbled off into the swamp. Prof. Aho and his wife survived the ordeal with only minor bruises and scratches. The music-powered engine, however, was completely destroyed. Prof. Aho's notes, which he kept in the glove box of the truck, were consumed by the flames. Contained in those notes was the mathematical formula upon which the principle of the audio-electrical converter was based. Sadly, due to a blow on the head sustained during the his leap from the truck, Prof. Aho can't remember anything about the formula, although he is fairly certain that it had a bunch of numbers in it. He has decided to abandon the project for the present and move on to his next project, the development of an effective formula for moose repellent. ∎

TRIVIA

How twisted are you?
Take this simple test and find out.
Answers & psychiatric profile on page 20

Twisted Trivia Questions
(Hint: Think *really* stupid!)

1. How many people are in the world?
2. What are their names?
3. Who was the city of Marquette named after?
   A. Bishop Baraga
   B. Father Marquette
   C. Bob
4. Who is the oldest guy in the world?
5. In what year was the blizzard of '76?
6. Who farted?
7. Why is one side of a Goose flock longer than the other?
8. Where are you?
9. How long does it take a tree to grow?
10. When do fish swim fastest?

How to keep 'em Whipped!

Gravel Gertie's
Husband Training Tips

Dear Gravel Gertie,
I am having a terrible husband problem, and hope that you will help save my marriage. After twenty years of marriage, I finally managed to get indoor plumbing installed in our house. The first time I used our new facilities, I fell right in because my husband had left the seat up (good thing I had only gone Number One)! I have patiently tried to teach him to put it down, and my friends tell me to just look before I sit, but my nerves are darn near worn out! I have to watch where I sit everywhere else in the house because of his fishing hooks and bear traps and hunting dogs—I should at least be able to let down my guard in my new bathroom! I hope you can help me Gertie; I've been watching Ann Lander's column, but I don't think she got my letter.
Seatless in Seattle

Dear Seatless,
The best thing to do is to keep him out of your bathroom altogether. Here's how I handled it. I hid a small tape recorder behind my toilet and rigged it up so that when Eugene lifted the seat, it played a tape of my mother laughing hysterically. It was such a traumatic experience for him that he never sets foot in my bathroom anymore. Now he goes out in the back yard and whizzes in the rose bushes.
Gertie

Dear Gertie,
Whenever my husband is working in the back yard and he has to go, he doesn't take the time to come into the house. He just tinkles in my rosebushes. My poor roses are withering and dying. How can I save them?
Rosebud

Dear Bud,
It didn't take long to cure Eugene of that habit. I cut the cord off an old lamp that I was throwing out. I stripped the wires back so about an inch of bare wire was exposed. Then I taped the cord to a branch right in Eugene's favorite whizzing area, leaving the two bare wires about a quarter inch apart. I ran the other end of the cord through the garage window and plugged it in. It took Eugene a few tries before he hit those bare wires just right, but he finally did. That was three months ago, and his hair is still standing on end. I don't know where he goes to take a whiz now. Maybe he gave it up altogether.
Gertie

Dear Gertie,
My husband has been on the couch for 23 years. He sits there with his remote in his hand and a blank look on his face. Our lawn looks like a jungle and the garage hasn't been cleaned in years. The last time he took me anywhere was when he let me go with him to the dump in 1979. I can't stand it another day. What should I do?
Fed Up

Dear Fed,
Aha! The old corpse on the couch problem. I had the same Problem with Eugene. Here's what I did. I had some moving men come in and pry him off the couch and move him out to the garage with the other useless junk. I left the remote control in his hand, so he's perfectly happy sitting out there thinking he's actually in control of something. I go out once a week or so and dust him off, but other than that, he needs little or no maintenance.
Gertie

Always remember:

No one, on their deathbed, ever looked back on their life and said, "Gosh, I wonder what cowpies taste like."

Another summer, which we are certain began only a week or two ago, enters the twilight of its life. It has not yet completely given up the ghost, but if you listen closely on a quiet night, you can almost hear the stirring of Heikki Lunta, the god of snow, turning over fitfully in his sleep. Yes, it was a good summer—any summer in Yooperland is a good summer—but it has definitely seen its better days. If there is any doubt that the summer is a thing of the past, that doubt is dispelled by the appearance of the slow and obtrusive yellow school buses along the autumn colored byways of Yooperland. They gobble up the neighborhood children and spit them out in a laughing and screaming mob onto the asphalt parking lots and playgrounds of our primary learning institutions, much to the relief of nerve-weary parents. School's in. The little recruits are once again handed over to the field generals of learning, who patiently wait behind their huge desks, serenely going over final details of their battle plans for the conquest and banishment of ignorance and illiteracy. Though all share the same objective, each uses different tactics.

Fanny B. Johnson's approach is somewhat Pattonesque—full force assault, little regard for casualties, no quarter asked, none given. Built wide and low like a tank, her lumbering, slow-moving appearance is deceptive. It is rumored among school children that she has discovered a way to transport herself instantaneously through space. She can be standing at the blackboard or sitting at her desk one moment, and the next instant lifting a slacker from his desk by the short hairs. She just pops out of existence and pops in again directly behind enemy lines. But even more devastating is the frontal attack. When you know you've been spotted committing an infraction of the rules (such as playing drums on the back of your

cousin's head with two pencils) the sight of Fanny B's full frontal assault advancing down the aisle toward you is as horrible as the actual attack. It has been many years since I have been subjected to that horror, and I still have nightmares.

Mrs. Warnberg was known for her quick and deadly ruler strikes. Thin and quick like a wasp, she would silently cruise the room, ever-watchful for note-passing, comic book reading, or worst of all, daydreaming. There is no quicker or more decisive ending to a school day afternoon fantasy than the sting of Mrs. Warnberg's metal edged ruler. A silent killer, she would attack on the fly, never uttering a word, never slowing from her cruising speed. By the time you realized that she had struck, she would be halfway across the room, already zeroing in on another target. Because of her constant and unceasing dedication to battle, Mrs. Warnberg has been credited with amassing the highest body count in the schoolroom battlefield.

The most fearsome and effective of all the schoolroom generals was the imperturbable Mrs. Magnuson. Substantial but stately in build, presidential in demeanor, she was the George Washington of the war for the minds of the children. What others could not accomplish by brute force or implied threats of extreme torture, Mrs. Magnuson could accomplish with a disapproving glance. She projected an aura of benevolent but unyielding omnipotence. Like the Fonz, who could intimidate the most dangerous hoodlums with a snap of his fingers, Mrs. M. could quiet the rowdiest class by merely entering the room. No one in recorded history remembers Mrs. Magnuson ever having to unleash the awesome destructive power she obviously possessed. Of all the generals in the war, she alone attained god-like status, and probably with good reason. No one ever saw, or heard of, or ever knew anyone who ever saw or heard of Mrs. M. ever going to the bathroom. That's proof enough for me. They don't make teachers like that anymore. ■

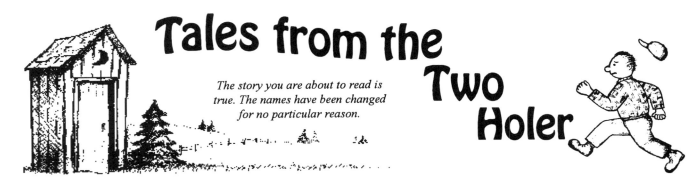

Tales from the Two Holer

The story you are about to read is true. The names have been changed for no particular reason.

Rudy and Tauno were the best of friends. They went bar-hopping together, went to Packer games together, and played cribbage on many a lazy Sunday afternoon. There was only one area where they were at odds. Rudy was a dedicated game warden; Tauno was a devout poacher. Rudy, being a man of principle, swore that if he could ever catch Tauno in the act, he would bring him to justice. Talk around town was that whenever Tauno stayed at his camp, which he often did, he would go out in the early mornings in search of out of season deer, and he was often successful. Rudy had sworn to put an end to it, so he began to sneak out to Tauno's camp in the early mornings. 4:00 a.m. would find him crouched out in the swamp near Tauno's camp, shivering, teeth chattering from the morning chill. He would perk up when he'd finally hear the creak of the door opening, certain that Tauno was headed out for some early violating. But to his surprise and puzzlement, Tauno would shout out to him, "Come on in for Coffee, Rudy. You must be freezing out there." So Rudy would go in to sit by the camp stove and sip hot coffee. He was sure no one could have

warned Tauno of his presence. He had told no one about his early morning stakeouts. He figured he'd made too much noise coming through the swamp and Tauno had heard him coming. He'd have to be much quieter the next time. So he would regularly steal through the swamp to Tauno's camp and sit, cold, wet, and miserable in the pre-dawn hours. And every time Tauno would stick his head out the door and call him in to warm up and have a cup of coffee. Over the years, Rudy tried his best to get the goods on Tauno, always with the same result. No matter how early he went out to the swamp and waited, no matter how careful and quiet he was, Tauno would stick his head out the door right around dawn and tell Rudy that he was getting to old to be sitting out there in the morning chill, and that he should come in and warm up with a cup of coffee. And of course, every time, Rudy took him up on it. A warm fire and a hot cup up coffee was just the ticket to warm his cold, aching bones. Though he kept at it for years, he never did catch Tauno poaching deer. Finally, on the day of Rudy's retirement, after

the party broke up and he sat sharing a pint of Kessler's with Tauno, he broke down and asked. "Tauno," he said, "You and I both know you bagged a lot of illegal deer over the years. And all along I did my best to catch you at it. All those mornings I waited in the swamp—you gotta tell me—how did you always know I was out there?"

At that Tauno laughed long and hard, then he said, "I knew you were trying to catch me at it. So every morning around dawn, just to be safe, I'd stick my head out the door and call you in for coffee. I never knew if you were out there or not, but every time you were you came in. On the mornings you didn't answer, I went hunting."

Top 10 reasons
why aliens would land on earth

10. Nothing better to do on a Saturday afternoon.
9. The only place they could find tasty deer ticks.
8. Intergalactic YMCA was closed.
7. The only place where dumb old guys rule.
6. Fresh cowpies!
5. Saw sign that read, "Last rest stop for 47,000 light years."
4. Peggy Bundy's hair.
3. Needed a reading from a certified professional psychic.
2. Rescue Toivo Maki from muskrat trap.
1. In search of their leader, Judge Ito, creator of all that is good.

Crossword Puzzle
Dog Daze

Across
2. A 60's Rock Group
   "Three ___ Night"
3. A popular food at baseball games,
   "Hot _____"
4. Lassie, Rin Tin Tin, and Benji are what kind of animal?

Down
1. Who farted? "The ___ did."
2. What your first blind date looked like.
3. Superman's animal friend,
   "Super ___"

Answers on page 20

.********************

...***SPLAT!*** The last thing that went through Toivo Maki's mind before he hit the rocks was *Holyowha! I bet dis is gonna hurt!* It did. A sharp pain shot through his head along with a sensation of being plunged into cool dark water on a hot day. Then everything went black. It seemed to Toivo that he was gone far away for a long time. It was sort of like the time he stuck his head down in a peat bog to see what it looked like under there and passed out from a lack of air. He was dreaming about that when consciousness began to seep back into his brain. He opened his eyes. A strange fuzzy image shimmered in the air in front of him. He rubbed the crusties out of his eyes and the image came into focus. It was the face of the little blue guy who had revealed his destiny to him, the same one that had taught him the difference between little green guys and little blue guys.

"Glrp zerg plrx duh," Toivo said.

"Whoops!" said the little blue guy. He stuck an instrument that looked like a glass corkscrew into Toivo's ear and gave it a twist. "Try again," he said.

"Where da heck am I?" Toivo asked.

"You're in the stupid human ward of our ship's hospital," the little blue guy said. "We scraped you off the rocks and put you back together."

Toivo sat up and looked around. The other little blue guys milled around the room, tinkering with beakers and glass tubing and ominously sadistic looking small appliances. They were the same little blue guys he'd met before, all right. He could tell because they were little and blue.

"We intended to put a metal plate in your head to replace a piece of skull that we couldn't find," the little blue guy continued, "but we ran out of plates so we had to put in a salad bowl instead,"

"Oh," Toivo said.

"But we've never installed a salad bowl in a human's head before, so we couldn't possibly have foreseen this problem."

Toivo didn't like the sound of that. "Problem? What problem?"

"Well—We've tried everything we could think of. It seems that the salad bowl in your head acts as an antenna through which you receive the 24 hour Hee Haw channel," the little blue guy said.

The life annd times of
Toivo Maki
known by
evil-doers and bad guys as...
YOOPERMAN

"And," he added with a tone of finality, "we don't know how to turn it off,"

Toivo's couldn't quite comprehend what the little blue guy was saying. He closed his eyes to try to concentrate. Suddenly Buck Owens jumped up out of a cornfield. Toivo screamed. It was such a horrible sight that it paralyzed him. He couldn't open his eyes. The Buck Owens monster grinned like a Stephen King version of Howdy Doody, and all Toivo could do was stare at it and scream. Then the little blue guy gave him a slap that made the salad bowl rattle in his head.

"Get a grip!" the little blue guy snapped.

Toivo's eyes popped open. "Holyowha!" he exclaimed. "What a rush!"

"I know," said the little blue guy.

"We've been monitoring Hee Haw transmissions for quite some time. The first time I saw it I almost crapped my shlrzles."

An idea popped into Toivo's brain all by itself. "Couldn't you fix it so I get Gilligan's Island instead?" He asked. "You guys must be smart enough to do that."

"Sorry," the little blue guy said. "It doesn't matter how intelligent *we* are. You can only receive transmissions compatible with *your* intelligence level. Gilligan's Island is just too sophisticated for the salad bowl implant default parameters, which are selected by your own brain waves."

"Oh," Toivo said.

He tried hard to understand it all, but it was too confusing. He took a chance and closed his eyes for a moment. A jug band was hooting away on a front porch. The Buck Owens monster was nowhere in sight. He opened his eyes.

"I'm hungry," he said. "Do you guys eat?"

Whack! The little blue guy slapped Toivo alongside the head. "Idiot!" he snapped. "Try to stay with me for just a minute longer."

"Ouch." Toivo said.

"Now that we've got you put back together, let's go over the details one more time," the little blue guy said. "You obviously need a little more help getting started. We have already given you your superpowers." He slid a box out from under the table and began rummaging through it. "But you are going to need a superhero costume—ah, here it is." He pulled out a pair of red flannel longies and held them up in front of Toivo. Sewed on the back, serving as a cape, was Toivo's blue baby blanket. His diaper was pinned onto the longies in the appropriate place.

"Well," the little blue guy said, "try it on."

Toivo struggled into the outfit

with the little blue guy's help. It fit perfectly, sort of. There was even some extra room in the seat to carry potatoes and stuff. The little blue guy led Toivo over to a mirror on the wall. Toivo looked at himself and was pleased with what he saw. This was the best outfit he ever had. It was the only outfit he ever had.

"Of course it's not quite complete yet," said the little blue guy. "It needs an emblem on the front to brighten it up, and also to show who you are."

Toivo had his second idea of the day. "I got it! Let's put my picture on the front!"

The little blue guy made a sour face. "Please," he said, "one face like that is enough for anybody. No, I think it should be the first letter of your name. Have you chosen a name for your superhero identity?"

"No."

"Okay, think of a name."

Toivo thought hard. He was careful not to close his eyes. Buck Owens could be lurking anywhere.

"Let's see... he mumbled. "A name...think of a name." He found it hard to think with his eyes open, and he was afraid to close them. Finally he gave up. "Nope," he said. "No luck."

The little blue guy looked like he wished he had hair to tear out. "All right," he said "let's use logic. You are to be the champion of your race. Your name must reflect that fact. From what race of beings do you come?"

"Uh—Yoopers," Toivo said.

"Yoopers, "the little blue guy repeated. Okay, now we're getting somewhere."

Toivo smiled proudly. "This is fun," he said.

The little blue guy chose to ignore that. "Now," he continued,"as a member of this race of Yoopers, to what sub-classification do you belong?"

Toivo stared blankly.

"Okay, let me put it this way—besides being a Yooper, what else are you?"

"Hungry?"

WHACK! The little blue guy rattled Toivo's salad bowl with a quick slap.

"NO!" he screamed, "A man!" His face began to get blotchy all over. "You're a man! You're a YOOPER...You're a MAN! Get it? YOOPER... and MAN! Now does that suggest a name to you?"

Toivo thought hard and suddenly a light went on in his head. He snapped his fingers.

"Bob!"

This time the little blue guy slapped himself in the head. He walked away shaking his head and mumbling to himself. When he reached the wall he walked through it and disappeared. All the other little blue guys continued to mill around, doing what seemed like some important work. They paid no attention to Toivo, so he just closed his eyes and watched Hee Haw. The monster was nowhere in sight. Grandpa Jones was talking about dinner. It made Toivo so hungry that he couldn't watch anymore so he opened his eyes. The little blue guy came back through the wall. He held up a big yellow "Y" made of some shiny fabric.

"Y," he said. "Y for 'Yooperman. That is your name." He slapped it on Toivo's chest and it stuck there. "Now remember," he said, "No one must know that Toivo Maki is Yooperman. So don't go changing clothes where anybody can see you." He handed Toivo a brown paper bag. "Here is your everyday wardrobe."

Toivo checked the contents. A flannel shirt, blue jeans, and a pair of ragged high tops.

"Now it's time for you to go," said the little blue guy.

"Before I go," Toivo said, "can I ask you—do you have a name?"

"You probably couldn't pronounce it. Just call me Benny."

"Benny," Toivo repeated. "I like that." He looked around at all the other little blue guys. "Benny and the Blue Guys. You could start a band."

"You have to get going," Benny said. He took Toivo by the arm and led him to a glowing spot on the floor.

"Are you gonna beam me down?" Toivo asked.

"Yeah, right," Benny said. He went to the wall and pulled a lever. The floor opened up and Toivo landed with a thud on solid rock. They had dropped him back on the top of the bluff that he had fallen from. He jumped to his feet in time to see Benny stick his head through the hole in the under side of the space ship. "Get a job!" Benny yelled. Then Benny's face disappeared and the hole closed up. With a sudden blast of hot air the space ship shot up into the sky. The impact blew Toivo off his feet and over the edge of the bluff. He reached out in desperation and just barely managed to catch hold of a tiny ridge of rock with his fingertips. He dangled from the edge of the sheer drop and watched the space ship carry Benny and the Blue Guys up, up, and away.

"Now what do I do?" he yelled after them, but they were already out of sight. Toivo was truly on his own now. He clung to the tiny ridge of rock for a long time. His fingers were getting sweaty and were starting to ache. He looked down. Yup, same old rocks as before. He closed his eyes.

Buck Owens grinned at him from the cornfield, reminding him that there were some things worse than death. Toivo's fingers began to slip...

Will Toivo ever get a grip and really get started on his super-hero career? Will he lose his grip and fall to his death? Will he someday trade in his salad bowl for a satellite dish? And most important of all, do duck turds float?

For the answers to these and other burning questions, turn to page 24 for the next mildly interesting episode of YOOPER-MAN!

Hairold

"Get set for a real thrill!
You're about to see the last red-tailed
tree swallow in existence!"

A Portrait In Pine

The little shack covered in a small clearing, looking lost and alone among the towering jack pines. It wore a tattered coat of tarpaper, its pine board ribs showing through in places, its only window peeking timidly though the branches of a young sugar plum tree. In the gathering dusk the heavy, perpetual sigh of wind and treetops sang in intimate harmony with the distant, primal roar of the mighty Escanaba whitewaters. In contrast, the small stillness of the shack seemed to create a silent disturbance in the wilderness. Nearby, the sad, slow melody of a swamp sparrow mourned the death of the day and quickened my last few steps to the cabin door. Rusty hinges squealed. Tired gray boards groaned underfoot. A small dark blur skittered across a ragged patch of linoleum, popping into a black spit where wall and floor had once met. The last faint glow of twilight through the grimy window pane dimly silhouetted and ancient kerosene lamp , the sole inhabitant of a barren, dust covered table top. I took three cautious, creaky steps to the table. A few minutes of tinkering, some whispered words of encouragement, and a half a book of matches brought the lamp flickering to life. The tiny flame grew, pushing back the darkness with a warm yellow glow, revealing a small square room sparsely furnished with a wooden table and chair, a small rusty pot belly stove, and, attached to the wall opposite the door, a crude pine plank bunk. On the wall above the bunk, Jayne Mansfield smiled down from a majestic pose on a faded calendar dated October, 1949. Beside her was a shelf consisting of a single pine board supporting one rusty, unlabled, and unopened tin can. In a corner near the stove a wood box held a treasure of dry hardwood blocks. After considerable cursing and clanking I persuaded the cantankerous little pot belly to swallow a few of the blocks. The stove belched a small puff of smoke from the crack around its door, and a few minutes later it rumbled and crackled happily, sending out a steady wave of warmth that felt as friendly as the yellow lantern glow looked. I creaked back into the old wooden chair. As the little room gathered warmth the chilled odor of damp wood was overpowered by an aroma of warm metal and wood smoke. A gray spider, residing somewhere beneath the stove, abandoned ship and made his escape up the side of the wood box, disappearing over the edge. The stove pipe clinked and popped as it expanded from the sudden heat, and soot and ashes rattled upward inside it, carried along by the superheated air. Enticed into a state of drowsy comfort by the warmth and the domestic sounds of the fir, I shuffled over to the pine slab bed and stretched out on it. As I watched the slow, lazy undulations of the cobwebs clinging delicately to the rafters, my eyelids began to lose ground in their battle against gravity. Just before sleep came I caught a glimpse of Miss Mansfield's faded smile flickering in the lamp light. I smiled back.

Madame Brewsky's
News that ain't happened yet

The Gazette's resident Certifiable Professional Psycho brings you the news before it happens.

The other day one of my fans wrote to me, asking me if I would pick out some winning lottery numbers for her. She thought, what with me being psychic and everything, I could look into my crystal ball and see what the winning numbers were going to be. I'd like to take this opportunity to clear up some misconceptions about psychics and fortune telling.

First of all, it would be unethical for a fortune teller to use his or her power for such things. To look into the future and see lottery numbers or the outcome of sports events like horse races or football games, and to use that knowledge for the purpose of monetary gain, well that would be just plain wrong. Besides that, it seems like some of us psychics have been shorted a little in that department. I mean, I don't know who hands out the psychic power in the first place, but whoever it is obviously didn't think I'd have any use for the ability to see winning horses coming across the finish line, or lottery numbers that would bring millions of bucks rolling in, because I sure didn't get the power to see that stuff. Different psychics can see different kinds of things in the future. Some can see a few years into the future and some can see centuries. Some can see nations rise and fall. Some can see natural disasters of global proportions. I can see Oscar Aho's bunions flaring up tomorrow morning. Or Puffy Pascoe's hemorrhoid surgery next week. Or some idiot spilling my beer this afternoon. That's about all I get to see.

So to whoever hands out the psychic ability, thanks a lot! And to the fool who wrote in asking me for the lottery numbers, you're on your own, honey. If I could see that kind of stuff, do you think for a minute I'd be wasting my time writing a column in a cheesy little rag like this? Hell no! I'd be on easy street. I'd be giving Bill Gates lessons in money management. I'd be the big winner of every lottery in the country. And then I'd come back and buy this ratty little hovel that I'm forced to work in and I'd burn it to the ground. But the grim reality is that I'm stuck here in this hole because I'm a small time fortune teller who can barely see past the end of her nose! So if you want winning lottery numbers, call one of those high-priced 900 numbers, and just stay off my back! By the way, I predict snow. ❈

Martha's Summer Kitchen

Hi again from my Summer Kitchen. Well, it was a beautiful summer. The gardens were plentiful and the berries were in abundance. Lots of canning this year. I entered my favorite tomatoes and my wild blueberry pie in the Marquette County Fair and I won blue ribbons for both. I'm sure my sister will do better next year. I think she needs to water her garden more often, I noticed her plants looked a little droopy. This issue I chose a Finnish recipe, **Korppuja**. This is one of my grand-daughter's favorites, I hope you like it as much as she does.

This is Martha signing off. (I've always wanted to say that).

Korppuja

2 cups scalded milk
1 stick oleo
2 unbeaten eggs
1 pkg. yeast dissolved in ½ cup warm water
1/4 cup sugar
2 tsp. salt
6 ½ to 8 cups of flour

Pour milk on oleo, sugar and salt. Cool. Add eggs and yeast mixture. Add enough flour to make batter. Beat well. Add more flour and knead gently. Let rise, about 2 hours.

Grease 2 cookie sheets, divide dough into 4 parts. Make rolls the length of cookie sheets and flatten with palms. Cover. Let rise 1 hour. Spread lightly with oleo, sprinkle with cinnamon and sugar. Pat down slightly. Bake 15-20 min. at 375 -400 degrees.

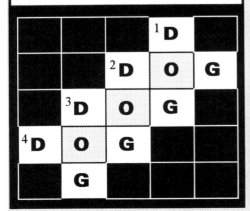

HOME SWEET HOLE

Answers to the crossword puzzle on page 16

Dog Daze

			¹D	
		²D	O	G
	³D	O	G	
⁴D	O	G		
	G			

Answers to Twisted Trivia

1. All of them.
2. I don't know.
3. Father Marquette.
4. Some really old guy.
5. '76.
6. It wasn't me. ("The dog did" is also correct)
7. There are more geese on that side.
8. Wherever you go, there you are.
9. Pretty long.
10. When they are in the water.

See below your score and evaluation

0-Correct
I'm OK, you're OK.
1-3 Correct
This is as normal as you can get.
4-6 Correct
You shouldn't be allowed to handle sharp objects.
7-9 Correct
You shouldn't be allowed to handle dull objects.

ALL 10 CORRECT
Be ready when the mother ship returns.

Hey, you shot my cow!

November 1, 1995 | **DEER CAMP** | Yellow Snow, Michigan

YOOPERLAND INVASION PLOT EXPOSED!

A Yooperland Defense Department spokesman announced today the impending invasion of Yooperland by armed gunmen from surrounding states, including downstate Michigan. Clothed in uniforms of blaze orange and armed with deer rifles of every make and model, this army of terrorists is preparing for a mass assault on our borders. Intelligence reports say the attack will begin on November 15. Observers have detected troop movements and military exercises, as well as the purchasing of supplies for the attack. Sales of rifles, ammunition, and cold weather clothing have skyrocketed in preparation for the assault. Tons of rations are being purchased by these terrorists, who cleverly explain away these rations as "deer feed." Movement of advance scouts into Yooperland has been detected by Yooperland Army Intelligence. It is believed that the terrorists have already established base camps throughout Yooperland. They are stocking these base camp with supplies, including vast amounts of beer, which they probably plan to give to the natives in order to win their trust. It is sad that these terrorists have such a disregard for the principles of civilized warfare that they will stoop so low as to corrupt the morals of our citizens with strong drink in order to gain a military advantage. Intelligence sources say that the strategy of the terrorists is to deplete the deer population of Yooperland and starve its people into submission. The terrorists believe that once the citizens of Yooperland have been transformed into a bunch of hungry drunks, they will gladly sell out their homeland for cheeseburgers, pizzas, and hot pasties. Yooperland authorities urge citizens to remain calm, stay out of the woods during the last two weeks of November, and don't take beer from strangers. The Yooperland military has the situation under control. Members of the Yooperland Resistance have been in the woods since early July stockpiling enough fresh deer meat to last through the winter. The President of Yooperland, in a speech to the Congress Bar in Ishpeming, assured customers that the Yooperland government had the situation well under control. The President received a standing ovation in response to his closing words, sure to live forever in Yooperland history books, "The only thing we have to fear is beer itself." ∎

Great Moments In History!

Historians doing research on General George Armstrong Custer have discovered that he was actually a Finlander from Houghton, Michigan. Born George Armstrong Kustermaki, he later changed his name to Custer. According to eyewitness accounts by Indians who took part in the battle at the Little Big Horn, Custer's last words were, **"Holyowha! Dese sooz are killing me!"**

King of the Jokers

by Gary Massey

1995 Camp Story Contest Winner from Flint, Michigan.

Some hunters like to entertain themselves with practical jokes. And sometimes these jokes backfire. One year a group of five of us spent a week at my dad's camp near Curtis. On our third day at camp my brother Tim got his buck, as he usually does every year. After hanging it up on the buck pole and gutting it, he proceeded to celebrate with a few drinks. Since he seldom drinks, Tim's elbow got tired early and he crawled into bed and went to sleep. The rest of us continued to play cards and celebrate into the wee hours of the morning. Then someone came up with the idea of having a little fun with Tim, whose loud snoring reverberated throughout the camp. After some debate it was decided that, since it was unusually warm outside for this time of year, Tim might be more comfortable out there. We decided to carefully pick Tim up, mattress and all, and move him outside. I knew that on those rare occasions when Tim drank, he slept like a rock and we could probably ☞

Page 21

do it without waking him up. So we picked up the mattress with Tim on it and, giggling all the way, we carried him outside and left him in the woods about fifty yards behind the camp. We covered him with an old army blanket and then tip-toed back to the camp, snickering as we went. We continued our card game until our eyelids started to droop, and then we went to bed. Suddenly, just as it was getting light outside, we were awakened by a blood-curdling scream from behind the camp. We jumped out of bed and rushed out to the sound of someone screaming bloody murder. I didn't want to believe it, but I knew it was Tim's voice. By the time we tumbled out the door the screaming had stopped. We rushed through the woods to where we had left Tim. To our horror, all we found was Tim's mattress, and a few yards away, the army blanket that had covered him, now stained with blood and torn to shreds. Frantically we searched the immediate area, but there was no sign of Tim. We ran back to camp, almost hysterical, planning to go and get some help. When we came around the corner of the camp, there was Tim, sitting on a stump and laughing so hard he was crying. He had woke up just before dawn and realized what we had done, so he had decided to pay us back. He had shredded and torn the army blanket and smeared it with deer blood. Then all he had to do was scream bloody murder until he heard us scrambling out of the camp. Our imagination did the rest. Tim just circled around back to camp and sat listening to our panic-stricken commotion out in the woods and laughing his head off. His only regret is that he didn't have a video camera to catch our reaction as we came around the corner and saw him sitting there. To this day Tim is still the undisputed champion of practical jokers. But we're working on it.

How to keep 'em Whipped!

Gravel Gertie's
Husband Training Tips

Dear Gertie,
My husband has been going deer hunting for 20 years and he has yet to bring home a deer. Every year he spends the entire season at the camp with his hunting buddies. He says he hunts faithfully from dawn to dusk every day, but he always comes up with some lame excuse for not getting a deer. I'm beginning to suspect that he doesn't really hunt as seriously as he says he does. How can I find out?
Deer Hunter's Widow

Dear Deer,
Simple. My Eugene did the same thing for years. I suspected that he wasn't hunting as feverishly as he claimed, so here's what I did. One deer season when I was helping him pack for his trip to deer camp, I slipped fifty dollars and a note into his gun case. The note read, "I thought you might need a little extra poker or beer money." When he came home two weeks later with his idiotic excuses for not getting a deer, I just checked his gun case. The money was still there. I know now that he never even opened his gun case, but I won't let him know that I know until I figure out how to use the knowledge to really make him look foolish—as if he needs any help.
Gertie

Dear Gertie,
Every Saturday night my husband goes out bar-hopping with his friends. He stays out until all the bars are closed, and then he comes stumbling in smelling like a brewery and in a romantic mood. By that time all I want to do is sleep. I don't know what to do. Can you help me?
Married to the Slob

Dear Slob,
What an amazing coincidence! I had that same problem with my Eugene. This is how I cured him. One

evening after he left for the bars I called a bunch of my girlfriends over and we repainted my living room a different color. I also traded living room furniture with one of them. I took all of the family pictures off the wall and put up pictures of strangers. When we got through the place looked completely different. Later, when I heard Eugene stumbling up the driveway, I hid in a closet and watched. He only made it a few steps in the door before it hit him. He looked even more confused than usual. He turned and tiptoed out of the house. I went on up to bed, but twice more that night I heard him come in, look around, and leave again. My Eugene was so confused that he wandered the neighborhood for three days looking for his home. Meanwhile, my friends came over and we changed the place back to the way it was. When Eugene finally came home, I gave him a good long lecture on what booze does to your brain cells. He never even touched a beer for six months after that, and he still won't leave the yard unless I go with him.
Gertie

Dear Gertie,
My husband is five foot eight and weighs 235 pounds. He loves to eat. He especially loves fried foods, like hamburgers dripping with grease. Everything he likes is full of fat and cholesterol. I can't get him to eat anything that is healthy for him. I'm afraid he's going to eat himself into an early grave. What can I do?
Mrs. Butterball

Dear Butterball,
Is the life insurance paid up? Feed him!
Gertie

Better luck hunting this year Eugene. Remember, shoot a buck, not your Truck!
Gertie

The Hunter's Ball

The main recreational event in Yooperland during deer season, besides lounging around the camp in your underwear, playing cards, drinking beer belching as loud as you want, scratching anywhere you want, telling dirty jokes, and stretching the truth about your hunting abilities, is the Hunter's Ball. What Hunter's Ball, you may ask. Any Hunter's Ball, I may answer. Check with any Yooperland bar of any consequence and chances are they'll have one on the calendar. It has been my experience that this event is as much fun to observe as it is to participate in. To really catch partying deer hunters in a natural setting, look for a small town bar with a rustic decor. There's a cozy warmth in knotty pine walls and hardwood floors that is noticeably absent in chrome, glass, and tile. If there is a slight odor of stale beer in the air when you walk in, you've probably found the right place. Beer spilled over the years soaks into the wood, and no amount of cleaning will ever completely eliminate the aroma.

For music, don't look for a band with brand new clean and polished equipment and instruments, decked out in white tuxedos and playing champagne music, because you probably won't find one. If you do, move on to another bar. Look for a band whose well worn equipment shows signs of many barroom parties. Beer stains and cigarette burns on the amplifiers are a good sign. Sometimes the name of the band can be a tip-off. Stay away from bands with names like *The Avant Garde Jazz Review*, or *Trash Metal Pubescent Skinheads In Heat*. Look for names like *Oogie and the Deaftones*, or *The Redneck Hippie Polka and Blues Band*. These names suggest that the band will probably attempt to honor any request, whether they know the song or not.

When the band begins to play, you may note an unusually high women to men ration on the dance floor. In fact, earlier in the evening, the dancers may be all women. Some visitors to the area my think it strange for women to dance with each other, but the practice is common in Yooperland. They want to dance, but the men are still warming up at the bar, so the girls dance with each other. A simple problem, a simple solution.

Meanwhile, the hunters (and the men dressed like hunters) stand four deep at the bar, swapping stories, telling jokes, buying each other beers, and generally getting loosened up enough to ask a girl to dance. This process can take up to three hours, at least for the local hunters. The downstate and out of state visitors are usually the first to break away from the pack and hit the dance floor. These hunters are slightly different from the locals in that they tend to be dressed up a little more, and they spend more money. The locals usually come dressed in their regular hunting garb. They are not out to impress anyone. They are just here for the fun, the comradery, and the beers. As the night goes on, shots of Kessler's and beers come across the bar at an increasing rate.

The women sitting at their tables will order four or five drinks at a time. Breaking through the defensive line to get to the bar to order is no easy task, so it is best to order several drinks, thereby reducing the number of trips. As the night progresses, the music gets louder to drown out the noise of the crowd, and the crowd gets louder to be heard over the music. Somewhere around the end of the third set or the beginning of the fourth, the band and the crowd reach a compromise. Or possibly both have reached the upper limits of their decibel levels and can get no louder. By this time the Yooper hunters who have been warming up for three hours or so are ready to dance. One of them breaks away from the bar and heads for the tables near the dance floor. By this time coordination is nothing more than a word that he now lacks the ability to say on the first attempt. But once he gets going, he's a dancing fool. One by one the rest join in, and for the first time during the evening, there are as many men as women on the dance floor. The band, inspired by the activity on the dance floor, will pull out all the stops and crank out their hottest tunes, working the crowd up to a fever pitch. Then, when the last song is over and the band is wrapping up cords and putting guitars into cases, the guys who stood at the bar until the last set, now just getting into the dancing mode, will chant "One more, One more, One more!"

The chant will soon peter out, however, with the realization that last call is not too far away, and there is beer to be bought to take back to camp. Slowly the crowd will thin out and soon will be reduced to a bartender, two old bucks who have been perched on bar stools all night nursing shots of Kessler's and draft beer, and one lone hunter sleeping peacefully, face down at the bar.

Cartoon Caption Contest

The winner of the cartoon caption contest in the September 1995 Issue is **Mrs. Margaret Roberts** of Germantown, WI.

"By the way, when is the one 'who is going to take you away from all of this' going to show up?"

In the last episode.... *Toivo Maki was scraped off the rocks and put back together by the little blue guys, who gave him his superhero costume, the name "Yooper man," and the salad bowl in his head that receives the 24 hour Hee Haw channel. They deposited our hero back on the top of the bluff, but when their spaceship took off, the blast knocked Yooperman over the edge. He managed to catch hold of a tiny ledge and now he dangles above the rocks below, and his fingers begin to slip...*

As Yooperman plunged through space toward the rocks below, everything seemed to happen in slow motion. His life flashed before his eyes, but it was a rerun, so he didn't watch it. He closed his eyes and watched Hee Haw until the Buck Owens monster popped up out of the corn field and scared him. He opened his eyes and looked down. The rocks were rushing up at him, but everything still seemed to be in slow motion. He knew from experience that it was going to hurt when he hit bottom. He started to search his pockets for a bottle of aspirin, but then realized that his Yooperman costume had no pockets. He recalled that he had stuffed the bag containing his change of clothes into the extra room in the seat of his costume, but he didn't feel like trying to dig it out now. In desperation, he clicked his heels together three times and whispered, "There's no place like home." It didn't work. The slow motion effect was really beginning to annoy him. He yawned. He scratched an itchy spot under his arm. He picked at a zit next to his nose. This falling business was really getting to be a tedious task. Just then everything went fast again. The rocks rushed up at him and he braced himself for the impact. Then a really fat deer hunter stepped out from the bushes.

SPLAT! Yooperman landed on the really fat deer hunter. It was like landing on a waterbed. Of course, Yooperman had never landed on a waterbed, so he didn't know that landing on a really fat deer hunter was like landing on one, but it was like that just the same.

"OOF!" the really fat deer hunter said, and his gun went off. There was a scream from a nearby clump of cedar trees and a big buck that had been lurking there giggling under its breath came tumbling out, dead as a doornail. We can only assume that this means the deer was pretty dead, since no one really knows what a doornail is anymore, or how dead a doornail is. The deer might just as well have been dead as a handful of pocket lint. Who can say? Either way, the deer was dead.

"I got one, I got one!" The really fat deer hunter, who was knocked on his formidable backside by the impact of Yooperman's body and the kick of the rifle, jumped to his feet. "Twenty years without a deer, and I finally got one! Wait till I show the guys back at the camp!"

Yooperman sat on the ground, stunned, watching little birdies and stars spin around his head. The really fat deer hunter helped him to his feet and dusted him off.

"Gee, thanks, mister," he said. "Because of you I shot the biggest buck I've ever seen. No one at our deer camp has ever got a deer. I'll be a hero!"

"No problem," Yooperman said. "It's my job."

The really fat deer hunter crinkled his chubby brow. "Your job? Going around falling on people is your job?"

"No," Yooperman said. "Good deeds. Doing good deeds and help-ing people is my job." He stepped back so the really fat deer hunter could get a good look at his superhero costume. "I'm Yooperman, the world's greatest super-hero."

The really fat deer hunter looked Yooperman up and down and made sort of a snorting sound. "Uh huh," he said. "And I'm the King of England."

Yooperman held out his hand. "Pleased to meetcha," he said. He thought it was pretty cool that someone as important as a king would come out here and do his own deer hunting, just like a regular guy.

The really fat deer hunter looked puzzled for a moment, then he shrugged and shook Yooper-man's hand. "Uh—okay," he said. "Now come on, give me a hand with this deer." He slung his gun on his shoulder and began to hack down a young maple tree. It only took a few minutes to cut a pole and tie the deer to it. Then they hoisted the pole up onto their shoulders.

"The camp is about a mile over this way," the really fat deer hunter said, motioning toward the north. Big fluffy snowflakes began to fall as they toted the big buck off toward the camp.

The camp was not much more than a tarpaper shack, perched on the edge of a small clearing under the branches of a stand of tall jackpines. Next to it was a small woodshed, and back in the trees was a small one-hole outhouse clothed in green tarpaper, with a well beaten path leading to it. As they approached the camp the door flew open and a mob of about a dozen un-shaven and unwashed deer hunters poured out. Some-one must have seen them coming. They flocked

Hairold

ERP!

"I finally shot that trophy buck! It's right behind these trees!"

around the really fat deer hunter, hooting and hollering and asking questions about how he came to bag such a magnificent buck. The really fat deer hunter promised to tell the whole story over a few beers, so everyone helped to string the deer up between to trees and gut it. This task was carried out without delay, and there was a feeling of impending celebration in the air as they all tromped back into the camp. The really fat deer hunter introduced Yooperman to the rest of the hunters and told them how he had happened along just after the big buck was shot, and was kind enough to help carry it back to camp. They all looked at Yooperman a little strangely, but this was deer camp. Who could say what was normal or unusual or strange? So they passed the beers around as the really fat deer hunter began to tell the story of the shooting of the big buck from beginning to end—how he had stalked the buck all day, and finally tracked it into a cedar swamp, where he brought it down with a one-handed hip-shot (the other hand busy catching Yooperman as he fell) as the buck made a break for it. Yooperman was impressed. No wonder the really fat deer hunter was made King of England.

Another round of beers was passed out, and then another. Yooperman was glad that among his super powers was the ability to drink 32 beers without puking. As the night wore on, hunters began to drop out of the celebration. The first one dropped out after 12 beers, another crawled into his bunk after his sixteenth, and two more slid under the table after twenty. Yooperman took every beer that was handed to him, and even drank a couple extra in between rounds. Proficiency in beer drinking never goes unnoticed at the camp, and soon the hunters began to look at Yooperman with a little more

respect. When everyone else was on their eighteenth beer and beginning to feel a little fuzzy, Yooperman was starting on his twenty-fifth and still standing straight as a jackpine. He did have a pretty good buzz going, though, and he got into the spirit of the party by demonstrating his ability to burp and fart at the same time without his chest caving in. This impressed the hunters so much that they forgot all about the really fat deer hunter and his trophy buck. And when Yooperman invited them all outside and showed them his ability to write his name in the snow without using his hands, there was a gasp of sheer awe from the crowd, and then a round of applause. They went back inside and had another round of beers and then another, and hunters kept crawling off to bed or falling face down on the table, or sliding under it, until only Yooperman and the really fat deer hunter were left. They sat across the table from each other and drank their beers quietly. The really fat deer hunter just sat with a silly smile, watching Yooperman. After a while he reached back into the cooler and brought out a can of beer.

"This is the last one," he said. "You want it?"

Yooperman let out a little burp. "I dunno."

The really fat deer hunter pushed the beer across the table. "Go ahead, drink it," he said. "You earned it."

Yooperman popped the beer open and chugged it down. "There," he said. "All gone." He looked at the really fat deer hunter, who began to look a little fuzzy around the edges. Then he began to sort of shimmer and melt. Yooperman rubbed his eyes and looked again. The really fat deer hunter looked like silly putty that was left out in the sun too long. He began to wiggle and droop around the edges, and he appeared

to be shrinking.

"Are you really the King of England?" Yooperman asked, but it came out more like "Roorly da knga ingln?"

"Of course not," said the really fat lump of silly putty.

"Den hoodaheckarya?" Yooperman wondered what he had just said.

Suddenly there was a sizzle and a pop and a flash of light, and Benny the little blue guy sat where the really fat deer hunter had been.

"Benny!" Yooperman cried and jumped to his feet. The room spun around really fast and he sat down again. "Wutdaheckryoodoonere?" he said. He had no idea what he was saying, but Benny seemed to understand.

"It seems that I've been assigned to you," Benny said. He looked slightly disgusted. "Since I keep having to come and get you out of trouble, the Council of Galactic Busybodies decided that I should stay with you. I'm sort of like a supervisor." He looked even more disgusted. "Actually, more like an assistant," he said. Then he blew out his breath, making a sound like a beer fart, and he buried his face in his hands. "Okay, a sidekick. I've been assigned to the position of ☞

Yooperman's sidekick until further notice."

"Holyowha!" Yooperman cried, and jumped to his feet again. The room spun around even faster than before, and his stomach began to turn in the opposite direction. He leaned forward and planted his hands firmly on the table, but everything just kept on spinning. He tried to focus his eyes on Benny.

"Benny"

"What?" Benny said from behind his blue hands.

"How mny burzh dud I drnk?" Yooperman asked.

Benny peeked out from between his fingers. "Counting the last one I gave you," he said, a sly smile crossing his face, "thirty-three."

Something gurgled down in Yooperman's stomach. It sounded like someone trying to unplug a toilet with a plunger. His stomach went into a series of spasms, and out of his mouth came the sound of someone priming a dry hand pump, and having some success at it. He clapped both hands over his mouth and looked around for a place to deposit the mother lode.

Benny jumped up. "Not in here, you idiot! The outhouse!" He led Yooperman to the door and shoved him out. Yooperman ran, stumbled, staggered, and finally crawled to the little tarpaper one-holer, flung open the door and made a dive for the hole. Unfortunately, his foot caught on the step and he fell forward, plunging headlong into the hole. He remembered the familiar feeling of falling and a comfort in knowing that at least this time it would be a soft landing just before everything went black.

Will Yooperman survive the fall down the outhouse hole? Will Benny survive his assignment as Yooperman's sidekick? Where do really fat deer hunters come from? What color is your car?

For the answers to some of these questions, turn to page 37 for the next amazingly clever and entertaining episode of **YOOPERMAN!**

Professor Eino Aho
Science Department

Deer Baiting: Fair or Foul?

An Analysis of a controversial issue by Yooperland's foremost intellectual, **Prof. Eino Aho,** *head of almost everything at National Mine University.*

I recently read a DNR deer hunter survey on deer baiting. Until I read the report I had no idea that the subject was so controversial. Hunters on both sides of this issue are equally steadfast in their beliefs, each side in strong and sometimes militant conflict with the other. I personally think it unwise to have two such strongly opposing factions lurking in our forests armed with deadly weapons, so I, with the clear and calm objectivity that only a scientific mind can offer, will inject a voice of reason into this volatile issue. First and foremost, we must define our subject. For this purpose I turned to the Webster's Dictionary.

Bait: *to tease, provoke*

There was more to the definition, but it was obliterated by a glob of ketchup that fell from my pasty onto the page. But this is enough to give us a clear idea of what we're dealing with. The question is, should the teasing or provoking of deer for the purpose of more easily shooting them be banned? Is this practice unethical, immoral, or even cruel to the animals? Having never hunted deer myself, and having never teased or provoked a deer, I cannot know from experience how baiting deer can improve chances of success in hunting. However, I can well imagine how repeatedly taunting a deer with insults and crude remarks could cause the deer to become extremely angry, and to charge out of its hiding place at the insulting hunter where it could be easily shot.

This practice in itself does not seem unfair to the deer. But perhaps there should be restrictions on the kinds of insults that may be used to bait deer. For instance, unsavory remarks about a deer's parentage might be allowed, but remarks that tend to demean deer as a race or to stereotype them unfavorably might be disallowed. An example of the latter might be a joke about the minimum number of deer required to perform the task of screwing in a light bulb. Such a joke might imply that all deer are of a predetermined limited mentality and that as a group or as individuals they are incapable of rising above that limitation. Insulting a deer's father, however, might be allowed, as in "Your father was shot by a flatlander" or "Your daddy was a spikehorn." On the other hand, since motherhood is sacred, baiting a deer by insulting its mother, as in "Your mama would do anything for a buck," would be strictly forbidden.

Insults and jokes of an adult nature could be used in the presence of adult deer, but should be avoided when young deer or fawns are present. An example of such an insult would be:

Q: How do you circumcise a buck?
A: Kick his sister in the jaw.

Reaching an agreement on what kinds of insults or crude remarks may be acceptable in baiting deer will surely be difficult, and may well be impossible. If an agreement cannot be reached, I submit that it may be wise to throw out the whole idea of baiting deer altogether and adopt some other method. Perhaps, instead of baiting, it might be a better idea to just put food out for them.

A YOOPER MYSTERY

DA CASE OF DA MISSING CASE

It was a beautiful summer Saturday in Yooperland, so with a case of beer and his deer rifle in the back of his truck Pirto Johnson decided to head out to camp. Like most Finlanders Pirto was feeling very thirsty and after about 10 minutes and 3 beers he felt the need to answer nature's call somewhere along South Camp Road. Being the classy guy that he was, Pirto couldn't just relieve himself right out in the open so he headed into the brush about 20 feet until he found a nice dirt clearing hidden behind some trees. After writing his name in the sand a few times, Pirto zipped his fly and headed back to the truck to grab another cold one and hit the road. What happened next has been recounted in bars all over the U.P. ever since.

As Pirto approached the truck he began to sense that something was wrong. According to Pirto it was as if there was a sudden emptiness in his stomach "as big as da biggest caving pit." When Pirto looked in the back of his truck he found out why. His beloved case of beer (minus 3 cans) was missing. Only a man with a true love for beer could feel such a loss before knowing it. Pirto, being that kind of man, realized that there was only one right thing to do. He drove to the nearest bar and (after filling the emptiness in his stomach with a few glasses of tap) he called for help.

"Two Men and a Twelve Pack Detective Agency, dis is Eino, how can we help you?"

"Ya, dis is Pirto Johnson. I'm at da Big Buck Bar. Someone stole my case of beer! I don't care how much it cost, you gotta help me!"

"We'll be right dere," was

Eino's professional reply, "Just as soon as Toivo gets his thumb outta da beer can."

A few hours later the two detectives arrived at the bar. They ordered a beer and sat down with Pirto to discuss their price.

"Ya know Pirto, we ain't cheap. If we find da case of beer, it's gonna cost ya a six pack for me and a six pack for Toivo."

"Ya," said Toivo, "detectives like us ain't cheap."

"True," said Pirto, "a six pack fer each of ya ain't cheap, but I gotta find dat beer, and from what I heard, you'se guys can really get da job done."

Pirto spoke the truth. Just a few weeks before Eino and Toivo were called out on a similar case. The two detectives were sitting in their office playing a game of 'Who can spit a lugie da furthest' ("I won," insists Toivo) when they received a frantic call from Ralph Heikkela whose fridge had been cleared out of all it's Goebels. After some grueling detective work they were able to crack the case. Eino, having a particularly keen mind, and Toivo, known for his ability to smell beer a mile away, put their heads together and discovered that Ralph's wife had poured out the Goebels while Ralph was at work. It was cracking cases such as these that gave the

Two Men and a Twelve Pack Detective Agency its excellent reputation, and allowed Eino and Toivo to command such a big fee.

Having settled on their price Eino and Toivo followed Pirto to his truck. The two detectives rummaged through piles of empties, cigarette butts, and garbage in search of clues. The only thing they found of interest was a woman's bra which, as it turned out, belonged to Pirto's old girlfriend and had nothing to do with the case at all. However, Eino, having a most perceptive mind, was quick to point out, "She sure ate a lotta pasties!"

Realizing that this was taking them nowhere, the detectives decided to inspect the scene of the crime. Pirto rapidly drove them to the nearest convenience store where they purchased yet some more beer to drink along the ride. By the time the less than sober trio reached the scene of the crime, all were hearing the same call that Pirto had heard many hours (and many beers) earlier. Pirto went off to mark the territory he had claimed earlier while Eino and Toivo stumbled across the road to find a spot of their own. After finishing his duty Toivo started back to the road but tripped over a tree stump and passed out. Eino was immediately concerned when his partner did not return so he comforted himself by finishing off the rest of the beer with Pirto. Then he went in search of Toivo.

"Toivo, wake up, we haf to crack da case." Eino shook Toivo who quickly came to.

"Ooooh," moaned Toivo as he stood up, "I feel like a big buck poked his antlers in my belly, Ooooh."

Eino Looked down at the spot on the ground where Toivo's stomach had been.

"Look Toivo! Dat beer can on da ground! Dat's why your stomach hurt. You musta landed on dat beer can! You didn't bring your beer wit when you left to take a pee. Dis must be one of da cans from da missing case!"

Eino was even more thrilled when he saw that

I wish these fools would get outa my way! I gotta get to the river!

Trip, Toivo, trip!

All I gotta do is out run Eino!

Continued on Page 30 ☞

DEER CAMP BULLETIN BOARD

Booger,
This is all you get for two beers!

2 beers
6 pack
12 pack reward
to whoever finds my truck Keys!

Booger

What a Babe!

Whoever is wearing my 'em... socks-keep 'em!

TINY EATS 5+

MISS DEER CAMP 1995

Miss Deer Camp Data Sheet

NAME: *Millie "Moose" Millimaki*

BUST: *52-2S* WAIST: *42* HIPS: *54*
HEIGHT: *5'10 1/16"* WEIGHT: *210*

BIRTHDATE: *None of your damn business*
BIRTHPLACE: *The big blueberry patch out south of Ishpeming*

HOBBIES: *Small engine repair, arm wrestling, beer drinking, dwarf tossing.*

FAVORITE MUSIC: *Da Twedy Point Buck, Second Week of Deer Camp, Flintstones Theme Song*

FAVORITE DRINK: *A shot and a beer*

FAVORITE FOOD: *Pasties, cudighis, pizza, cheeseburgers, beans, spaghetti, lasagne, french fries, chocolate cheese cake, venison, pepperoni, potato sausage, juicy T-bone...*

SING ALONG WITH MILLIE
THE SECOND WEEK OF DEER CAMP

LYRICS BY JOE POTILA & JIM DECAIRE
RECORDED BY DA YOOPERS

It's the second week of deer camp. I got a swollen head
I'm lying with the dust balls underneath my bed
An icy breeze is blowing in through the tongue and groove
My pants are frozen to the floor and I'm too sick to move
I didn't drink too many only thirty cans of beer
It must have been that last shot that put me under here

(Chorus)

It's the second week of deer camp and all the guys are here
We drink play cards and shoot the bull but never shoot no deer
The only time we leave the camp is when we go for beer
The second week of deer camp is the greatest time of year

I remember playing poker that weasel musta won
He's wearing my new swampers and sleeping with my gun
He's snoring like a chain saw the camp smells like a dump
Someone's dirty under wear is hanging on the pump
Mukku's in the woodbox Eener's passed out on the stove
His flannel shirt is smoking I wonder if he knows

(Repeat Chorus)

eclairs, raspberry turnovers, pigs feet fried in bear fat, washed down with a couple beers.

PERSONAL NOTE:

I was working as a dancer and bouncer at da Wayside Bar when I heard about da Miss Deer Camp contest. Right away I thought, Millie, dat's for you, so I went and signed up right away. Some of youse guys might tink a girl has to put out a little to win votes from da judges. Well, once I let it be known dat I could kick da crap out of any one of dem judges or all of em put together, I won by a unanimous decision. I got so excited when I won dat I almost peed my drawers. I can't tell ya how trilled I am to be Miss Deer Camp for 1995.

Millie "Moose" Millimaki

Thanks to the
Yellow Snow Gazette
for sponsoring me.
Millie

HOOSH IT?

Imagine that you died and went to heaven. Would you choose to spend eternity at the Deer Camp? We know a lot of yoopers who would. But suppose you went the other way and found yourself trapped for eternity in...

The Deer Camp From Hell
Camp Rules

1. No cussing
2. No drinking
3. No gambling
4. Wake up call at 5:00 a.m.
5. Hunters must be out hunting by dawn
6. All meals will be cholesterol free and fat free
7. Hunters must tell the absolute truth at all times.
8. Hunters must be clean shaven at all times
9. Lights out at 9:00 p.m.
10. Snoring hunters will be permanently transferred to The O.B. Ward from Hell.

10 EXCUSES FOR NOT GETTING A DEER

A list of ten lame all-purpose reasons why you didn't bring home that big buck this year. May be used singly or in combinations.

1. Wife forgot to pack bullets
2. Couldn't shoot straight because gloves didn't fit
3. Lost gun in poker game (The other guys cheated)
4. Someone guys cheated)
5. Wounded a deer but followed false blood trail planted by DNR
6. About to shoot deer, but was suddenly abducted by UFO
7. About to shoot deer, but deer was suddenly abducted by UFO
8. Too sick from eating bad stew
9. Didn't want to show off
10. Got one but it was too small so I threw it back (This one works better for fishing)

Gubba was here

Riddin' Believe It or Shut Up!

Strangest Suicide Attempt

Tapiola, Yooperland USA - Heikki Heikkinen dressed himself up in a deer costume and wandered the woods of Yooperland in a deer costume. During the through the season of 1989 in a During the deer season he was during the deer season attempt. Mr. bizarre suicide attempt! Mr. Heikkinen all misses. "I never knew two weeks of deer season all misses. "I never shot at 337 times all misses." I Heikkinen commented. "Here were so many downstate hunters there here." out there."

Words of whizdom:
Don't do this!

Who died in the outhouse?

the can was the beginning of a trail of empties. Together the detectives followed the trail hoping that the culprit would be at the end. As they neared the 20th can Eino and Toivo heard a loud growl. Eino felt a sudden urge to relieve himself. Toivo puked in the bushes.

"Eino," he said when he was done, "let's get outta here. Dis ain't worth no six pack."

"No, Toivo. What would da people think if we quit now? We gotta protect da reputation of da Two Men and A Twelve Pack Detective Agency!"

Eino and Toivo continued to follow the trail of beer cans, which ended abruptly behind a large rock. They peeked around the rock and received the shock of their lives (second only to the time that Toivo tried his electric razor on the dog while Eino was giving it a bath). Up stood the largest, hairiest, ugliest bear they had ever seen. It had no teeth and one paw missing and a beer can in the other. The bear opened its mouth and let out a humungous, putrid belch. Eino and Toivo did not stick around to question the bear about the missing case. They ran back to Pirto who was "sleeping" in the truck and drove back to town so fast that they eluded two police cars.

The next evening, the news was all over the bars about Old Toothless One Paw, the beer stealing bear, and Eino and Toivo were treated as heroes for having survived the encounter. Pirto didn't even mind that his case was never recovered. In fact he received many free beers long after in exchange for telling his story. As for the Two Men and a Twelve Pack Detective Agency, they are still in business. A few days after the case of the missing case they received another frantic phone call.

"Two Men and a Twelve Pack Detective Agency, dis is Eino how can we help you?"

"Ya, dis is Ralph Heikkela. You gotta help me! When I came home from work I found dat my Hustlers was missing! I don't know what coulda happened to dem!"

"Don't worry Ralph. We're on da way, just as soon as Toivo gets his thumb outta da nail he was poundin...." ■

Martha's Summer Kitchen

Today I was thumbing through my recipe books and I found an error so I promised myself that I would proofread all my recipes. It does remind me of my sister when she did our church cookbook. She typed all the numbers of the table of contents in wrong. So if you were looking for deserts you found meat dishes instead. She was so embarrassed. Our granddaughter is going hunting for the first time. She insists that she is as good as her brother. She always was a little spunky. In this issue I have chosen my favorite Finnish pancake recipe. It's easy and it really tastes good too! My husband's friends really enjoy my pancakes so he makes them every year at deer camp. Good Luck Ensio, and have a safe and fun time hunting. I'll get my venison recipes ready.

Finnish Pancakes

Ingredients

1/4 cup butter
3 eggs
1 tea. salt & sugar
1 cup sifted flour

Preheat oven to 400 degrees. Pour 1/4 cup of butter in a 9 X 13 pan and melt.

Beat 3 eggs. Add 1 tea. salt and sugar, 3 cups of milk. Spoon in 1 cup sifted flour, 2 table-spoons at a time. Beat by hand until smooth. Pour into very hot pan and bake 30-40 minutes. Pancake will fluff very high, then flatten as it cools. Serve with butter, jelly, syrup, etc.

Answers to Twisted Trivia

1. On the outside.
2. Because then Green Bay would want one too. (No hate mail, please -we're only Kidding!)
3. That's when Yoopers run out meat from the deer they shot in July.
4. Get wet.
5. All his life.
6. Six, including the spare tire & steering wheel.
7. For a long time.
8. The one nearest the top.
9. It's too far to walk.
10. We had to make sure you'd get at least one right.

See below your score and evaluation

0-Correct
Your mom would be proud.
1-3 Correct
Maybe not.
4-6 Correct
We're beginning to worry about you.
7-9 Correct
No more beer for you.

ALL 10 CORRECT
Just sit quietly and eat your flies.

December 1, 1995 | **Christmas** | Yellow Snow, Michigan

ORIGINAL DICKENS MANUSCRIPT FOUND!

Reprinted here is the original draft of the Dickens classic, A Christmas Carol The manuscript was found in an abandoned outhouse in Bruce Crossing, where Dickens is said to have spent a winter. After returning to England and drying out, he rewrote the story. Had he left it as originally written, it might have become a great piece of literature.

Old Barley was as dead as a doornail. That has to be understood before any of this story makes any sense. Old Barley was a ghost, and you have to be dead to be a ghost. That's the law according to Casper. Barley was dead. And Old Stooge was hung over. I mean really hung over. After killing a fifth of Old Barley the night before, who wouldn't have a rip-roaring case of the cotton-mouth heebie-jeebies? Stooge was in a dark mood, partly

Believe It or Shut Up!

Strange Santa

On Christmas Eve of 1970 Rudy Kempinen of Baraga drank two fifths of Kessler's while assembling a bicycle for his son, without looking at the instructions! On Christmas morning the bicycle was fully assembled and there were enough parts left over to build a blender!

because of the hangover, but mostly because it was his nature. Old Stooge had a heart as cold as a well digger's derriere. That could be pretty cold, unless the guy was digging the well in Arizona or somewhere on a hot day. Of course, if he was digging the well in someplace like northern Canada in January, his butt would be really cold. But then, who would try to dig a well in a place like that when the ground was all frozen? Wouldn't he wait until summer? Besides, if he wanted water in January, all he'd have to do is melt snow. But I digress. Let it be sufficient to say that Old Stooge was a cold-hearted dude.

Stooge ran a lumber company that was doing some cutting just north of Ishpeming. On this day, December 24, he sat in his office, a two room tarpaper shack, trying to figure out how to short his employees on their wages. He couldn't come up with a way to do it that he could get away with, and that made him even crabbier. His clerk, Bob Catshit, hunched over his desk in the next room trying to look industrious, shuffling papers and sharpening pencils. A small icicle hung from his nose, and he shivered constantly. Old Stooge allowed him one stick of hardwood a day for the pot belly stove in the corner. As Stooge liked to say, wood doesn't grow on trees. Besides, a cold worker is more likely to stay active. Bob Catshit looked busy, but Old Stooge suspected that the shiftless no-account had one eye on the clock at all times. As soon as the clock ticked quitting time, Bob Catshit walked over and knocked at the open doorway that separated the two rooms.

"Don't tell me," Old Stooge snarled, "you'll be wanting the whole day off tomorrow, right?"

"Well--it is Christmas," Bob Catshit said, his voice trembling slightly. "And it's only one day a year."

"Christmas!" Stooge exploded. "Bah--uh--ah--er--," he groped for a word.

"Humbug, sir?" Bob Catshit offered timidly.

Old Stooge's neck veins popped out. "Humbug?" he roared. "What kind of a silly word is that? #X@&*%>!" Now there's a word! That's what I meant to say! Bah, #X@&*%>!"

Bob Catshit had never heard of such a word, and he hoped he'd never have to spell it. Old Stooge stood up and shook a skinny finger at the quaking clerk. "I suppose you must have the whole day tomorrow! But be in to work all the earlier the next day!"

"Okay, boss," Bob Catshit called over his shoulder as he ran for the door, "and Merry Christmas!"

"Christmas!" Old Stooge spat. "Bah, #X@&*%>!"

Old Stooge climbed into bed early that night, hoping to get a good night's sleep and recover from the effects of the fifth of Old Barley. He endured the usual spiders and snakes that crawled over him as he tried to relax. He had learned from watching *Lost Weekend* on the movie channel that the spiders and snakes weren't real. They were just tricks that this mind played as he went through Old Barley withdrawal. But just as he was about to drift off to sleep, he began hearing things.

"Pssst," a hushed voice said. "Hey, you!"

Stooge sat up in bed. "Who is it?" he whispered. "Where are you?"

"Over here by the fireplace," the voice answered.

Stooge peeked out between the bed curtains, expecting to see some horrible disembodied spirit. He was somewhat relieved to see a big California raisin perched on the hearth.

"What do you want?" Stooge snapped. "Can't you see I'm trying to sleep?"

The raisin waddled over to the bed. "Sorry," he said. "We got business."

"Business?" Stooge repeated. "What business?"

"Well, first of all," the raisin said, "I must warn you that I'm sort of a beginner at this." He hopped up on the edge of the bed. "Usually our company sends three spirits for a job like this. But we've had some budget cuts and downsizing. All the spirits have been let go."

Stooge stroked his chin thoughtfully. "Downsizing--of course! Why didn't I think of that?"

"Pay attention," the raisin scolded. "We don't have all night." He jumped off the bed. "Come with me," he said. "I want to show you something." He pulled Stooge out of bed and led him over to the couch. Then the raisin plopped his wrinkled butt down and picked up the remote control. "Now watch," he said. "Here are a few scenes from Christmas past."

He punched the play button and a picture came onto the screen of Stooge's big-screen TV. A small boy sat in the corner of a bare room pulling the wings off of flies and repeating, "She loves me, she loves me not..."

"Hey, that's me!" Stooge said.

"Right," the raisin said. "And, I recall, it ended in 'she loves me not.' You never recovered from the heartbreak." He fast forwarded through a series of commercials. "Here you are a few years later," he said. "This is where you met Old Barley." On the screen was a young but dirty and unshaven man dressed in rags, lying against the curb outside the Ruptured Moose Tavern. He was tipping a fifth of Old Barley. "You spent the last of your inheritance on that bottle," the raisin continued. "Then you had to go to work, so your uncle got you a job in the lumber business, where you schemed and cheated your way up to where you are now."

"So what's your point?" Stooge was getting impatient.

"Let's fast forward to Christmas of the present," the raisin said.

There appeared on the screen a small tarpaper shanty cowering in a stand of lofty jackpines. A small outhouse perched in the snow about fifty yards behind the shanty. As they watched, the outhouse door flew open and Bob Catshit lurched out, bent almost double under the burden he carried. On his shoulders sat a short but very round little boy who laughed cheerfully as Bob Catshit stumbled through the snow. Attached to the little boy's leg just below the knee was the decaying remains of a raccoon, its teeth buried in the boy's flesh. The raccoon appeared to have been deceased for quite some time.

"That's my clerk, Bob Catshit, and his son, Tiny Otto!"

"Yes," the raisin said. "Tiny Otto, as a small child, wandered away into the woods one day and was attacked by a belligerent raccoon. The animal attached itself to the boy's leg, and in attempting to remove it, the boy's father beat it to death. In death, the animal's jaws locked up. Now only a trained taxidermist can remove it, but Bob Catshit can't afford to have it done on the wages you pay."

"So what?" Stooge said. "The boy is not so bad off. At least he has a pet that can't run away. He even gave it a name--Skipper, I think"

"It is not uncommon for people to give names to their handicaps," the raisin said. "It somehow makes them easier to live with. I believe you named yours 'Mr. Happy,' didn't you?"

Old Stooge scowled and turned a little red around the ears. "Now watch," the raisin continued, fast forwarding once more.

Now on the screen was the interior of the tarpaper shanty. A tired looking woman was busy making pasties, doing laundry, overhauling a snowblower engine, and trying to control a herd of screaming kids. She glanced out the window.

"All right, kids," she said, wiping her hands on her apron, "here comes your father with Tiny Otto and Skipper. Clothespins, everyone." The kids obediently lined up like brave little soldiers. Mrs. Catshit pulled clothespins out of her apron pocket went down the line, clamping a clothespin on each little nose. Then she clamped one on her own.

"Why does Tiny Otto stink so?" asked one of the little rug rats.

"It's not Tiny Otto, dear," the woman answered. "It's Skipper. And he seems to be getting worse every day." She sighed heavily and went back to her pasties.

"Okay," Stooge grumbled, "So the kid has a B.O. problem. I'll buy him a Mennen speed stick. I hope this show gets better. So far the plot has been pretty weak."

"Hey, lighten up," the raisin scolded. "This got two thumbs up from Siskel & Ebert." He motioned to the screen. "Now watch these scenes from Christmas yet to come."

A woman stood among a cheering and applauding studio audience. As the applause died down she spoke:

"Good morning and welcome to 'We'll Do Anything For Ratings.' On today's show our topic is 'Children Who Have To Wear Clothespins On Their Noses Because Their Brother Has A Rotting Raccoon Attached To His Leg'. Let's say hello to our guests today, the Catshit family."

The audience cheered and applauded. On one end of the stage was a row of chairs in which all the Catshit children sat, clothespins in place. On the other end of the stage sat Tiny Otto and Skipper.

"First, I want to get some thoughts from our studio audience," the woman said. She stuck the microphone in the face of a pimply faced girl who chewed a big wad of gum. "What is your reaction?" she asked.

"Well," the pimply faced girl said, "Like, if he wants to have a dead raccoon on his leg, y'know, that should be his right, y'know—like, I mean, doesn't it say something about that in the Decoration of Independence?" She blew a bubble and twirled her hair around her finger as the studio audience erupted into a rehearsed chorus of boos, hoots, and howls.

A big guy in a Love it or Leave it T-shirt jumped up and grabbed the mike. "Instead of all this complaining and whining," he shouted, pointing a finger at the Catshits, "why don't you all get jobs and pay taxes like me!?"

A skinny, sharp-nosed woman in a business suit snatched the microphone from his hand. "I think you are all suffering from an acute case of raccoon envy!" she screeched. Then everyone started yelling at once.

Old Stooge's eyes grew wide in horror as he watched. Other audience members got up and voiced their learned opinions, some in favor of wearing a dead raccoon, some opposed, and some unable to make a commitment. Tiny Otto and Skipper and the rest of the Catshit children sat on stage like sideshow freaks. Stooge began to feel sick to his stomach.

"Why?" he asked. "What could possibly make the Catshits want to degrade themselves like that? No one deserves that kind of humiliation, not even them!" Stooge turned away from the screen, shielding his eyes. "No more, please," he begged. "Turn it off!"

The raisin punched the power button and the screen went blank. "They had to go on that show, and many more like it," he said. "It's the only way they could make enough money to pay the taxidermist to remove Skipper."

"No!" Old Stooge cried. "This must not be!" He dropped to his knees and clasped his hands together. "Please," he begged. "tell me that I can change what I just saw!" He collapsed on the floor in a fit of sobbing. "I'll pay for the taxidermist!" he cried, pounding on the floor with his fist. "I'll pay...I'll pay...I'll pay..."

Epilogue

Old Stooge was as good as his word. He went to meetings to exorcise Old Barley's ghost, and became a new man. He not only paid to have Skipper removed from Tiny Otto's leg, he even had a coonskin cap made, which he gave to Tiny Otto as a Christmas gift so that Tiny Otto would always have Skipper with him and would never be alone. Stooge also paid for nose jobs for the entire Catshit family, whose noses had become hideously deformed from wearing clothespins on them for so long. He even gave Bob Catshit a raise and a promotion and he bought Mrs. Catshit a brand new used snowblower. And that is the story of how Old Stooge found the spirit of Christmas. May all of our hearts be full of the joy of Christmas this year, and may we never have to go on daytime talk shows to raise money for cosmetic taxidermy—and God bless us every one!

How to keep 'em Whipped!

Gravel Gertie's
Husband Training Tips

Dear Gertie,
My husband informed me that we have several business Xmas parties to attend this year. So he surprised me and brought me a new outfit. It is the most awful looking outfit I have ever seen. I love my husband and I don't want to hurt his feelings, but I can't go out in public wearing that horrible outfit. Please help me out of this situation.
Ronald McDonald Look-alike

Dear Ron,
My Eugene once bought me a checkered dress that looked like it was made out of a tablecloth. When I tried it on I looked like a walking kitchen table. I used Eugene's own ignorance against him to solve the problem. I made up a phony tag that gave instructions for washing the dress and I sewed it inside. The instructions said to wash in very hot water with 6 cups of bleach. Then I asked Eugene to put the dress in the washer for me and to follow the washing instructions on the tag. He had no idea that the instructions were false. Naturally, the dress was ruined. I made sure I was there at the end of the wash cycle so he couldn't sneak out and buy another to replace it. Not only did I get rid of the dress, I also had the added pleasure of making Eugene feel like a total idiot for ruining it. He felt so low that he gave me some money to go and buy an outfit for myself.
Gertie,

Dear Gertie,
Every year at Christmas my husband's brother comes to visit and he always stays for a week. I don't think he takes a bath all year, and he just lounges around, drinking beer, smoking cigars, and sweating all over my furniture. I can't say anything because my husband is always so happy to see him. What should I do?
Ready to puke

Dear pukey,
Set him on fire.
Gertie

Dear Gertie,
My husband John is driving me nuts. He wants to buy a Christmas gift for his boss, but the man seems to have everything. John is no good at making decisions and he has given me the total responsibility of picking out a gift. His boss is single and lives in a $250,000 home with a four car garage, and four new cars to go in it. He dresses in tailor made suits and seems to already have the best of everything. What could I possibly get for him that he doesn't already have?
Stumped

Dear stump,
Are you nuts? Wrap yourself up and have yourself delivered! As for your loser husband, get him a Christmas card that begins with "Dear John..." But if you have grown used to the bum and don't like that idea, here's another option. Buy the guy a gift subscription to The Yellow Snow Gazette. That'll make him think your old man actually has some sophistication and taste. It might even mean a promotion or a raise.
Gertie

Dear Gertie,
My husband argues with me about everything. No matter what we talk about, he always disagrees, and before long we're in a heated argument. The only way I can end an argument with him is to give in and agree with him. How do you win an argument with a husband who just won't listen to reason?
Wanna Win One

Dear Wanna,
The same way I win arguments with my Eugene—a haymaker to the jaw.
Gertie

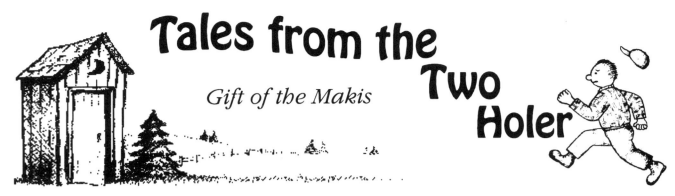

Tales from the Two Holer

Gift of the Makis

Heikki and Alma Maki had been married for thirty years, and at war for twenty-nine. At first, after hearing some of their fights, the neighbors, the nearest of which lived half a mile away, wondered how long they would last together. But over the years they decided that Heikki and Alma must get some kind of happiness out of their relationship, because no matter how often or viciously they fought, they always stuck together and defended each other against any criticism from outsiders. A few days before the Christmas of their 30th year together, Heikki perched on the pot, reading his Yellow Snow Gazette and thinking about Alma. Times had been pretty tough. His unemployment had run out and the flooring mill wasn't hiring. The mines were laying off people left and right, and Heikki was not interested in any aeronautical engineering or computer programming positions. So he sat, thinking. How to buy Alma something nice for Christmas? Then it hit him. Sell something! But what? Everything Heikki had was at the bottom of the hand-me-down chain. Except for one thing. His old 28-gauge shotgun. It was a Sears and Roebuck model that he bought brand new many years ago. It was beaten and worn, but his brother had offered him twenty-five bucks for it not too long ago. So Heikki resolved to sell his shotgun to buy Alma a footstool, so she could put her feet up when she sat in her favorite armchair to rest her bad back. He'd seen a fancy footstool with flowers on it in the window of the second-hand store downtown. It was the perfect gift. He could buy it and have enough left over for a few beers at the Buck Snort Bar. He went to the closet and got his shotgun. Then he bundled against the cold up and headed down the road toward town.

As Heikki headed up the driveway, Alma sat in her favorite armchair, smoking her Camels and drinking her coffee, thinking about how she could manage to get something nice for Heikki. She had no money, and she wasn't good at knitting so she couldn't make him anything. So she thought and thought and finally it came to her. Sell

"Ho Ho... HOLYOWHA!"

something! But what? She thought and thought some more and finally she remembered that every time her sister came to visit, she would plop down in Alma's favorite armchair. Even though it was well worn and the stuffing was falling out in places, she said it was the most comfortable chair she ever sat in, and if Alma ever wanted to get rid of it, she'd give her twenty-five bucks for it. It was hard for Alma to think about giving up her favorite chair, but she had the Christmas spirit, and she finally decided that she would sell the chair to buy a gift for Heikki. And she knew just what to buy. She'd seen that genuine simulated leather gun case in the window at the sporting goods store downtown, and it would be perfect. Heikki loved that old shotgun of his, and he'd be thrilled to get a new genuine simulated leather case for it. She could buy it and have a little left over for Bingo. So she called her sister and asked if the offer still stood. Her sister agreed to the price, saying that Alma could come and pick up the money tonight if she wanted to, and her sister's husband would come an haul the chair in the morning. So Alma put on her good coat for the walk into town.

Heikki walked along the icy sidewalk from his brother's house toward the second-hand store. The only problem was that to get there, he had to walk right by the Buck Snort Bar. It was cold outside, and the warm glow emanating from the window looked pretty inviting. Heikki decided that he'd stop in and warm up with a shot and a beer before continuing on to the second-hand store.

Alma counted her money as she walked from her sister's house toward the sporting goods store. She couldn't wait to see Heikki's face when he found the brand new genuine simulated leather gun case under the tree. The only problem was, to get to the sporting goods store from her sister's house, Alma had to walk right past the Bingo Hall. It was awfully cold out, and she decided to go in and warm up, and maybe play a card or two before continuing on her way.

Hours later, Heikki stumbled out the door of the Buck Snort Bar. He was really depressed. He hadn't meant to have the second or third round, or the fourth or fifth. He really hadn't intended to buy a round for the house, but when he had Kessler's and beer in him, his self-control seemed to fly out the window, and all his money right along with it. As he plodded along through the snow toward home, cursing himself for his stupidity, he spied Alma. She was trudging along on the other side of the street with her head down, muttering to herself. Then she noticed Heikki. Upon seeing him, she was overcome by guilt and confessed that she had blown his Christmas gift money at the Bingo Hall. Not to be out done, Heikki told her how he had spent the money for her gift at the Bar. Since each was equally guilty, they couldn't even fight about it, so they trudged homeward silently. After a long silence Alma turned to Heikki and said, "You know, It's he thought that counts."

"You're right, old woman," He agreed, "It's the thought that counts. So, as Heikki thought about Alma being run over by a cement truck, and she thought about him being trampled by a big, nasty bull moose, they hummed a little Christmas carol all the way home. ■

How twisted are you?
Take this simple test and find out.
Answers & psychiatric profile on page 40

Twisted Trivia Question?

(Hint: Think really stupid)

1. Where is the North Pole?
2. If it doesn't snow in Hawaii, what makes the snow fall in Yooperland?
3. What was President Andrew Johnson's wife's name?
4. Who was the first white man to be buried in Yooperland?
5. Why does Santa Claus say, "Ho, Ho, Ho?"
6. Why does Santa wear red?
7. How many grains of sand would you guess there are in the world?
8. What color is blue?
9. What is that spot on your chin?
10. How would you smell after a month without a bath?

The Night Before Christmas

T'was da night before Christmas in dis Yooper house,
en nutting was stirring, not even our mouse.
Da rest of da family was all fast asleep,
wit visions of pasties delivered by jeep.
Da swampers was hung by da chimney wit care,
in hope dat St. Nikkola soon would be dere.
En in da far corner, was lovely to see,
da Bosch cans en cabbage dat hung from da tree.
Ma home from da mine, me out on parole,
she was snoring in bed, I was perched on da bowl.
Den all of a sudden da house starts to shudder,
Some nut's on da roof en he broke da rain gutter!
He jumps down da chimney en swears cause it's tight.
I hide behind beer cases way outa sight.
He lands in da fireplace en singes his hair,
on some busted up orange crates still burning in dere.
He climbs from da fireplace en I take a look.
He's just like dey show him in my coloring book.
Wit vodka-glazed eyes en a gut like a bubble,
a five day old beard en dere's soot on da stubble.
His teeth when he smile look like grampa's swede saw.
He wears tennis shoes big as grizzly bear's paw.
Dis old Yooper elf gives me nutting to fear,
as he heads for da kitchen for cookies en beer.
He kills off a six-pack den belches en smirks,
en grabs his potato sack, ready to work.
Now under da tree he is starting to set,
da most beautiful presents us Yoopers can get.
A new pasty-matic en snowblower for mudder,
a brand new chain saw en some choppers for brudder.
Some mud flaps, a CB, en a new used weed wacker,
a helmet en nightshirt dat says Green Bay Packer.
He close up da sack en jumps back in da coals,
en hollering, "OUCH!" up da chimney he rose.
He grunted en groaned as he tossed out his bag,
en he cracked such a beer fart, I'm startin' to gag.
I must watch him leave so I rushes outside.
I looks up at da roof while in bushes I hide.
En what does I see when I looks troo da twigs?
Dis rusty old car body, pulled by eight pigs!
Santa jump in en he give 'em all hell,
"Let's go all youse pigs, don't just sit dere en smell!
On Rudy, on Heikki, on Lempi en Joe,
en alla youse udders what names I don't know!
Fly over Negaunee, den turn to da right!
We make Houghton-Hancock before I get tight!"
Den I heard him exclaim wit a cynical sneer,
"Pull in at dat Bosch sign—I run outa beer!"

SCIENCE DEPARTMENT

NMU Prof. Discovers Space Age Fruitcake

Excerpts from the notes of distinguished NMU Professor, Eino Aho, on his latest scientific discovery, printed by permission of National Mine University.

One day as I dug through my closet looking for Christmas decorations, I saw a string of lights on the top shelf, barely out of reach. I stretched and reached and finally managed to grasp it. As I pulled, something hard and heavy came down on my head, rendering me unconscious for quite some time. When I regained consciousness I discovered that the object in question was a fruitcake given to me for Christmas by my sister-in-law last year. The fruitcake was made from her own special recipe. It was in a petrified state that seemed to keep it from decomposing. This made me curious, so I took the fruitcake to my laboratory at National Mine University to run some tests. In attempting to break a sample off the fruitcake for analysis I used every method known to man, but I was unable to cut it. Saws, drills, cutting torches, even lasers were unable to make a mark on it. Intense heat, frigid cold, even explosives had no effect. Somehow, my sister-in-law had invented the hardest material known to man. I contacted her and she gave me an old shopping list, upon the back of which she had scribbled the recipe. She cautioned me that it was the only copy she had. I immediately notified my colleagues at NASA, informing them that I had discovered a space age material that may be of immense value to the space program. They immediately sent a team of scientists to verify my claim. After extensive tests, they concurred with my findings. Something in the fruitcake caused it to become petrified after a short period of curing and aging, and no force known to modern science could destroy or damage it. We calculated that a spacecraft constructed of the fruitcake material one thousandth of an inch thick would have the strength of the hardest steel three feet in thickness, but would weigh only 120 pounds. Our excitement grew as we discussed the possible uses for the new space age fruitcake. Its benefits to mankind would be immeasurable. Plans were immediately put into motion to build facilities for mass production of the material. Teams of engineers, chemists, and physicists were assembled to work on the project. There was even talk around the scientific community of a possible Nobel prize nomination. Then disaster struck. While driving to the laboratory to deliver the formula, my stomach began to gurgle and churn. I had to make an emergency bush call. I pulled over and made a dignified dash for the bushes. After finishing my business there, I realized that I had not brought along my emergency roll of paper. Luckily, I found in my pocket an old shopping list that served me well. After completing the paperwork I continued on to the laboratory. Upon arriving there I discovered to my horror that the fruitcake formula was nowhere to be found. I was sure I had it in my pocket when I left home...

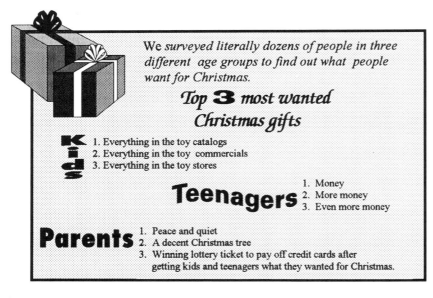

We *surveyed literally dozens of people in three different age groups to find out what people want for Christmas.*

Top 3 most wanted Christmas gifts

Kids
1. Everything in the toy catalogs
2. Everything in the toy commercials
3. Everything in the toy stores

Teenagers
1. Money
2. More money
3. Even more money

Parents
1. Peace and quiet
2. A decent Christmas tree
3. Winning lottery ticket to pay off credit cards after getting kids and teenagers what they wanted for Christmas.

Profound and Inspiring Poetry Section

Little birdie in the sky
dropped some
whitewash in my eye
I don't worry, I don't cry
I'm just glad that cows
don't fly

In our last episode... *Yooperman survived his fall by landing on a really fat deer hunter, who invited him to the deer camp, where Yooperman drank just one too many beers. He ran for the outhouse to hurl his lunch and every other meal he had ever eaten. But as he made a dive for the outhouse hole, he caught his foot on the step and fell headlong down the hole. Mercifully, before he hit bottom, everything went black...*

When Toivo first woke up, he thought he was back home with his muskrat family. Maybe it was all a bad dream. Maybe he had never left muskrat mama to go out into the world to seek his fortune. Maybe there were no little blue guys, and Benny was just a ghost that inhabited his dreams, along with Buck Owens, Minnie Pearl, and all the rest of them. He sat up an shook his head to clear the cobwebs. There was a small rattling sound. He closed his eyes and saw a cornfield. No one popped up out of it. They must still be asleep, he thought. It was real, all right. He was in a cave of some sort. Next to him was a little pile of glowing coals, and covering him were a few mangy, moth-eaten animal skins. Just then there was a rustling, scraping sound from the mouth of the cave and Benny appeared, bent under the weight of a bulging burlap sack that he carried on his shoulder. His little blue face was almost purple from the effort. He threw the sack down with a sigh of relief.

"Oh, you're awake," he said. "I thought you were gonna sleep until June"

Yooperman yawned and stretched. "How did I get here?" he asked. "How long did I sleep? Where are we? Whatcha got in the bag? Where do babies come from—?"

"Hold it!" Benny commanded. "The answers to your questions are, in order, I brought you here, you haven't been sleeping, you've been in a coma for five weeks, we're in a cave, stupid, and I've got food in the bag. As for the last question, you don't wanna know." Benny proceeded to empty the contents of the sack. There were a few dozen jars of pickled herring, about five dozen twinkies, and a paper bag full of rubber bathtub stoppers.

Yooperman picked up one of the bathtub stoppers and looked it over. "What are these for?" he asked.

Benny snatched it away and took a bite out of it. "Those are for me," he said as he chewed. "They're the only earth food that seems to agree with me, except for beer." He reached into the sack and pulled out a twelve pack of Pabst Blue Ribbon.

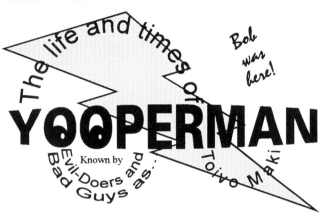

Yooperman's stomach flip-flopped. "None for me, thanks," he said. "I'll just have these." He began to wolf down the pickled herring and twinkies.

As they ate, Benny filled Yooperman in on what had transpired since the fiasco at the deer camp. Benny had followed him to the outhouse, and just as Yooperman tumbled into the hole, Benny had fired the anti-gravity gun that he now carried, since Yooperman seemed to have a real problem with falling. He had snagged Yooperman with the anti-gravity field just in the nick of time. Yooperman, after just one too many beers, had passed out. Benny had brought him to the cave and made him comfortable, and had been watching over him for the last five weeks.

"Wait a minute," Yooperman said. "If you have an anti-gravity gun, how come you didn't use it on that heavy bag?"

"Because I drained the batteries using it to carry you here," Benny said. "And you know how it is when you need batteries. The only size nobody has in stock is the size you need. I looked everywhere, and nobody has size ꝏꝏꝏ plutonium alkaline batteries."

Suddenly Yooperman cocked his head and listened. "Did you hear that?"

"What?" Benny listened. A voice, muffled by the heavy winter snow, was faintly audible, coming from outside. It sounded like an angry voice. Though they couldn't make out any words, the unmistakable tone of cussing came through clearly. They crawled to the mouth of the cave and peeked out. In the snow covered clearing outside the cave stood a very fat man dressed in red, cursing a bunch of deer who seemed to be milling around in confusion. They were attached to a big sled, and they appeared to be tangled in their traces. Some were having trouble staying on their feet, and one with a big red nose was curled up in the snow, fast asleep.

"Well," Benny said, "here's your chance to do a good deed. It looks like he could use some help."

Yooperman got up and brushed himself off. "I'll handle this," he said. "You wait here." He stepped out of the cave and approached the fat guy in the red suit. "Can I help you?" he asked.

The fat guy in the red suit turned, startled, and his mouth dropped open. "And I thought I dressed funny," he half whispered to himself. Then he regained his composure. "Who the heck are you supposed to be?" he snapped.

Yooperman stood up straight and puffed out his chest. "I'm Yooperman, the world's greatest superhero," he said proudly.

"Ya, and I'm the King of England," the fat guy in the red suit said.

Yooperman was puzzled, but he held out his hand anyway. "Pleased to meetcha," he said. If England wanted to have two kings, he figured that was their business.

The fat guy in the red suit shook his head. "No—," he said, "I didn't mean that literally—I'm Santa Claus." he peered at Yooperman over the top of his wire-rimmed glasses. "Don't you know Santa Claus?"

Yooperman felt sorry for the fat guy in the red suit. He had been struggling with an identity crisis of his own, and it was no picnic. He went along with the old guy. "Oh, ya, Santa Claus," he said, slapping himself in the head. "What was I thinking? Of course I know Santa Claus!" He looked back toward the cave and made an idiot face at Benny, then he turned back to Santa. "What seems to be the problem here?"

"It's these blasted reindeer," Santa said. "They got into the root cellar and gorged themselves on the wife's pie apples just before we took off. Well, those apples must have been fermented pretty good, cause after about an hour, my reindeer started weaving all over the sky. I finally had to make an emergency landing. So here I am stranded, with my reindeer falling down drunk, and me with a load of toys to deliver." He sat down in the snow and held his head in his hands. "I don't know what I'm gonna do," he sobbed. "I've never missed a delivery before. I can't bear the thought of all those little children waking up on Christmas morning and finding that old Santa had let them down." He turned his tear-stained face up to Yooperman. "What am I gonna do?" he sniffed.

Yooperman was a sucker for a sad story, and soon he was blubbering right along with the old guy. He knew he had to help. He thought hard for a moment. It hurt a lot, but this was important, so he ignored the pain and kept on thinking. It didn't work. "Wait here," he said. He bounded through the snow to the cave entrance where Benny sat munching on a bathtub stopper and sipping a beer.

"What's up?" Benny asked.

Yooperman explained the prob-

lem. Benny listened, and as the story went on his face began to brighten. He had studied earth customs and legends and knew all about Santa Claus. "This is a great opportunity," he said. "Of all the good deeds you could do, helping Santa out of a jam is the best. This will make you a hero for sure."

"But how can I help?" Yooperman asked.

Benny grinned. "With a little help from our advanced technology, it'll be easy," he said. "Here's what we'll do. We are going to deliver the toys for Santa."

"How?" Yooperman scratched his head.

"Just leave it to me," Benny said. He went to a boulder near the back of the cave and pulled a suitcase from behind it. He opened it up and

Hairold

began rummaging through it. "Ah, here they are," he said finally, and held up two small objects. They looked to Yooperman like shiny metal long neck beer bottles.

"What are they?" he asked.

"Plutonium propulsion modules," Benny replied. "Strap these babies to the runners on the sleigh and you could fly it to the moon if you wanted to.

"But how do you steer?" Yooperman asked.

"With this," Benny said. He held up what appeared to be a TV remote control.

"Holyowha!" Yooperman exclaimed. "Let's do it!"

They hurried back outside where Santa sat in the snow. He looked up when he heard them coming. "Oh, you again," he said glumly. "Who's

the smurf?" he asked motioning to Benny.

"This is my sidekick, Benny," Yooperman said. Benny made a sour face. "We have solved your problem," Yooperman went on. "We'll deliver your toys for you."

He explained the plan to Santa. At first Santa wanted to deliver the toys himself, but when Yooperman told him how dangerous it was for deer in the woods of Yooperland, it was decided that Santa would stay and keep the reindeer in the cave to protect them from violators. While Santa shooed the drunken herd into the cave, Benny strapped the plutonium propulsion modules to the sleigh and he and Yooperman climbed aboard.

"We'll be back in the morning," Yooperman called to Santa. "If you get hungry, help yourself to some pickled herring and twinkies."

"The bathtub stoppers are mine," Benny added. "and I know just how many there are!" Then he grabbed the remote control from Yooperman, who was fiddling with the buttons. "I'll drive," he said. He punched a button and the propulsion modules whined, then roared and shot out purple flame. The sleigh shot into the sky and was out of sight in seconds.

All through the night Yooperman and Benny flew, stopping on every rooftop, delivering toys to every good little boy and girl. Since they didn't have a list of which children were naughty and which were nice, they just delivered gifts to all of them. Yooperman made sure he ate all the cookies and drank all the milk that the children had put out for Santa. Benny was a little disappointed at how few households use rubber bathtub stoppers anymore. They made good time with Benny's propulsion system, and in record time they were finished with the deliveries and headed home.

"Hey, look," Yooperman cried suddenly, "there's still one gift left in this bag. I thought we emptied it." He pulled out a small package. It was wrapped in silver paper with gold ribbons, and there was a small tag attached. "Hey," Yooperman exclaimed, "it says 'To Yooperman from Santa!' I wonder what's in it?" He held it up to his ear and gave it a shake.

"It seems logical that the best way

to find out would be to open it," Benny replied.

"Good idea," Yooperman agreed, and tore open the package. "Wow!" he cried excitedly, "It's a remote control." Then he scratched his head. "Gosh, I wish I had a TV to go with it."

"Let me see the box it came in," Benny said. He grabbed the box and pulled an instruction booklet out of it. "According to this," he said, "what you have there is a brain-wave descrambler. With that you can unscramble your brain waves so that you'll be able to receive any channel you want through the salad bowl in your head."

"Cool!" Yooperman exclaimed. "I'm gonna try it." He shut his eyes and punched a button on the descrambler. Instantly a beer commercial popped into view. "It works!" he cried. He flipped through the channels until he found the 24-hour Gilligan's Island channel. "Let me know when we get home," he said. He put the descrambler on the seat and settled back to watch Gilligan.

Dawn was still hours away when Benny went into a holding pattern at about a thousand feet above the cave. He set the cruise control on the plutonium propulsion modules and put his remote control on the seat next to him. Then he sat back to take in the scenery. The moon was bright, and the snowy wonderland below glowed in its light. Benny was accustomed to the cold, steady glare of the stars in outer space, but here on this world, on this night, the stars twinkled and seemed to flicker with a warm candle-like glow. The night was still, not with the stark, empty silence of space, but with a warm sort of quiet that made him feel strange inside. He'd never felt quite this way before. The inhabitants of this world may be backward, even primitive, he thought, but they had something here.

"Hey, Benny?" Yooperman interrupted his mood.

"What?"

"You didn't get a gift."

"Yes, I did," Benny said.

"Oh, Good." Yooperman felt around on the seat for his brain-wave descrambler. "I'm gonna see what else is on," he said. In the darkness he grabbed Benny's remote control by mistake.

"No, you idiot!" Benny screamed, but it was too late. Yooperman had already punched the button, and the sleigh suddenly did a barrel roll. Benny and Yooperman were both thrown from the sled and found themselves falling through space.

Rusty Chevrolet

Dashing through the snow in my rusty chevrolet
Down the road I go sliding all the way
I need new piston rings   I need some new snow tires
My car is held together by a piece of chicken wire

Rust and smoke the heater's broke the door just blew away
I light a match to see the dash and then I start to pray
The frame is bent, the muffler went, the radio it's OK
Oh what fun it is to drive this rusty chevrolet

I went to the IGA to get some Christmas cheer
I just passed up my left front tire and it's getting hard to steer
Skidding down the Highway right past the Negaunee cops
I had to drag my swampers to get the car to stop

Rust and smoke the heather's broke the door just blew away
I light a match to see the dash and then I start to pray
The frame is bent, the muffler went, the radio it's OK
Oh what fun it is to drive this Rusty Chevrolet

Bouncing through the snowdrifts in a big blue cloud of smoke
People laugh as I drive by I wonder what's the joke
I got to get to Shopko to pick up the layaway
Cause Santa Claus is coming soon in his big old Rusty Sleigh

Rust and smoke the heater's broke the door just blew away
I light a match to see the dash and then I start to pray
The frame is bent, the muffler went, the radio it's OK
Oh what fun it is to drive this Rusty Chevrolet

"I'm beginning to see a pattern developing here!" Benny shouted to Yooperman as they plunged toward the earth a thousand feet below...

to counseling? If a giant meteor destroyed the earth tomorrow, how would that affect our plans for next weekend?

What, again? Oh well...will Yooperman survive the fall? Will Benny? Will they ever find some bad guys' butts to kick? Will Santa's reindeer admit they have a problem and agree

For the answers to some of these questions, ask someone really smart. For the rest, turn to page 47 for the next barely believable episode of YOOPER-MAN!

Martha's
Summer Kitchen

I like making my home-made paper bows from leftover pieces of wrapping paper. Ensio helps me put my bows on packages and decorate the house with them. I noticed my sister used hers last Christmas for covering up her mistakes —like the 2 inch gap where the wrapping paper didn't quite meet together. She told her grandson it was a new recycling idea she had. I think my sister should write a book about recycling tips. Who knows, it could be a best seller. During the holidays we bake cookies and make candy and lots of goodies. But I like to make Cardamom loafs and give them away for gifts. Everyone seems to really enjoy getting bread instead of fruit cake. Have a Merry Christmas and a Happy new Year. Martha & Ensio

Christmas Paper Bows

1. Collect a small pile of wrapping paper scraps. (the key is to use high-quality paper otherwise they may tear.)

2. Cut the scraps into strips about 4 inches to 6 inches long and 1/2 inch or less wide. Different width will give the bow added texture.

3. Take one of the strips of paper and lay it across another at a right angle, attaching the two in the center with a staple gun or glue gun.

4. Keep adding strips, attaching each at the center, until you have made a star. The more strips you add, the fuller the bow will be.

5. With the edge of a scissor, curl each strip as you would a ribbon. Good luck and have some fun too.

Cardamom Loaf

1 loaf or 1 dozen rolls

Scald 2 cups of milk
Stir into milk, cool to Luke warm
   3/4 cup Sugar
   1/4 cup butter
   1 tsp. salt
Stir and let stand for 5 minutes.
   2 pkg. dry yeast
   1/4 cup warm water

After milk mixture is cooled add yeast mixture. Add 2 eggs and 1 tsp. crushed cardamom seeds (optional) and 2 cups flour. Beat until smooth, continue adding flour (about 4-5 cups) until the dough leaves the side of bowl. Knead 8-10 minutes, cover dough with Crisco, let rise until double, 1 to 1½ hours. After shaping let rise until double. Bake at 375 degrees for 25 min.

Words of Whizdom:
The more you think the less you know— I think.

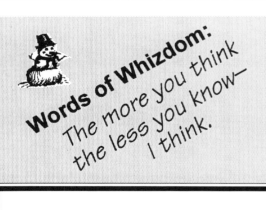

"I don't know—it sounded sort of like 'Ho, ho, splat' to me!"

Answers to **Z Twisted Trivia**

1. North.
2. Gravity.
3. Mrs. Johnson.
4. Some dead guy.
5. If he said, "Hee, Hee, Hee" he would sound like a pervert.
6. He didn't want to be mistaken for Kermit the frog.
7. If you took a guess, you're right, if you know why, add an extra point.
8. Blue -(if you missed this one subract an extra point.
9. If you wiped your chin, subtract a point (if you think we can really see you, you need help)
10. With your nose.

See below your score and evaluation

0-3 Correct
You are incredibly normal.

4-6 Correct
You are normally incredible.

7-9 Correct
Pull up before you crash!

ALL 10 CORRECT
Donate your brain to science.

Heikki Lunta Awakens! Snow God Dumps on D.C.

Residents of Yooperland prepare for the long stretch of winter weather that follows the awakening of Heikki Lunta, the legendary God of Snow. In Yooperland folklore, the mythical snow god awakens and does his snow dance, bringing snow for the snowmobilers, skiers, and those few children who would still rather go sledding than play Nintendo games. This year, Heikki seems to be doing the snowshoe shuffle in earnest, dumping mass quantities of the white stuff all over Yooperland. Apparently, he had a lot of snow left over for other areas of the country. The god of snow dumped a heavy load on Washington D.C., giving the people on Capitol Hill another excuse for not doing anything, as if the economic shut-down of the government was not reason enough. The fact that a little snow has brought the government to a halt shows how ill-equipped the federal government is to deal with an emergency. If we had more Yoopers in Washington, their wives would have had the snowblowers out before the first snowflake fell, and would have had the situation well in hand. And economic shut-down? What is that? Yoopers have been functioning in an economic void ever since the Great Depression, from which Yooperland has never recovered. People here know how to stretch a buck. Put a bunch of Yoopers together in a room with some crayons and a few cases of beer and they'll come up with a balanced budget before the beer is gone. Foreign relations? No problem. We'll send a delegation of old farts from the Paradise bar to parley with the old farts from all those other countries. Our boys will drink a few beers and shoot the breeze about fishing, hunting, chain saw maintenance, and the weather until those other guys cry uncle and will agree to anything just to shut 'em up.

One of the best things we could do for this country is to kick everybody out of congress and replace them with unemployed Yoopers. Most Yoopers do more work while on unemployment than our congressmen do on the job. They could do the same job for a fraction of the pay. Just slip 'em a few bucks in untraceable tax-free cash and you'll get a good day's work. And after a hard day on Capitol hill, a Yooper will go down to the garage and help out with limousine maintenance, just to relax. No need for vacations to the Bahamas or such silly exotic places. A Yooper congressman needs only a six-pack, a couch, and a remote control, and maybe a chain saw engine to tinker with. And in session, you'll never find better bullshitters, which seems to be an important quality in politicians. Get a bunch of Yoopers together to shoot the bull and they'll come up with more ideas by accident than our present representatives of the people do on purpose.

Most of the problems of governing this country could be solved by some good old common sense, something that Yoopers possess in abundance. For instance, would a Yooper wade through a mountain of paperwork and bureaucratic red tape to appropriate $2000 with which to buy a pipe wrench to have a leak in the congressional john fixed? No, he'd borrow a wrench from his neighbor Rudy and go and fix the damn thing himself. And how would he negotiate with the leader of a hostile country? He'd invite the guy to camp, get him puking drunk, then take a snapshot of him on his knees hugging the toilet. A little good-natured blackmail can accomplish wonders.

The snow dumped on the nation's capitol has served to force the government to take a look at reality. Maybe Heikki Lunta, in his infinite wisdom, dumped on D.C. to show the people of the United States just how helpless and ineffective their government really is. And

"You're right, father, God does want me to live! I'm coming in!"

the lesson is not lost on the citizens of Yooperland. Already a plan is in the works to stage a Million Maki March on Washington. One million Yoopers, with snow shovels in hand, will be marching on Washington to demonstrate the effectiveness of direct, no-nonsense action as the best solution to any problem. So far, twenty-five guys have signed up. The rest have bad backs, but are willing to sign their wives up. The date of the march will be announced as soon as logistical problems are worked out, such as how to transport the beer needed to fuel an undertaking of such magnitude, and figuring out where all these Yoopers are going to pee. The Yellow Snow Gazette will report on any new developments as they occur. ■

News Briefs

Local Man Wins Lottery!

Elmer Ostola, 93, of Yellow Snow, Michigan, won the $1,000,000 jackpot in the Yellow Snow Lottery yesterday. He will receive payments of one dollar per year for the next million years. Mr. Ostola, who is a janitor at the high school, plans to save his winnings for his retirement. He purchased the winning ticket from the Buck Snort Bar.

Rintala's

Believe It or Shut Up!

Yooperland Winter Olympics

In the 1912 Yooperland Winter Olympics, Mrs. Saima Kangas of Ralph, Michigan, won a gold medal in the snow shoveling competition. Mrs. Kangas, aged 93, shoveled a path three feet wide from Bruce Crossing to L'Anse in 32 hours, 12 minutes, 43 seconds, beating the record set the previous year by her sister Irma. When asked how it felt to be a champion, Mrs. Kangas remarked, **"I can't talk now, I gotta go home and shovel the driveway before Taisto gets home."**

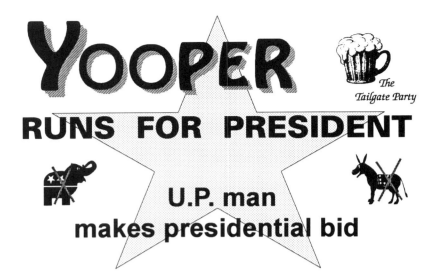

YOOPER
RUNS FOR PRESIDENT

The Tailgate Party

U.P. man makes presidential bid

At a press conference held at Bartanen's Muffler & Tire Shop yesterday, Waino "Wedgie" Kempinen, a lifetime resident of Yooperland, announced his candidacy for the office of President of the United States. "After seeing all those other yohos who think they're qualified for the office," Kempinen said, "I think I have a good chance. It's about time we had a man of the people in the White House." Asked about specific qualities he felt he had that made him presidential material, Kempinen replied, "I can be as charming as Kennedy, I can fall down as well as Ford, and if need be, I could lie like Nixon." Kempinen says he intends to run a clean campaign that focuses on the issues. He deplores the smear campaigns and mudslinging that have become so common in politics. He is confident that political enemies would be able to find no ammunition in his past conduct to use against him. "The only thing my opponents might try to use against me is the fact that I chewed tobacco in high school, but let me state for the record that I didn't spit."

Mr. Kempinen begins his campaign this weekend with a bar-hopping tour through western Yooperland and northeastern Wisconsin. He feels that the bars are the best place to hear the griping and complaining of the populace, and there might even be a few free beers in it, if not votes. Although Kempinen has never been elected to public office, he does not see that as a problem. "All through history there have been people who rose to positions of power without ever being elected to public office," he told reporters. "For example, look at Attila the Hun, Alexander the Great, and my wife, Helga."

Mr. Kempinen advocates a return to the basics in America, back to a simpler, common sense approach to the nation's problems. The economy is one of his main concerns. "I'm gonna start cutting expenses right at the top," says Kempinen. "The first thing I'm gonna do when I get in the White House is put in a wood stove. Then I'm gonna lay in about ten cords of hardwood and start saving on those heating bills. And then there's all those empty rooms. All our kids are grown up and gone, so there'd be just me and Helga. I'll bet you could sleep ten or twelve in each one of those rooms. I'll just bring in a lot of army surplus cots and we can start getting some of the homeless off the streets, starting with my relatives. They can earn their keep by doing some painting and plumbing and such."

Some of Mr. Kempinen's critics charge that because he has never served in the military and has never seen combat, he is not qualified to serve as commander-in-chief of the armed forces. To these charges Kempinen replies, "They oughta try living with Helga for thirty years. Besides," he adds, " they should look at my record before they judge me. I've been dodging the DNR in these woods for forty years, and they ain't caught me yet. I think I could show those Green Berets a coupla things."

At the end of the press conference, Mr. Kempinen issued an open invitation to all the other candidates to meet him in a debate on the issues. "Any time they wanna argue," he says, "they can find me at the Buck Snort Bar."

Waino "Wedgie" Kempinen is a candidate of the newly formed Tailgate Party of Yooperland.

How to keep 'em Whipped!

Gravel Gertie's
Husband Training Tips

Dear Gertie,
I'm one of those women who doesn't work outside the home. I spend my days washing dishes, doing laundry, sewing, sweeping, scrubbing, mopping, waxing, grocery shopping, cooking, paying the bills, and generally providing a good home for my husband to come to after a hard day's work. It's a full time job to keep a household running smoothly, but my husband thinks that all I do is sit around drinking coffee, talking on the phone, and watching TV all day. What should I do?
Totally Insulted

Dear Insulted,
Sit around, drink coffee, talk on the phone, and watch TV all day.
Gertie

Dear Gertie,
My old man goes into hibernation every January 1st, and doesn't come fully awake until sometime in April. He only leaves the house to go to work, and the rest of the time he hibernates on the couch with the remote control. I can't stand to have him lying around underfoot. He's driving me crazy. What should I do?
Mama Bear

Dear Mama,
My Eugene used to turn into a sofa spud every winter, too. One day while he was gone to work I bought a brand new couch and had the old one hauled away. When Eugene came home and tried to get comfortable, he just couldn't seem to settle down. You see, couch potatoes must have their own scent to wallow in or they just can't feel at home. The new couch didn't fit his body, and it didn't smell like sweat, smoke, and beer farts, so

he didn't feel at home there. Every time Eugene begins to get the couch broken in and starts to look comfortable, (which takes about a year) I just have it hauled away and have a new one delivered. So he's still around all winter, but he's miserable, and that's good enough for me.
Gertie

Dear Gertie,
My husband likes to drink beer. The trouble is, he doesn't like to clean up after himself. He'll go to the fridge and get another beer, but do you think he'll bring the empty can with him? No! He just leaves the empties wherever he happens to be. My living room is littered with beer cans every night, and on weekends it's like a dump. How can I get him to clean up after himself?
Tin Can Annie

Dear Annie,
My Eugene used to put away a twelve pack every night, and he'd leave the empties lying around everywhere. The situation called for drastic measures. One day when he went to the bathroom I doctored up the beer that he had just opened. I took the shavings from my electric razor and dumped them into his beer. For good measure, I also threw in a cigarette butt and a little something I found stuck to the underside of a chair. He took a good slug of that beer and he spent the next two hours in the john, hacking and retching. I don't have a problem with empty beer cans anymore because Eugene still can't stand the sight of a can of beer. He can't even watch a beer commercial without turning green and making funny gurgling noises.

Gertie

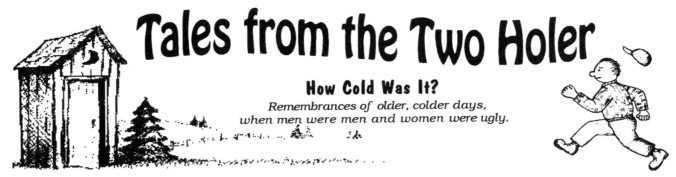

Tales from the Two Holer

How Cold Was It?

*Remembrances of older, colder days,
when men were men and women were ugly.*

On the news the other day I heard about some cold weather warnings where they predicted dangerously cold temperatures, with chill factors as low as minus 50 degrees. Every time I hear "chill factor" it sets me to thinking. When I was young, we didn't have chill factors. We had a thermometer outside the kitchen window and that was enough. And 50 below zero, "dangerously cold?" Well, maybe it is to some these days, like those kids I see jumping into their cars and driving off with no gloves, no hat, nothing but a light jacket and tennis shoes. In my day we wore more than that to go to bed on a cold winter night. And when we went out, we were dressed for it. 50 below, when you're dressed warm, ain't all that cold. In fact, it never seems to get cold like it did in the old days. I remember more snow when I was a kid than we ever get now. Maybe the snow seemed deeper because I was shorter, but I don't think so. But I know for a fact that we had colder winters back then. I don't need to look at a thermometer to tell that. You can see the signs in nature. That's the way we used to do it. It wasn't really that long ago. The old days are simply those days when things seemed better than they are now. That could mean as far back as when gas was twenty-nine cents a gallon, or as recently as just before the last insurance rate hike. But let me get back to whatever the hell it was I was talking about before you let me start rambling. Oh, ya—cold weather.

I remember one day in particular, the coldest day I ever saw. How cold was it? Well, I couldn't say exactly, 'cause the mercury in the thermometer went down clear outa sight. But it was damn cold. I remember I went out camp that day, and I left my truck home 'cause it was so cold that the rubber tires were frozen solid and would shatter if I hit a bump. It was about a five mile walk out to camp. During the walk to camp my breath froze and fell to the ground in clumps of ice. I had to be careful not to trip on them. As I walked, I picked frozen chickadees off the branches of the trees along the way. I use the feathers for tying flies. It was just like picking little apples, except that their little frozen claws held tight to the branches and sometimes you had to really yank hard to get them off. My uncle told me about one time on a real cold day back in the forties when he saw a gray squirrel frozen in mid-air, quick-frozen in the middle of a leap from tree to tree. I don't really believe that. Gray squirrels are too smart to go out when it's that cold. Anyway, once I made it to camp I had to get a fire going, so I filled the kitchen stove with wood and lit it with a kitchen match. Then I threw the match out the window. I stayed at camp for a couple days of ice fishing. It was pretty easy fishing. All I did was take my double bit axe down to Flopper's Creek and chop those trout out of the ice where they had been trapped when the creek froze up solid. I had a couple of days of enjoyable fishing, and then I went home. When spring finally came, I decided to go out camp and do some fly fishing. I drove out and was dismayed to find nothing but a pile of ashes where the camp had been. I poked through the ashes to try to figure out what had happened, and finally came to a conclusion. The only way I could figure it was, when I threw that burning kitchen match out the window on that cold day in February, the flame had frozen solid as soon as it hit the cold air. When spring finally came the flame thawed out, started the camp on fire, and burned it to the ground. How cold was it? Pretty damn cold. ∎

Top 10 reasons why U.P. men are good catches

by Jessica Kerkela

10. Don't feel like grocery shopping? Dinner's already hanging in the back yard.

9. They don't require much foreplay—just put on a Hank Williams album and shave your legs.

8. At your wedding reception everyone will be too drunk to remember that you danced naked on the groomsmen's table and barfed on the wedding cake.

7. You'll never catch a yooper man wearing a silk bathrobe, drinking evian water, and playing backgammon with a guy named "Drew."

6. If you give birth to a son you can name him cool names like *Gubba, Booger,* or *Pouch.*

5. You don't have to shop Maurice's men's store—you can do all his clothes shopping at Moose's Yard Sale.

4. Got a broken chain saw? He can fix it.

3. Can't afford a waterbed? Just jiggle his beer gut.

2. You're guaranteed separate two-week vacations every November.

1. You'll never have to worry about what to do with all your money—you won't have any!

Hairold

Science Department

The High Cost of Heat: A Gastric Solution

A proposal by Professor Eino Aho, head of just about everything at National Mine University

There is an answer to high heating costs. There is an alternative to expensive and rapidly depleting fossil fuels. All we need to do is use an intelligent scientific approach to the problem.

One day last month, while making out checks to pay the monthly bills, I became outraged by the extremely high cost of heating fuel. Living in a part of the country where heat is required for most of the year, I am acutely aware of the problem of high heating bills. Being a person of high intelligence and great ingenuity, I decided to do something about the problem. Clearly, the solution to the problem would be to find and abundant, low cost fuel source. I immediately set my mind to finding a solution. First of all, I would have to find a substance that was flammable. Secondly, this substance must be plentiful. As I often do when wrestling with a dilemma, I decided to take a walk down to the Buck Snort Bar. Its atmosphere is often conducive to creative thinking, depending upon how much one imbibes.

As I sat at my favorite table wrestling with my problem, a few of the regulars at the bar were engaged in some kind of raucous activity. They were consuming vast quantities of peanuts, popcorn, and potato chips, which they washed down with gallons of beer. Occasionally I would hear a muffled explosion, followed immediately by cheers and howls of laughter. I was puzzled by this behavior until I realized that it was Friday night. At the Buck Snort Bar, Monday is pool night, Tuesday is darts, Wednesday is cribbage, Thursday is arm wrestling, and Friday is fart lighting night. Contestants on each team would bend over and ignite their gastric emissions, and the length of the flame would be measured with a yardstick. Though I don't follow the competition closely, I know that the Buck Snort Bar boasts a fart lighting team that has been undefeated since 1989.

Suddenly, with a flash of light and a muffled *boom* the

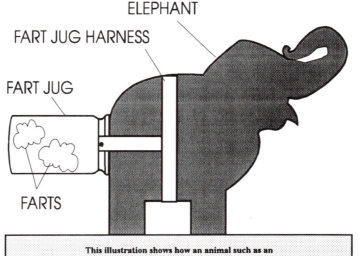

ELEPHANT

FART JUG HARNESS

FART JUG

FARTS

This illustration shows how an animal such as an elephant could be fitted with a fart jug for collection of gastric emissions.

solution to my problem presented itself. Of course! Gastric emissions! An abundant source of flammable gases! I rushed back to my study to begin work on the idea. I gathered all the statistical information that I could find on gastric emissions. At first I was somewhat disappointed to find that the average person releases only about half a cup of gas in each emission, and that, during the course of a day, only about two cups are emitted. Given the number of people in the average household, which I estimated to be about 3.5 people, the amount of flammable gastric emission available for heating fuel would be only about seven cups per household per day. This is not nearly enough to heat a home. According to my calculations, the amount of gastric emission needed to heat the average home would be 43,200 cups per day. Even trained professionals such as those on the Buck Snort Bar fart lighting team could not produce that much. Clearly, a more productive source would have to be found. Logically, since people who live in warm climates do not need to heat their homes, they do not need their farts. If we imported farts from the warmer regions of the world, the amount of gastric emissions available for heating fuel would be greatly increased. Unfortunately, after further calculation, I found that the amount of fuel available from those sources still fell far short of the requirement. Some of this deficiency could be remedied by the saving of farts during the summer months, to be used for heating during cold weather. Of course, people would have to be taught to fart responsibly, diligently capturing each emission to be stored away for future use. So many of us fart carelessly during times of plenty, never giving a thought to the valuable resource we are squandering away. Then cold weather comes and we complain about the cost of heating. It reminds me of the story of the grasshopper and the ant. The grasshopper lounges around all summer, farting indiscriminately, never thinking of the future, while the industrious ant carefully captures and stores away each emission, even the silent ones, in diligent preparation for the cold winter to come.

An abundant source of flammable gastric emissions is animals. Elephants release gas in much greater amounts than do humans. According to my calculations, 1,127.2 elephant farts could heat the average home for up to four hours. Elephants and other large animals, such as hippos and water buffalo, could supply large amounts of gas. Closer to home, horses are notorious for their farting and could contribute significantly. In my ozone report, printed in the June 1995 issue of this publication, I reported that 909,646, 408,000 farts were released by cows yearly in the United States. I have called in a team of engineers to begin work on designing a fart jug, which will make the collection of these gastric emissions easy and efficient. If all of our cattle and other animals were fitted with fart jugs, imagine the amount of heating fuel that could be harvested!

I have applied for a grant with which to finance research and development in this important area. Hopefully, the day will soon come when we will no longer be dependent upon expensive fossil fuels to heat our homes. The remedy I propose here may lead to the perfect solution to the problem of skyrocketing heating fuel costs. My solution to the problem is a fart in a jug. ∎

The Secret Room

There's a secret room in our house we don't tell no one it's here
My mother in law was cleaning it and she just disappeared
I came in here to search for her with a baseball bat
I need it for protection against those bedroom rats

There's pizza on the dresser growing fungus hair
Lichen growing on those socks and dirty underwear
2000 dirty dishes, glasses, cups and bowls
Cemented all together with dry milk and cheerios

On the floor I find a mess of rock and roll CD's
They're all glued to the carpet with macaroni and cheese
Freaky rock musicians are staring from the walls
Keith Richards on the closet door is scariest of all

A dozen pair of blue jeans are scattered on the floor
among the black banana peels and dried up apple cores
There's something growing on the sheets I can't identify
I sprayed it with some DDT and still it wouldn't die

I just felt something slimy crawl across my feet
I hope it doesn't think of me as something good to eat
The curtain's smeared with something red I hope it's pizza sauce
And something's growing on the wall It must be Spanish moss

There's something underneath the bed I thought I heard it groan
I think it was a big mistake to come in here alone
It's about as cheerful here as midnight in a tomb
No place on earth is spookier than our teenager's room

There's a secret room in our house It's our teenager's room
It's like another planet it's stranger than the moon
If I get out of here alive I never will return
This place is just to hard too clean It's easier to burn

KEEP OUT OR DIE!

In our last episode... Yooperman and Benny take Santa's place on the toy
route while Santa keeps his drunken reindeer safe in the cave. After emptying Santa's bag, Yooperman finds a gift for himself. It turns out to be a brain wave descrambler, with which he can receive any channel he wants through the salad bowl in his head. But the remote control for his descrambler looks a lot like Benny's plutonium propulsion module control panel, and Yooperman inadvertently grabs the wrong remote. He punches the button and the sleigh does a barrel roll and dumps them both out in the sky high above their cave. We now join our heroes as they plunge through space toward the earth a thousand feet below...

Just then Santa stepped out of the cave. "OOF!" came out one end, and something like "FHLRRRRP!" came out the other as Yooperman landed on him and knocked him on his elfin butt. Yooperman thought that landing on Santa felt a lot like landing on a really fat deer hunter, only more embarrassing. Santa wasn't in the jolliest of moods, not after spending the night in a cave with a herd of puking reindeer. And then Yooperman and Benny were late getting back—out joy riding with his sleigh, no doubt. Then he steps outside for a smoke break and this idiot comes out of the sky and knocks the crap out of him. No, Santa was not jolly. He gathered up his reindeer, recovered his sled from where it had crashed in the swamp, and flew off northward in a huff. Yooperman watched him go, hoping that Santa wasn't the kind to hold a grudge. He had hopes for an electric train set next year.

"Toivo," a voice said. It came from above.

"Huh?" Yooperman said.

"Toivo," the voice said again.

Who is it?" Yooperman asked. "And how do you know my real name? Where are you?"

"Up here, stupid," the voice came again. "In the tree!"

Yooperman looked up. In the top of a forty foot jack pine sat Benny, scratched, bruised, and very unhappy looking, but alive.

"Benny!" Yooperman cheered, "I'm glad ya made it!"

"Well, I haven't made it yet," he grumbled. "As you can see, I'm still some distance from the ground. And I don't know how to get down."

"Don't worry," Yooperman called. "I'll get you down!" He grabbed a big handful of snow, packed a good, solid snowball, and flung it at Benny, catching him in the side of the head. Benny was caught off

guard and fell out of the jack pine, landing in the snow with a little *flupp!* He came up out of the snow spitting and sputtering, and cursing in some language that made Yooperman think of 300 turkeys choking on rubber bands while

The life and times of Toivo Maki known by Evil-doers and bad guys as...

YOOPERMAN

listening to Nirvana tapes played backwards. But the message came across that Benny was not happy, and Yooperman decided to stay away from him for a little while and let him get over his crabbiness. However, it became difficult to stay very far away from Benny, because that day, and every day for weeks thereafter, great, gusty winds swooped out of the north, bringing one blizzard after another. Yooperman and Benny were forced to take refuge in the cave. The storm raged on and on, and eventually their provisions began to run low. They had not anticipated the possibility of running out of rations, so they made no effort to conserve. The day came when they sat across the fire from each other at dinner time, Yooperman with his last twinkie and Benny with the last of the rubber bathtub stoppers.

"Well," Benny said. "Here we are." He turned his last rubber bathtub stopper over in his hands. "We're down to the last of our food, and the weather shows no signs of letting

up. There's no way we could make it to civilization in this weather, and hunting for food is out of the question. Got any ideas?"

"Ya, let's eat," Yooperman said, and he gulped his last twinkie down.

"You—-!" Benny began, then stopped. "Oh, what's the use?" he said. He popped his last rubber bathtub stopper into his mouth and washed it down with his last beer. "Now we're out of food," he said. "And it's months until spring. What'll we do for all that time?"

"I don't know about you," Yooperman replied. "I lost my brain wave descrambler in the snow, and my salad bowl is stuck on the 24-hour Gilligan's Island channel, so I'll be watching a lot of TV."

Benny sat cross-legged by the fire with his head cradled in his hands. "It's going to be a long winter," he mumbled. The snowstorm raged on. To fill the time, Benny and Yooperman talked. They talked about everything they could think of. Yooperman was finished in five minutes. Benny began to tell Yooperman stories of his adventures throughout the galaxy, but Yooperman kept falling asleep, and his snoring was really obnoxious, so Benny gave it up. There was a period of a few days when they played tic-tac-toe to while away the time, but then Yooperman hit a lucky streak and started winning heavily, so Benny quit, not because he was a sore loser, but because he really didn't want to have to murder Yooperman, who treated every win as if it were the jackpot lotto. After that they each began to withdraw to opposite corners of the cave, each to withdraw deeper into his own private thoughts. Boredom was their enemy, but hunger was also beginning to join in the attack. Yooperman's hunger became so great that his brain was unable to generate sufficient power for reception on the salad bowl in his head, so he could no longer watch Gilligan's Island. Inevitably, the need for nourishment of mind and body reached a critical point, and this was when the last vestige of sanity left our heroes. This was when Benny spent a whole afternoon trying to figure out what the sound of one hand clapping might taste like, and Yooperman began saving his farts in an empty beer can, hoping to find some use for them someday. Their bodies began to waste away, and the gnawing ache of hunger began to eat at their minds as well. Benny often sat silently, gazing at Yooperman, hoping to find somewhere on him a Rubbermaid seal or B.F. Goodrich insignia that he might have overlooked before. Yooperman began to notice how closely Benny resembled a blue twinkie, and how he smelled a lot like pickled herring. And still the blizzard raged outside, with no end in sight. Benny began to cut strips of rubber from his boots, to gnaw on them, absorbing whatever meager sustenance he could. But he immediately ceased this practice when Yooperman pointed out that he wasn't wearing any boots. Yooperman used a piece of charcoal from the fire to draw pictures of juicy bugs on the cave wall. Then he would lick them off. It didn't really relieve his hunger, but he could pretend that it did. He even drew a rubber bathtub stopper for Benny—or at least he thought it was rubber. He inadvertently drew a picture of a nylon bathtub stopper, and when Benny licked it off the wall he almost died of nylon poisoning. After that, Yooperman would draw no bathtub stoppers, and out of fairness to Benny, he stopped drawing bugs, too. He made an attempt to draw a cellular phone with which to order a pizza with onions, mushrooms, and stoppers, but his drawing skills were inadequate. The best he could do was a picture of two tin cans connected by string. So they took turns calling. First Benny would be Little Caesar's Pizza, and Yooperman would call in and order 600 pepperoni pizzas. Then Yooperman would be Rubbermaid, and Benny would call and order a truckload of used rubber bathtub stoppers, heavy on the soap scum.

Then Yooperman accidentally drew a phone bill that was 6 months behind, and the phone company disconnected the tin can phone. A terrible argument followed, Benny and Yooperman each blaming the other for not keeping up on the phone bill, after which each retreated again to his own private corner of the cave to sulk.

Yooperman whiled away the days and nights by counting his toes. Benny passed the time by stacking particles of dust on top of one another. Even in their deranged state, they both realized that they were in severe danger of extinction; their bodies had wasted away to mere shadows of their former selves; their minds were prone to fewer and fewer bouts of lucidity; hallucinations were the norm rather than the exception; and still the unrelenting winter dragged on. Yooperman finished counting his toes, but couldn't remember how many he was supposed to have, so he gave up the whole idea. Benny's condition worsened. He seemed to have slipped into some kind of delirium, and he crawled about the cave turning over rocks and digging holes, apparently in search of his belly button. Benny's mind had apparently gone away, and it was up to Yooperman to figure out a way to save them both.

While he thought, he doodled on the wall with the charcoal. He drew a hot, steaming pasty, and licked it off the wall. He could actually taste the rutabagas in it. He drew a blueberry pie for dessert, and a hot cup of coffee to go with it. The pie turned his tongue blue and the hot coffee burned it. But now that he had eaten something he could think more clearly. He hit upon an idea, and immediately went to work on it. He began to draw frantically, occasionally stepping back to assess his work, then flinging himself back into it again. A building began to take shape. It was not a large building, but it seemed to fit whatever Yooperman had in mind, for he kept on drawing without erasing at all, as if he knew exactly what he wanted the end result to be. His hands were a blur as he put on the finishing touches. Finally he stepped back to admire his work. Before him on the wall stood a small building of charcoal-

drawn bricks, glass, and steel, sporting a sign that read *Woody's Sub & Stopper Shop*. Yooperman wasted no time, knowing that Benny was fading fast. He opened the door he had drawn on the building and stepped into the wall, and everything went black...

Is this the end of Yooperman and Benny? Will they starve to death before spring? Will Benny ever find his belly button? Will Yooperman ever regain consciousness? Did he ever have it to begin with? What am I asking all these stupid questions for? Should I get out more?

For the answers to these and other ridiculous questions, either consult your encyclopedia or trun to page 55 for the next quasi-cerebral episode of **YOOPERMAN!**

★★★★★★★★★★★★★★★★★★★★★★
★ **Words of Whizdom:** ★
★ No man, on his deathbed, ever ★
★ looked back on his life and said, ★
★ "Hey, rewind that, I wanna see the ★
★ hemorrhoid surgery again!" ★
★★★★★★★★★★★★★★★★★★★★★★

How twisted are you?
Take this simple test and find out.

Answers & psychiatric profile on page 50

Twisted Trivia Questions
(Hint: Think *really* stupid!)

1. Which way does the Michigamme River flow?
2. If you nailed your feet to the floor, how could you Polka?
3. What tool does a Yooper most often use for snow removal?
4. What is the leading cause of divorce in the U.P.?
5. What should you always add to deer meat when you cook it:
6. What can horses do that no other animal can do?
7. Chose one of the following numbers: 3 3 3.
8. Is this a rhetorical question, or what?
9. How many pine trees are there in Yooperland?
10. How many morons does it take to change a light

SPECIAL CABIN FEVER REPORT ━━━━

This is part of a comprehensive YSG report on the psychological effects of the harsh Yooperland winters. The following are entries from a journal found among the personal effects of Onni Ostola of Perkins, Michigan upon his admission into the Sulo Lempinen Home for the incurably insane. Mr. Ostola agreed to allow publication of his journal on the condition that he remain anonymous.

Jan. 13 The weatherman has predicted heavy snow. The kids are excited.

Jan. 14 A foot of snow fell during the night. I thought they said heavy snow. This is more like a moderate frost.

Jan. 15 Three more feet of snow last night. That's more like it.

Jan. 16 Went out this morning and couldn't find the snowblower to clear the driveway. Couldn't find the driveway either.

Jan. 17 It snows all the time now. Managed to shovel a path to get the Chevy out to the road. Made it to the store to buy beer, coffee, and frozen pizzas. Bought enough to last for the duration of the storm, I hope.

Jan. 20 Had to climb out the upstairs window to go and check the mail. Couldn't find the mailbox.

Feb. 3 The snow has continued to fall for three weeks now. We can no longer get out of the house to buy provisions, and will have to conserve what we have if we are to survive until spring. Fortunately, we have a dozen frozen pizzas in the freezer.

Feb. 4 Unfortunately, we have two teenage boys. The last of the frozen pizzas were cooked and eaten today. We are down to one can of stewed tomatoes and another can with no label. I found three navy beans on the floor in the pantry. I think tomorrow I will make three bean soup.

Feb. 6 The unlabeled can turned out to be white hominy. Are you kidding? Nobody can get that hungry.

Feb. 7 We are out of food. We have started rationing out the dog's food. The dog seems nervous.

Feb. 9 The dog food is all gone. So is the dog. I think he ran away.

Feb 10 Made water soup today. We had icicles for dessert. Didn't taste too bad, but not very filling.

Feb. 12 Searched under the couch cushions. Found a piece of peanut shell and a few cracker crumbs. Made soup. Eat your heart out, Al Bundy.

Feb. 13 Sat around staring at each other. Later the kids went to their rooms to hunt for small rodents and insects.

Feb. 14 The kids are still hunting. My wife and I are spending quality time, starving together. I am having hallucinations. Today, for a moment, she looked like Sharon Stone. I'm not hungry anymore.

Feb. 15 Today my wife looked like Arnold Schwarzenegger with whiskers. I ate my socks.

Feb. 18 The kids found a petrified rodent of some kind under a bed. We boiled it for hours. It turned out to be a rubber toy. Hard to chew, but not bad tasting.

Feb. 20 Still snowing.

Feb. 22 My birthday. My wife made me a cake out of snow. Don't know where she found the yellow food coloring.

Feb. 24 Wanted to make water soup again, but couldn't remember the recipe. Ate the wife's leather purse instead.

Feb. 26 Getting weaker. Had a dream about giant hot dogs and hamburgers waging war against humans. What a food fight.

Feb. 28 My belly is rubbing against my backbone and the squeaking sound keeps me awake.

Mar. 2 Celebrated our Anniversary. Had a candlelight dinner, minus the dinner. Didn't have candles either—ate them last week.

Mar. 4 Saw a large round yellow object in the sky. Called everyone to come and look, but it was gone. They think I've lost my mind.

Mar. 6 It snowed today.

Mar. 7 It snowed today.

Mar. 10 It snowed today.

Mar. 13 Looked at pictures of food in a magazine. Glossy paper tastes like crap.

Mar. 14 Found a dead ant carcass in cupboard. Divided it up equally among us. I got a drumstick.

Mar. 16 Celebrated St. Urho's Day

Mar. 17 St. Patrick's Day storm came right on time. I counted fourteen snowflakes. One of them looked like Rutherford B. Hayes. It winked at me.

Mar. 20 Saw the big yellow round thing in the sky again. Kept it to myself this time.

Mar. 21 The sky cleared today. The big yellow round thing was back again. Looked it up in the encyclopedia. It's the sun! Snow is melting. I love winter! I gotta go now. I must hurry to the bank and get these toenail clippings into the vault before it's too late. Waiter, what's this fly doing in my soup? Oh, it's fly soup. Okay. That explains everything. Scented toilet paper? It's all so simple. Did I mention that I love winter?

Okay, take me away. I'll drive.

Martha's Summer Kitchen

Well, the snow is flying and our wood stove is burning away, keeping us nice and warm. Boy, we are getting a lot of snow this year. Ensio doesn't complain too much. But every February we visit family in Arizona and I think he has his suitcase packed before New Year's. Well, enough about that. It's time for me to get down to work. Some of us have a knack for cooking and are good in the kitchen. We can improvise with whatever ingredients we happen to have on hand, and can come up with tasty and nutritious meals. Unfortunately, there are those among us who are lost in the kitchen without our recipes and instructions. For my recipe in this issue, I chose an ice cube recipe for my sister who lost hers.

Ice Cubes

(Master recipe)

Ingredients: Water

Directions: Pour 2 cups cold water into standard size 16-cube ice cube tray. (some may experiment with other type of trays but we are going to use the standard size for this recipe) Place tray in freezer.

Freeze until water turns to ice. Be careful not to remove from freezer too early. When ice cubes are done, keep them in the freezer to prevent melting. If ice cubes are accidentally melted, they can be refrozen with no loss of flavor or freshness.

Freeze for 1 to 2 hours or until frozen.

Answers to Twisted Trivia

1. Downstream.
2. You couldn't.
3. His wife.
4. Marriage.
5. Heat.
6. Shit horse turds.
7. 3. If you chose 3 or 3, you're wrong.
8. You decide. (don't think about it too long-you'll hurt yourself.)
9. Oops! We mean to say palm trees. We'll give you this one
10. Duh, what's a light bulb?

See below your score and evaluation

0- Correct . . . . You're harmless.

4-6 Correct. . . . Do stretching exercises before attempting to think.

7-9 Correct. . . . Use your brain only in extreme emergencies.

ALL 10 CORRECT

Stop sniffing that paint right now!

I ♥ Mosquitos!

June 1, 1996 | **Summer** | Yellow Snow, Michigan

Killer Heat Wave Hits Area

The National Mine University Meteorology Research Center has been swamped with phone calls during the last few weeks from concerned citizens reporting sudden and extreme changes in local weather conditions. As temperatures soar into the 50's and sometimes even higher, area residents struggle to cope with the unusual weather. There have been scattered reports of panic, some fearing that the end is at hand. Law enforcement officials fear looting and rioting if the extreme conditions continue. NMU meteorologists issued a report on the condition, stating that there is nothing to fear. According to Professor Eino Aho, head of almost everything at NMU, this condition is what meteorologists call "summer." Although rare in this area, the phenomenon is common in other parts of the country. NMU records show that a summer occurred in Yooperland as recently as 1978, when temperatures actually reached the low 70's and the sun was visible for three days in a row.

Local emergency rooms have been filled to capacity with people seeking treatment for heat-related health problems, both physical and psychological. Many local residents, having little or no experience with the phenomenon of summer, are unable to make the transition from the usual winter conditions to the tropical conditions that have arisen. Public Health officials say that most of the problems are due to improper dress for warm weather. They urge the public to practice dressing for summer. Most people are unable to break the habit of bundling up in long underwear and three layers of outer clothing when they go outdoors. The Health Department is scheduling classes in local high schools to teach people how to deal with summer. Topics discussed will include dressing for warm weather, dealing with snowbank deprivation, and lawn mowing.

NMU Scientists in Disagreement

A fist-fight nearly broke out among meteorologists at NMU yesterday after a disagreement on the cause of the recent weather conditions got out of hand. Some of the scientists subscribe to the theory that the warm weather is in some way related to Global Warming. Others maintain that the cold, wintery conditions that usually prevail in the area are the product of Nuclear Winter, and that the recent warming trend is a return to normal climatic conditions. Reportedly, one scientist began to remove his coat, saying to another, "Global Warming, my ——! Are you prepared to back that up?" Then they chose up sides and began to remove their coats, mittens, scarves, sweaters, and other heavy clothing. By the time they had stripped down to comfortable fighting weight, they had forgotten what the argument was about. They adjourned ☞

Sports Report

Baseball Game Continues

The annual baseball game between the residents of The Yellow Snow Nursing Home and their long time rivals from the Al Z. Heimer Senior Citizens Facility in Gwinn continues to drag on. In the top of the first inning, the Gwinn Gummers lead by a score of 79-0, with nobody out and the bases loaded. Taisto Makinen, the 103 year-old pitcher for the Yellow Snow Yankers, has walked the first 82 batters and still shows no sign of throwing a strike. Play was held up for an hour today to conduct a search for Yanker left fielder Arvid Ahonen, who wandered off after a butterfly. Ahonen was found watering flowers in a nearby florist shop and returned to the game. Since the florist is an avid Yanker fan, no indecent exposure charges were filed. Play will be suspended for two hours this afternoon due to nap time. Tickets are still available at any Ticketmaster outlet.

Great Moments In History!

Mukku Millimaki, a Finlander from Skanee, Michigan, served with the Texas troops in the Texas war for independence, and was credited with causing the massacre of the defenders at the Alamo by Santa Anna's troops on March 6, 1836. According to the diary of Colonel William Travis, Santa Anna was on the verge of signing a truce when Millimaki suddenly yelled, *"Holyowha! Look at all dem taco-benders!"*

to lunch at the Buck Snort Bar for further discussion.

Killer Mosquito Invasion!

Along with reports of unusually warm temperatures in our area have come disturbing reports of attacks by a flock of killer mosquitoes. Although not related to the killer bees that have invaded the southwest in recent years, the killer mosquitoes should be considered equally dangerous. Local farmer August Helsten reported seeing a flock heading north over his cow pasture early yesterday morning. Mr. Helsten has been plagued with livestock disappearances over the last few weeks, in which five of his chickens, a cow, and two pigs have disappeared. Last week he discovered the dried up husk of his favorite beagle behind his barn. He suspects that the killer mosquitoes had something to do with it.

Another local resident reported that his wife was carried off by a large flock of killer mosquitoes yesterday afternoon. According to the man, who declined to give his name, the flock of mosquitoes attacked her as she worked in her garden. He hurried in the house to get his shotgun and when we came back outside an hour later, she was gone.

Entomologists from NMU have offered a $500.00 reward to anyone who can bring in a killer mosquito for study. So far, mosquito bounty hunters from downstate have brought in five partridge, three geese, two bald eagles, and a whooping crane. To prevent further mistaken identities, NMU has provided this artist's sketch of a killer mosquito, drawn from the descriptions reported by various eyewitnesses:

Many local residents are responding to the recent mosquito attacks with force. Hundreds of local hunters, intent upon wiping out the mosquito menace have taken to the woods with their guns. One local taxidermist is reportedly offering $10.00 apiece for killer mosquito

carcasses. He plans to stuff the mosquitoes and sell them to tourists. The Department of Natural Resources issued a statement that it will prosecute anyone who shoots a mosquito, or anyone who deals in the exploiting of their carcasses for profit. Says an official, "Remember, it is a criminal offense to shoot the U.P. state bird, except in clear cases of self-defense."

Members of a local militant group, the Yellow Snow Militia, maintain that it is their right to kill anything that threatens their homes and families. A dozen or so of the militant group have barricaded themselves into their deer camp a few miles south of Yellow Snow, vowing that they will not be taken alive. Local law enforcement officials plan no action, saying that it is not a crime to barricade yourself into your own deer camp. "Besides," said one officer, "they'll come out when they run out of beer."

Not all local residents are so militant. Heikki Nurmi, an elderly Finn living in a tarpaper shack in a cedar swamp south of National Mine, says he has found a perfect defense against killer mosquito attacks. "It seems that they have a low tolerance for alcohol," he told reporters. "I was sitting outside whittling and sipping on a fifth of Kessler's one day last week and one of them killer mosquitoes came along. It stuck its proboscis into my arm and started to draw blood. It only got about a teaspoonful and suddenly its eyes went crossed and it started to stagger away. It took off but it couldn't fly too straight. It crashed into a big jack pine tree and fell to the ground. Then it got up, shook its head, and staggered off into the woods. It comes back once in a while to draw another drink, but it ain't no bother as long as I keep lots of Kessler's on hand."

So far, researchers at National Mine University have been unable to come up with an effective killer mosquito repellent. Some scientists think there may be some merit in the Kessler's idea, and are pursuing research in that area. Their findings will be published as soon as the NMU cryptography experts can decipher their incoherent scribbling. For now, experts suggest that the best defense may be to enclose decks, porches, and patios with chain link fencing, which seems to be fairly effective in keeping the killer mosquitoes at bay. ∎

Learn to talk good with the help of the Yooperland Dictionary

Babysit: That yellow stuff in diapers.

Beer: Beer.

Bug Juice: Best-selling Yooperland cologne.

Bush call: A stop at a Yooperland rest stop.

Dandelion: The Upper Peninsula State Flower.

Fart: Someone who is very old or very little, as in "old fart" or "little fart".

Holyowha: Yooper expletive meaning, "Holy_ _ _ _!"

Junker: Yooper yard ornament.

Kits: Children. "How's da wife and kits?"

Mining urinal: Da paper (Mining Journal)

Nort: Opposite of sout.

Noseeums: Tiny gnats capable of driving strong men insane.

One-Holer: Private restroom

Smart Pill: Rabbit droppings, in Yooperland legend said to increase intelligence.

Socks: Devices to make your car or truck ride smoother. "I gotta get new socks on my truck"

Spring Fever: An illness that comes right after cabin fever.

Summer: The warm season in Yooperland. (The last one occurred in 1978)

Swampers: Rubber boots worn by Yoopers in the spring during the muddy season. (not a winter boot)

Terrorists: People who flock to Yooperland during the terrorist season.

Two-Holer: Public restroom

Gravel Gertie's

How to keep 'em Whipped!

Husband Training Tips

Dear Gertie,
My husband goes fishing every weekend, and he always brings home a mess of fish. I don't mind because I love fish. What I don't like is that he always expects me to clean them. How can I get him to clean his own fish?
Fanny Fishguts

Dear Fishguts,
First of all, get him to agree that you get to keep anything you find inside the fish you clean. Then, the next time he goes fishing, go to a rare coin shop and buy a valuable coin, maybe in the $100.00 range. Then when you're cleaning his catch, slip the coin down the throat of one of the fish. When you clean the fish and find the coin inside, make sure your old man is there to see it. It might be a good idea to have a coin catalog handy so you can look it up and show him the value. I used this technique on Eugene and now he goes fishing every day, and he won't let me touch the fish he brings home. If he ever gets tired of cleaning fish again, I just might find a diamond ring next time.
Gertie

Dear Gertie,
My husband never gets around to chores, like cleaning the garage or mowing the lawn. He always says he'll get around to it one of these days. Meanwhile, he spends whole afternoons sitting in front of the TV drinking beer. How can I get him moving?
Mrs. Unhandyman

Dear Un,
Hit him where it hurts. Start paying the neighborhood kids top dollar to do all those chores. When the old man comes to you to bum beer money, tell him you spent all your cash on wages to get the chores done. You'd be surprised ambitious a Yooper man can get for beer.
Gertie

Dear Gertie,
We own a 1974 Chevy Nova. It's the only car we own, and it's a piece of junk, but my husband loves it, and refuses to get rid of it and buy a newer car. This old clunker rattles, rumbles, and smokes, and it's embarrassing to ride in it. The muffler system is held together by baling wire, and you can see the road through the rust holes in the floor. How can I convince him to get rid of this junker?
Uneasy Rider

Dear Rider,
Do him a big favor. Take that car down to one of those automatic car washes, the kind that slaps the hell out of your car with those big brushes. Once the water dissolves the rust, which is all that holds the car together, those big brushes will slap that bugger into a useless pile of rubble.
Gertie

Dear Gertie,
My husband never wants to go anywhere on vacation. He'll go out to the camp and fish and drink beer, but that's as far as it goes. He never takes me away anywhere romantic or exotic. It's not like we couldn't afford it. We both work and make good money. I can't stand the thought of staying home for another vacation. What should I do?
Housebound in Houghton

Dear Housebound,
Send him a postcard from Maui.
Gertie

Are you a real Yooper?
Take the
YOOPER YARD TEST
and find out for sure
(Mark answers true or false)

T   F
☐ ☐ 1. Walking barefoot in your yard is not an option because of the abundance of dog dumps.
☐ ☐ 2. You have at least one tire-less non-working vehicle displayed in your yard.
☐ ☐ 3. You have at least one spot where grass won't grow because you can't be bothered with going in the house to whiz.
☐ ☐ 4. You have an oil slick in your back yard where you change oil.
☐ ☐ 5. You have at least one jack pine tree in your yard.
☐ ☐ 6. Your yard has more dandelions than grass.
☐ ☐ 7. You let snake rhubarb grow wild in your yard because it looks nice.
☐ ☐ 8. You could gather at least one ton of scrap metal from your backyard at any time.
☐ ☐ 9. Your yard borders on a swamp.
☐ ☐ 10. There is at least one half eaten deer leg buried somewhere in your yard

SCORING:
Give yourself 1 point for every "true" answer.

0-3 pts.   You are a non-yooper. Move to Gross Pointe.

4-6 pts.   You are trying but could use some help. Call the Yooper Yard Hot line at 1-800-DUMPSITE.

7-9 pts.   You are definitely "Keeping up with the Makis" but you might want to get some more dogs.

All 10 pts.   You are a True "Yooper" and have the right to capitalize on this title. Sell tickets to tourists and let them take pictures of your yard.

★★★★★★★★★★★★★★★★★★★★
★ **Words of Whizdom:** ★
★ *Death is nature's way of telling you* ★
★ *that your heart has stopped.* ★
★★★★★★★★★★★★★★★★★★★★

Politics Today

An Interview with
Waino "Wedgie" Kempinen

* * * * * * * * * * * *

Yellow Snow Gazette head writer Joe Potila met with the Tailgate Party's presidential candidate at his deer camp a few miles south of Yellow Snow, Michigan, where Mr. Kempinen fielded some tough questions on the issues.

Gazette: What is your position on the right of citizens to bear arms?

Kempinen: Well, for the biggest part of the year in Yooperland, it's so cold that everybody wears long-sleeved shirts anyway. And in the summer, the mosquitoes are so bad that you don't wanna go running around with bare arms either. But I figure if folks are set on having bare arms, I suppose they oughta have a right to do it. Of course, there are some people who should never go out with bare arms, like my mother-in-law. What a pair of flabby monsters they are. It makes you sick to look at 'em.

Gazette: No, I meant the right to bear arms—B-E-A-R. The right to carry weapons.

Kempinen: Uh—I knew that. It'd be kinda hard to bring down a buck without a gun, unless you got a good heavy piece of iron ore and a good throwing arm. And if your arm is all frozen or full of itchy mosquito bites, your aim might not be too good. So I guess you should wear a flannel shirt and carry a good deer rifle.

Gazette: What do you have to say about the economy?

Kempinen: I'm for it.

Gazette: You issued a challenge to your opponents to meet you in a debate of the issues. Have you had any takers?

Kempinen: Not yet. Bill Clinton's

secretary said he couldn't make it. Something about him having a lot of trouble with Bosnia or something like that. Maybe I'll send him a bottle of my wife's back pills. They work on my gout, and they might help his Bosnia problem. Bob Dole's people said they'd get back to me, but I ain't heard from them yet. He's probably pretty busy with all them pineapples. I'm working on a deal with Bruno down at the Buck Snort Bar to advertise free beer for the debaters. I figure that oughta bring 'em in.

Gazette: Women's rights groups are always lobbying for legislation that will give women equal opportunities to rise to positions of leadership in government and business. If you are elected, how will you deal with that?

Kempinen: I haven't made a decision on that yet. I'll ask da wife and then I'll let you know what I think.

Gazette: Are you pro-life or pro-choice?

Kempinen: Yes.

Gazette: What are your feelings on prayer in public schools?

Kempinen: Well, around exam time there's probably a lot of it going on. I suppose if you can't see your buddy's paper, you gotta do *something.*

Gazette: Your critics say that someone who completed only six grades of schooling lacks the education to handle the responsibilities of the presidency. How do you respond to that?

Kempinen: Well, maybe I only finished six grades, but it took me eighteen years to do it. So I got more years in school than some of them college graduates. I've had more years of American History than Clinton and Dole put together. Go ahead, ask me anything about American History.

Gazette: Okay. Who was Vice President under Rutherford B. Hayes?

Kempinen: Now that's a tough

question. That's the difference between me and them other guys. At least I got the guts to handle the tough questions. You watch those other guys at press conferences and you'll see how slick they are. They'll give you the run-around until your head is spinning so bad that you forget what the question was. Yup, they're pretty good at side-stepping hard questions. Usually they just slide on into some other subject that they're not afraid to talk about, like how bad a president Jimmy Carter was. He was the first honest man in the White House since Lincoln, and all he got for it was a lot of grief. But at least he didn't have to worry about being re-elected. So I plan to use the Carter presidency as a model for my term in the White House. I'll just be honest and deal straight with everybody and there's no way in hell I'll ever get re-elected. Then I can retire with a nice pension. And as an ex-president, I'll probably never have to pay for a beer again. Well, that's all the time I have right now. I'll grab a couple coat hangers and we'll wire up that muffler on your car. I gotta fix that damn pot hole one of these days. Say, can you give me a ride to town? I gotta pick up my unemployment check, and then I got a campaign strategy meeting at the Buck Snort Bar. ■

News Briefs

National Mine Woman Sets New Speed Record

A new record for the 100 yard dash was set during the Yellow Snow Senior Citizen's Track Meet held in Helsten's field on May 12. Elsie Erkkila, 92, streaked to victory with a time of 11 minutes 23 seconds, beating the record set by her grandmother last year. Times on the 1000 meter relay will be reported as soon as the event is completed.

In our last episode... Yooperman and his faithful sidekick Benny are snowbound in their cave. Their food has long since run out, and their physical and mental conditions are rapidly deteriorating. While Benny searches the nooks and crannies of the cave for his belly button, Yooperman doodles on the wall with a piece of charcoal. In his delirious state of mind, he formulates a desperate plan to save himself and Benny from death by starvation. He draws a picture on the wall, a building bearing a sign reading "Woody's Sub & Stopper Shop." He opens the door on the building and steps into the wall, and everything goes black...

The life and times of Toivo Maki known by evil-doers and bad guys as... **YOOPERMAN**

For a moment Yooperman felt a moment of panic, fearing that he might get stuck in the cave wall. He struggled to move forward, and a moment later he popped out of the rock wall into another room. A few feet in front of him was a rough stone counter. Behind the counter stood a stick man, like the kind Yooperman used to draw when he was a kid. He was never very good at drawing people. He was pretty good at muskrats. The stick man stared at him with unblinking eyes. His mouth was a single line, frozen into a perpetual smile, and his hair (Yooperman counted five of them) stuck straight out of his head.

"Welcome to Woody's Sub & Stopper Shop," the stick man said. "What can I do for you?"

"Hullo dere," Yooperman said. "You must be Woody."

"Nope. Nobody by that name here," the stick man said.

Yooperman was confused, as usual. "Well why is this place named 'Woody's Sub & Stopper Shop'?" he asked.

The stick man shook his head. "Beats me," he said. "You're the one who drew the stupid sign."

Yooperman had a little trouble remembering what he had come in for. Then it came back to him.

"Food," he mumbled. "I need food."

"You came to the right place," the stick man said. "We have sub sandwiches, and this week we're running a special on rubber bathtub stoppers."

"Okay," Yooperman said. "I'll take a dozen of each."

"What do you want on those?" The stick man asked.

Yooperman tried to think. "Uh—whattaya got?" he asked.

"Nothing," The stick man said. "I was just kidding. You take 'em plain or not at all."

"Okay, a dozen of each with nothing on 'em," Yooperman said. Then he eyed the stick man suspiciously. "Wait a minute," he said. "Does the nothing cost extra?"

"Nope. No extra charge."

"Okay, nothing on 'em," Yooperman said.

"All right," the stick man said. "Regular or fat-free?"

Yooperman was confused again. "Huh? Regular or fat-free what?"

"Nothing," the stick man said.

"Wait a minute," Yooperman said, tugging at his hair with both hands. "If you're not putting anything on them, why does it matter?"

"But I am putting something on them," the stick man argued.

"What?" Yooperman asked.

"Nothing."

"Okay," Yooperman said, "that's what I want."

"Regular or fat-free?"

Yooperman gave up. "Never mind," he sighed. "I'll take a dozen of each with the works."

"Coming right up," the stick man said. He reached under the counter and pulled out two large paper sacks. "That'll be $12.95."

Yooperman searched his pockets. He had no cash, but he felt the piece of charcoal in his pocket. "Do you take checks?"

"If you have some form of identification," the stick man said.

Yooperman quickly drew himself a small mirror and looked into it. "Yup. That's me," he said.

"Okay," said the stick man.

Yooperman drew a check with his charcoal and filled in the amount. He handed it to the stick man, who crumpled it up, popped it into his mouth, and swallowed hard. Then a slip of paper scrolled out from between his thin lips. He tore it off and handed it to Yooperman.

"Here's your receipt," he said.

Yooperman was anxious to get back to the cave. He was worried about Benny. He turned to leave, but found only a blank wall where he had come in. With his charcoal he quickly drew a door on the wall. He turned to the stick man. "Do you spell 'EXIT' with one or two T's?"

The stick man just stood there, drawn on the wall, behind the counter which was also drawn on the wall. Yooperman drew a sign

Hairold

"Oh, sure—I turn around to look and then you grab the last beer!"

above the door that said OUT. He pushed on the door for a few minutes before he realized it opened inward, then he pulled it open and plunged into the blackness of the wall. A moment later he popped out the other side into the cave. Benny sat in a corner, crying, mumbling something about not having any place to carry his lint.

"Okay, Benny," Yooperman said. "Let's eat!"
He tossed the bag of rubber bathtub stoppers to Benny, who tore it open and began to wolf down the contents. Yooperman tied into his sub sandwiches, and soon their hunger was satisfied.

Benny laid back against the wall, his blue belly bulging, a contented smile on his face. "That was great," he said. "Where did you get all that food?"

Yooperman told him how he had drawn Woody's Sub & Stopper Shop on the wall and had gone in to buy the food.

Benny's smile faded as he listened. "You idiot!" Benny cried. "You can't do that! It's not possible!"

Yooperman scratched his head. "It isn't?" He got up and went over to the drawing of the building on the wall. He ran his hands over it. It was nothing more than a charcoal drawing on the cave wall.

"See?" Benny said. "Take my word for it. It's scientifically impossible."

"Holyowha!" Yooperman said. "It's a good thing you didn't tell me that before we ate."

Benny stroked his chin with a blue hand. "Hm. You have a point there. But now what will we do for food? Who knows how much longer we'll be snowed in here?"

Just then a mosquito came whining along and landed on Benny's neck. It drilled into him and fed until it was bulging. Then its little eyes went crossed and it fell with a tiny scream to the floor of the cave, dead.

"Did you see that?" Yooperman cried. "A mosquito!"

Benny poked at it with a blue finger. "Is that what it is? It doesn't look very tasty."

"Do you know what this means?" Yooperman got up and ran to the mouth of the cave."I was right!" he cheered. " We're saved!"

Benny got up and followed him. They stood at the mouth of the cave. Outside the sun was shining. Birds were singing and blossoms and flowers bloomed everywhere. Yooperman looked at Benny. "I guess we shoulda looked outside once in a while," he said. "We might have been able to leave this cave weeks ago."

"Yeah, you're right," Benny said. "Let's not mention this to anyone, okay?"

"Okay."

They searched the area for Yooperman's remote control, which had been dropped when they fell from the sleigh. It was nowhere to be found. That was okay with Yooperman, since the salad bowl in his head was set to receive the 24 hour Gilligan's Island channel, which was his favorite. Then they gathered up their meager belongings and prepared to leave the cave. Yooperman put his regular clothes on over his Yooperman costume, assuming his secret identity of Toivo Maki. Benny dug a flannel shirt and blue jeans out of his suitcase and put them on. He looked like a yooper smurf, and Toivo had a hard time looking at him without laughing. They packed up their belongings and started off through the woods in search of civilization. Toivo Maki needed to take his place in society, a place where he could blend in among the ordinary mortals and remain ever vigilant, ever watchful for crime, injustice, and littering. Little did he know as he and Benny tramped through the north woods toward civilization that an evil plot was afoot in the land, and that the perpetrator of this evil would be a worthy adversary for even the world's greatest superhero ...YOOPERMAN!"

What sinister evil-doer will arise to become Yooperman's arch-enemy? What evil does he have in store for the weak and innocent? Does he have bad breath? Did he come from a dysfunctional family? Was he a middle child or an only child?

How dangerous is it to stand behind an elephant? How the heck should I know?

*For the answers to these confusing questions, turn to page 68 for the next disturbing episode of **YOOPERMAN!***

*For the answers to these confusing questions, turn to page 68 for the next disturbing episode of **YOOPERMAN!***

Hairold

"Thank God!
That stupid dog finally got tired of barking!"

TWISTED TRIVIA
How twisted are you?
Take this simple test and find out.

Answers & psychiatric profile on page 60

Twisted Trivia Questions
(Hint: Think *really* stupid!)

1. What color is Bob's dog and where does he sleep?
2. If you had a pet stick, what would you call it?
3. Where do black bears usually hibernate?
4. Who invented the indoor flushing toilet?
5. What is the main difference between a boy mosquito and a girl mosquito?
6. How deep do Yoopers dig their wells?
7. Where does a Yooper usually build his out-house?
8. When is the best time to fix the lawn mower?
9. In a beer drinking contest between Yoopers and Cheeseheads, who would win?
10. Why don't Yooper football teams ever play on artificial turf?

WAINO KEMPINEN:
A man of destiny

There are some amazing similarities between Waino "Wedgie" Kempinen and great presidents in history. Are they merely coincidence, or are they indications that this humble man of the people is destined for greatness?

When political analysts first began to take notice of the meteoric rise of Waino Kempinen on the political horizon, they laughed. Making note of Kempinen's humble beginnings, his deceptive image of crudeness and ignorance, his lack of formal education, and his utter failure in virtually everything he had ever attempted in his life, they tended to write him off as being no threat to the aspirations of the powerful high-profile opponents he faces in the political arena. In the 1990's, they say, an ignorant and uneducated unknown outsider who has no financial base, no political allies in high places, and no grasp whatsoever of the basic concepts of politics, has no chance of being elected dog-catcher, much less President of the United States. I would remind these "experts", however, that there is more to success in politics than money, power, and political savvy. Often, throughout the course of human history, the mysterious hand of fate has intervened, wiping away the mightiest plans and highest aspirations of political parties with a careless flick of a forefinger, thus paving the way for an ordinary man to keep an appointment with destiny.

How can one determine whether or not, despite all outward appearances, a man is destined for greatness? One must look for subtle signs, usually in the form of similarities shared with men of destiny throughout history. For instance, in Kempinen's case, one would look for similarities with former U.S. presidents. They do indeed exist. Some of the uncanny similarities are subtle, some more pronounced. For example, I point to the fact that George Washington,

our first president, was a tobacco grower who lived at Mount Vernon. Is it coincidence that Waino Kempinen was a chain smoker who once lived at Vernon Hintsula's camp? Perhaps not. And what about the time Washington hurled a silver dollar across the Potomac river? It is a documented fact that, while on the way home from a night of revelry at the Buck Snort Bar, Waino Kempinen once hurled his lunch across the Ely Creek. Coincidentally, the beer sausage that Kempinen ate for lunch that day cost him *exactly one dollar!* Add to that the legendary incident where George Washington, as a child, chopped down his father's cherry

tree. When asked who did it, young George said, "Father, I cannot tell a lie. I did it." George's father was so impressed with his honesty that he could not bring himself to punish the boy. When Waino Kempinen was eleven years old, he got into his father's homemade choke cherry wine. When the old man asked who drank the wine, young Waino could not lie. In fact, he could not speak at all, since he was passed out. But his brother Toivo said, "Father, I cannot tell a lie. Waino did it."

Waino's father, being a little less forgiving than Mr. Washington, gave the boy a sound trouncing after he regained consciousness. If one looks closely, one can see similarities in the two incidents. Is it coincidence, or something else?

One can also find striking similarities between Kempinen and another great president, Abraham Lincoln. Lincoln was born in a log cabin. Kempinen was born in a tarpaper shack. Lincoln had little formal schooling, yet went on to study law and become a successful lawyer. Kempinen skipped a lot of school, was involved with the law, and never said a word without consulting a lawyer.

Even some of the negative aspects of Kempinen's personality are similar to those of U.S. presidents in history. Ulysses S. Grant struggled with alcoholism, yet managed to serve two terms in the White House. Kempinen could probably drink Grant under the table and then polish off another case just for good measure. Gerald Ford fell down a lot, but Kempinen holds the record for falls, biting the dust 37 times while walking from the Buck Snort Bar to Big Debbie's Hot Oil Massage Parlor and Billiard Room. Ronald Reagan used to walk into the oval office and then stand dumbfounded, wondering what he was there for. Waino Kempinen often stumbles into the men's room of the Buck Snort Bar and stands there in a fog, unable to recall what he came in for.

The similarities go on and on. The name James Buchanan and the name Waino Kempinen both contain thirteen letters, the number of the original colonies. Calvin Coolidge's time in the presidency totaled six years, which is the number of toes on Kempinen's left foot. Using letters from the name Millard Fillmore, you can spell out Millie, which is Kempinen's mother's name. Kempinen's wife bears a striking resemblance to Martin Van Buren when she shaves her upper lip.

These amazing similarities are too numerous to be mere coincidence. The political analysts and prognosticators would do well to take these facts into consideration before they bet the ranch on their favorite candidates. They are liable to find themselves embarrassed and ranchless come election day, when the steady hand of fate places a true man of destiny in the White House.

Send Campaign contributions to Tailgate Party Headquarters at the Buck Snort Bar in Yellow Snow, Michigan.

Rintala's Believe it or Shut Up!

Breakfast of Champions!

Woody Maki, 1995 Yooperland Olympic beer drinking Champion from Yellow Snow, Michigan, drank 139 cans of beer at the Buck Snort Bar on July 4, 1995. Mr. Maki is unavailable for comment, as he is still in the men's room!

Martha's Summer Kitchen

Well, according to our local news we broke records this winter and we're all glad to see the snow go away . Everyone seems to be in better spirits this month. It's amazing what a little sunshine can do. I see my neighbors are raking and getting their gardens ready for planting. Ensio built me a very nice greenhouse a few years back so I start my garden early. On the north side I have a nice bunch of rhubarb plants and every year I bake my rhubarb pie for Ensio. My sister's husband must have a sixth sense because every time I cook rhubarb pie he just happens to stop in for a visit. One of these days I'll have to show my sister the right way to make rhubarb pie. I think she uses snake rhubarb in hers. Anyway, I hope you enjoy this recipe. Have a nice summer.

Rhubarb Pie

1 baked 9-inch shell

2½ cups sugar, approximately
1 cup of water
1¾ pounds rhubarb (5 cups cut)

6 tablespoons cornstarch
1/3 cup of water
1 cup heavy cream, whipped

Cool pie shell while preparing rhubarb filling.

Mix sugar and 1 cup of water; bring to a boil, stirring, and add rhubarb. Cook, stirring gently once or twice before rhubarb starts to soften. Continue cooking without stirring until just tender. Lift out rhubarb with a slotted spoon and reserve.

Heat syrup to boiling. Blend cornstarch with remaining 1/3 cup water; add to boiling syrup and cook, stirring, until thickened and clear. Add more sugar if desired. Add reserved rhubarb; cool 5 minutes and turn into pie shell. Chill.
Before serving, garnish with whipped cream. Sweeten if desired.

Cooking Hint:
Chimneys on a Pie: Keep fruit from boiling over by placing 1½-inch pieces of uncooked macaroni in the top. The juice boils up into these little"Chimneys" instead of boiling over the sides. May be used with a lattice topped or a two crust pie.

*Can intelligence be increased?
NMU Professor Eino Aho thinks so. In this report he chronicles
his experiment with a traditional folk remedy that could become
one of the greatest medical breakthroughs of all time.*

Smart Pills:
*Nature's best hope for
the intellectually
challenged*

By
Professor Eino Aho, head of almost everything at
National Mine University

In my studies of local traditional medicines I have seen many amazing, even miraculous remedies for everything from the common cold to cancer. Recently I was contacted by two brothers who lived in a rusted car body a few miles south of Skanee. They had heard about my research and claimed that they knew of a little known natural remedy for one of the oldest and most widespread afflictions to ever plague mankind—stupidity. I have been struggling with the problem of stupidity for many years, so I gladly agreed to meet with the brothers, who wish to remain anonymous. They agreed to deliver samples of the miraculous remedy to me at my laboratory in exchange for a case of Irish Rose wine. The very next day they arrived at my laboratory with a matchbox full of small brown pellets, which they called *smart pills*, gathered from a cedar swamp where they hunted snowshoe rabbits.

Because of the urgent need for an end to stupidity, I elected not to waste valuable time in laboratory analysis of the pellets. I decided to use myself as a test case. If they could increase the intelligence of a stupid person, imagine what they could do for someone who was already extremely high on the intellectual scale. A half hour before sitting down to write this report, I swallowed six of the pellets. I noticed no effect at first, so I decided to swallow the rest of the pills. As I sat down to write I experienced a slight queasiness of the stomach. The feeling soon passed, however, and was soon replaced by a period of shortness of breath and an increased pulse rate. This was soon replaced by a light-headedness, along with what

I believe to be an increased clarity of thought, an ability to focus my mind on a problem, excluding all external distractions. Even as I write, I am becoming increasingly aware of the amazing dexterity of my fingers. What wonderful tools they are. How gracefully they dance across the keyboard like little ballerinas, never faltering, never zzstumbling%, their little feet touching down as lightly as shadows. I suspect that this heightened sense of awareness is one of the positive effects of the smart pills. In order to be highly intelligent, one must be extremely aware and focused.

The process of thought is the main function of the intellectual mind in its search for solutions. It is like a train, remaining true to its course, never leaving the track until it reaches its destination. Of course, sometimes trains have accidents. Maybe a drunken engineer, or possibly a couple of foolish hot-rodding kids who think they can beat the train. Then you have a real mess on your hands. All those dead people lying around. And then some wino comes by and steals their shoes. No, not like a train. I can see that now. The smart pills are definitely taking effect. The thought process of the intellectual mind is more like a hungry stray dog, nosing through a garbage can, ignoring the useless bits of inorganic material, ferreting out the edible tidbits. But then he usually gets shot in the ass by some guy with a pellet gun. He yelps and runs out into the street into the path of a beer truck driven by a guy named Bill. Then the next day, when you're driving to work with a hangover, you see a big black crow picking his guts out and you barf all over your dashboard. No, I was in error in my earlier assumption. The intellectual thought process is not like a hungry dog after all. As the effect of the smart pills becomes more apparent, I find that I can think more clearly and concentrate better with each passing moment. My ability to focus, and to follow clear and logical lines of thought toward solutions to questions seems greatly enhanced. With the help of this miraculous aid to clear and focused thinking, there may be no problem that cannot be solved. Now that the smart pills

"Don't worry, there are no animals in these woods bigger than a rabbit."

have taken effect, I will put my increased intelligence and concentration to the test in reasoning out an answer to a difficult question.

Question: *If a tree falls in the forest and no one is there to hear it, does it make a sound?*

As I contemplate this question, I wonder what made the tree fall in the first place. Obviously, it was not cut down by lumberjacks, because they would have been there to hear it fall. Of course, it is possible that they were deaf lumberjacks, even though there is no record of any lumber camps ever hiring the handicapped. But then it would be stupid to hire deaf lumberjacks, because they would never hear when you yelled, "Timber!" and they would all eventually be killed by falling trees. Of course, they could have communicated by sign language, unless they were blind as well as deaf. But if they were blind they wouldn't have fingers to make signs because, being both blind and deaf, the only way they could tell if their chain saws were running would be to feel the chains to see if they were going. In no time at all, the whole bunch of them would be fingerless. And of course, if they didn't have any fingers, they couldn't operate their chain saws to cut down trees, so no trees would fall in the forest, and all the lumberjacks would be fired. Then they would probably all go to a bar to drown their troubles in strong drink, and then we would have a lot of deaf and blind fingerless drunken unemployed lumberjacks on our hands. A tragic situation indeed.

I think it is important that we do something for these poor souls who have sacrificed so much. We must find new jobs for them. But what can these men do if they can't see or hear, have no fingers, and are hopeless alcoholics? First we have to get them dried out. Although it may seem harsh, we could pass legislation to make it illegal to sell alcohol to deaf and blind fingerless unemployed drunken lumberjacks. Eventually they would recover from their alcoholism and they would thank us for it. Then, since they could not hear, see, or do any manual work because of their fingerless condition, they could be put to work as thinkers and philosophers. We could put them all in a room here at NMU and feed them a regular diet of smart pills, and they could just sit around and think all day. Maybe they could even come up with an answer to the question of the tree falling in the forest, if it is not too painful for them to think about it. Or maybe not. Frankly, I don't have time to worry about such trivia anymore. My face is melting and I just noticed several miniature television repairmen swimming around in my coffee cup. The colors are awesome! My dog , sleeping on the floor next to my desk, woke up and spoke to me, telling me to go and take a nap. He has a British accent. How strange. ∎

Top 11 fun things to do in the spring

1. Watch geese trying to land on frozen ponds.
2. Shovel snow left behind by "April Showers."
3. Hold pagan sun-worship rituals.
4. Sit in a lawn chair with a beer and cheer for the little patches of bare ground.
5. Build an anatomically correct snowman.
6. Go metal detecting for garden tools under the snow in the back yard.
7. Throw snowballs at neighbors returning from winter in Florida.
8. Put on shorts and wish it was warm enough to go outside.
9. Remove that embarrassing dried up Xmas tree from the snowbank by the back door
10. Cover bare patches of ground with show and turn calendar back to January.
11. Go back to sleep until July.

Twisted Trivia

Answers to

1. I don't know.
2. Why bother? It wouldn't come anyway.
3. In the woods.
4. Thomas Crapper. (It's true-look it up!).
5. One is male, the other is female.
6. To the bottom.
7. Outside.
8. When it's broken.
9. Who cares? The beer is free!
10. During half time there would be no place for the cheerleaders to graze. (Sorry, we couldn't resist this one)

See below your score and evaluation

0-3 Correct. . . . You're probably harmless.

4-6 Correct. . . . Someone should keep an eye on you.

7-9 Correct. . . . You should stop playing with dead things.

ALL 10 CORRECT

Turn yourself in before they come for you!

SUMMER REALLY SUCKED!

What do you say about a place where there is more heating fuel consumed during the month of July than in a whole year in most parts of the country? Summer really, really sucked, that's what you say. Although we did have two or three days where you could actually get a miserable sunburn, (which Yoopers usually do because they don't know how to deal with the sun) those days were the exception. There were altogether too many days of dark, dreary rain, with temperatures hovering around the mid forties, sometimes dipping lower. But we must take comfort in the knowledge that this was not the worst summer we ever had. This reporter seems to recall grandma dressing up our grandson in a snowsuit to go and watch the Fourth of July fireworks just a couple of years ago. The only reason it didn't snow on that day was because there was no precipitation. But had it come, it wouldn't have been rain.

Now we're well past halfway through the summer, and memories of last winter still linger even as we count down the days until this summer's garden dies of hypothermia. We unconsciously scan the trees for any trace of color. Although the autumn is glorious in this part of the country, the first tinge of color brings on a feeling of foreboding; a vaguely chilling feeling that nothing lasts forever, least of all summer in Yooperland. Of course, once the fall colors near their peak, we have gotten used to the idea that summer is over, and we turn our attention toward enjoying the autumn, and we try not to think about what comes next. Still, as jaded as one might get, there is that little bit of kid in most of us that just won't die. That's the part of us that actually feels excitement at the first snow. It's the magical first snow of the winter. Sledding, skating, building snowmen, building snow forts that put the Alamo to shame. Coming in with rosy cheeks and a cherry red nose to sip hot chocolate in front of a roaring fire. Christmas! Nice idea. Call me irresponsible. Call me a romantic.

Call me *stupid!* What about shoveling and snow-blowing every other day? What about humungous heating bills? What about cars that refuse to come to life once the mercury drops out of sight? What did I do with that Florida map? I wanna look at it again. That's it. I'll just sit in front of the fire with a double brandy and look at my worn and tattered Florida map. I'll just look at it and dream until next July.

Great Moments In History!

Wyatt Earp was actually a Finlander from Negaunee, Michigan. He was born Waino Erpala, but changed his name when he moved out west. His legendary clean-up of Tombstone, Arizona was not as a peace officer, but as a sanitation engineer. During his tenure as chief manure shoveler, not one citizen of Tombstone ever stepped in horse shit.

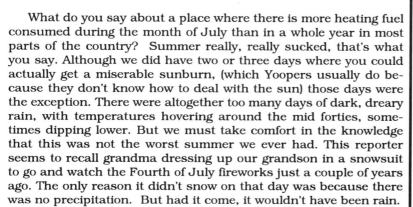

Campaign '96
The Tailgate Party

Kempinen Campaign Rally a Riot

A campaign rally held at the Buck Snort Bar by supporters of the Tailgate Party presidential candidate Waino "Wedgie" Kempinen ended in violence last Saturday night. A spokesman for the "Win With Wedgie" campaign told reporters in a press conference yesterday that the riot was the result of a simple misunderstanding. During a campaign strategy meeting, Kempinen's campaign strategists suggested that he kiss some babies, which is a long-standing traditional practice in politics. Kempinen's hearing aid was in the shop for repairs at the time, and he thought they said "kiss some babes." The resulting fist-fight between Kempinen's wife and Miss Barbie Bigguns at the campaign rally following the meeting sparked a free-for-all in which five people were hospitalized and one arrested. Candidate Kempinen issued a public apology for the incident. "It was an honest mistake," he said. "If I am elected president I'll carry a spare hearing aid with me all the time so things like this won't happen when I'm dealing with leaders of hostile countries. No problem." When asked if the incident would adversely affect his campaign tour of Yooperland planned for next month, Kempinen replied, "No, not at all. We're gonna keep up our aggressive campaign. Just like my campaign manager said at our strategy meeting, we're gonna hit the campaign trail and kiss some Syrian's butt." There will be a fund-raiser at the Buck Snort Bar next Saturday night to raise bail for Mrs. Kempinen.

Gravel Gertie's

Husband Training Tips

How to keep 'em Whipped!

Dear Gertie,
My husband has this big, ugly flea-bitten hound that he loves. I don't mind the dog so much, but he always does his business all over our lawn. I like to putter in the yard, but I'm constantly stepping in dog dump. I've complained to my husband but to no avail. What can I do?
Shingleton Shoe-scraper

Dear Shingle,
My Eugene had a big mongrel that used to dump all over our yard. I scooped up the doggy logs and put them in strategic places. I put a big one on the seat of Eugene's truck, and another in one of his shoes. I kept this up for a few days, and I had fun finding creative places to hide the goodies. Finally one day, when Eugene fired up the sauna and the big squishy pile of doggy do on the rocks began to heat up and spread its aroma, he gave up. He took the dog for a ride, and I haven't seen it since.
Gertie

Dear Gertie,
I read the YSG and I thoroughly enjoy most of it. But when I get to your column it makes me sick. You guessed it, I am a husband. Your continuous husband bashing is in poor taste. No, we're not perfect, but we don't deserve the kind of humiliation and ridicule that you subject us to in your column.
Hurt Hubby

Dear Slime,
Watch it, bub—I know where you live.
Gertie

Dear Gertie,
Every Saturday night I like to spend a few hours relaxing in the sauna. But my husband is a full-blooded Finn and he likes it hot. Once he gets the temperature up to where he likes it and gets through throwing water on the rocks, I look and feel like a boiled lobster. I can't stand it and I have to get out. I tried to talk to him about it, but he says I'm just a wimp. What can I do?
Steamed in Stambaugh

Dear Steamed,
My Eugene used to get the sauna so hot I could steam vegetables in it. Here's what I do. A couple of hours before we go into the sauna I eat a big plate of corned beef and cabbage and wash it down with a few warm beers. I just let the mixture ferment, and by the time the sauna is ready, so am I. It only takes about ten minutes for me to drive Eugene out and then I have the sauna to myself for the rest of the evening.
Gertie

Dear Gertie,
My husband has a terrible habit. He quit smoking last year, but now he chews tobacco. On weekends he plops down in front of the TV, puts in a big chew, and promptly falls asleep. He lies there with his mouth hanging open, drooling tobacco juice all over. All his shirts are tobacco stained, and so is my couch. Any suggestions?
Grossed Out

Dear Grossed,
The next time he puts a load of chew in and falls asleep, try running a bead of super glue along his lower lip. Then clamp his mouth shut for a few seconds. Your troubles will be over and his will be just beginning. Sometimes this will cure a man of chewing permanently.
Gertie

Science Department

UFOs: Fact or Fantasy?

Professor Eino Aho, head of just about everything at National Mine University, takes an objective look at those strange objects in the sky.

For a number of years now I have been conducting ongoing research into the phenomenon of UFOs. I have read much material on the subject, and I find that most people, when discussing UFOs, tend to lose their scientific objectivity. Virtually everyone who ever addresses the subject seems to have formed an opinion on UFOs. Even respected scientists have fallen victim to the tendency of the unenlightened to jump to premature conclusions. All their research, therefore, is geared toward proving their own pet theories, or disproving the theories of others. As a result, no one has maintained an impartial and open-minded method of study of this phenomenon. I, with my customary scientific objectivity, will present only the facts that I have discovered in my research and will leave it up to the reader to draw conclusions based on these facts.

First of all, I must clarify my subject. The term UFO could mean anything from "Uncouth Fascist Octogenarians" to "Unruly Farmyard Omnivores" to "Ugly Fat Outlaws." For the sake of exactness, I must specify that, in the context of this study, the term UFO will refer only to *Unidentified Flying Objects.*

Exactly what is an Unidentified Flying Object? It is an object that we cannot identify which is in the act of flying. This definition excludes from my study objects that are identified, such as rocking chairs or digital watches, and also objects that do not fly, such as—well, rocking chairs or digital watches. The key words in the term Unidentified Flying Objects are the words "Unidentified" and "Flying." The word "Object" simply describes a thing. A thing is always a thing except when it is not, in which case it is nothing and we cannot see it, and we therefore cannot determine whether it is unidentified or not, or whether it is flying or not, or indeed whether it is an object or not, except for the fact that it is not there. So, to avoid confusion, we will restrict our study to objects that do indeed exist. Now that I have cleared up this confusion, let us move on. If an object is flying through the air, but is clearly seen to be an airplane, a mallard duck, or a potato thrown by an

The object is in flight, but is identified as a cow, therefore it cannot be classified as a genuine UFO.

COOKIES

The object is unidentified, but is at rest upon a case of motor oil mistakenly labeled "cookies," therefore it is not a UFO.

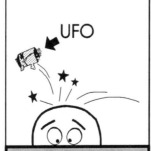

UFO

The object is in flight and is unidentified, therefore it can be classified as a bona fide Unidentified Flying Object.

angry wife, that object is flying, but it is also identified, and therefore it does not qualify as a UFO. By the same token, if an object is unidentified but is not flying, such as an unidentifiable object dragged in by the dog and left lying on the living room rug, it still cannot be accurately termed a UFO. However, if the unidentified object left on the rug by the dog were to be picked up and thrown out the window, it would for a short time be in the act of flying, and therefore could be termed an Unidentified Flying Object. The same is true of many unidentified objects that I find while cleaning my garage. They may be identifiable by someone, but I have no idea what they might be, so I send them flying into the garbage can. During their short flight into the can they become bona fide UFOs.

Another type of UFO is the flying object that we probably could identify if we had sufficient time in which to make an identification. For instance, during my lunch break at the Buck Snort Bar the other day, an argument broke out near the pool table. The argument quickly escalated into a free-for-all involving most of the patrons of the bar. At some point during the conflict, an object whizzed by my head and flew out the open window. From my brief glimpse of the object, I guessed that it must have been either a cue ball or Heikki Makinen's glass eye. But I cannot be certain of the identity of the object, so I must label it a UFO.

Some UFO observers have theorized that many UFOs may be space vehicles from other worlds. If any of these observers were to conclusively prove that the objects in question were indeed spacecraft, then these objects would be identified, and would no longer qualify as UFOs. We would be able to eliminate such objects from our research and thus significantly narrow our field of study. Then serious researchers such as myself would be able to concentrate our study on those mysterious objects that fly through our everyday lives, defying identification and explanation. Perhaps then I will be able to go to sleep at night without having to wrestle with disturbing questions like *was it a cue ball or a glass eye?*

Madame Brewsky's

News that ain't happened yet

As I sat down to my crystal ball and my fourth jumbo last Saturday night, I had a vision. I could see in my crystal ball an image of the Chicago Cubs playing in the 1997 World Series. I could not get a clear image of the other team, but I know the Cubs were playing because I kept hearing somebody yelling "Holy Cow!" over and over. Then the scoreboard came into focus and I could see that it was the bottom of the ninth inning and there were two outs. The Cubs were down by one run. I could also see that the bases were loaded. A batter was at the plate, and after a few swigs from my jumbo to clear my vision I could see that he wore a Cub uniform. He took a mighty swing at the first pitch, and I heard him swearing in Spanish as he missed the ball by at least a foot. The next pitch was a fast ball right across the middle of the plate, and the batter just turned up his nose and ignored it. The next three pitches went by and the count was full. The crowd was on its feet, hollering and screaming so wildly that I had to finish off my jumbo and open another one before I could continue. The pitcher wound up and let it fly, and the batter gave a mighty swing. There was a loud crack as the bat connected with the ball, which went sailing toward the center field wall. It was a high fly ball, so high that it went almost out of sight. The center fielder seemed to think he had a shot at it, because he kept running toward the wall, and when he reached it he leaped into the air, reaching over the wall with his mitt. I could see the grimace of effort on his face as he stretched his arm out. Unfortunately, at that moment, I got excited and spilled my beer all over my crystal ball. Sorry, Cub fans. I guess you'll just have to wait and see. In the next issue I'll have news that ain't happened yet about the second coming of Elvis. Don't miss it!

What I did on my SUMMER VACATION

The winning entry in our essay contest was submitted by Ed McKelvie of Ann Arbor, Michigan. Ed received a certificate and an authentic thing that we found in our garage but can't identify.

On my summer vacation I went fishing with my wife. She drove because I can't drive and drink at the same time without spilling my beer. When we got to the river I got out and shut the car door. Then I noticed that my shirt tail was caught in the door. I tried to open it but it was locked. I told the wife to open the door and get me loose, but she said oops she locked her door too, and she left the keys in the car. That wasn't bad enough, but she also left the car in neutral. All of a sudden the car started to roll down the hill toward the river. I had to run alongside the car because my shirt tail was still caught in the door. I yelled to the wife to help me and she yelled back, drag yer feet, drag yer feet. I tried, but I couldn't stop the car. It went over the bank into the river. I thought I was done for. Then I remembered I had my pocket knife with me. I took out my knife and cut myself loose just as the car sank to the bottom. I tried to swim to the bank, but the current was too strong and it kept washing me down the river. The wife hollered hold on, I'll go get a rope. She ran to a farm house back up the road and came back with a long clothesline. I hollered trow da rope, trow da rope! She threw the rope. It was a good throw and it got right to me. The only problem was she forgot to hold on to one end. So now I'm floating down the river all tangled up in clothesline and I'm starting to drown. So I started thinking, what would McGuyver do at a time like this? I couldn't think of anything, except maybe drowning. Then I saw up ahead a tree branch hanging out over the river. I threw the clothesline up over it and one of the clothespins got snagged in the branches. Trouble was, the rope got tangled around my neck and I started choking. The wife could see what was happening and she hollered, cut da rope, cut da rope. So I took out my knife again and cut the rope before I choked to death. Now I was back in the same trouble I started with, which was drowning. I thought maybe I liked choking better. The wife was running along the river bank hollering, swim Eddie, swim, and I hollered back I don't know how. Then she hollered hold on, I'll go call 911, and she ran off back to the farm house. While she was gone I got washed onto a sand bar. I walked back to the farm house where she was still talking to the 911 operator about some beauty parlor and I told her I was okay. She said be quiet, can't you see I'm on the phone. I decided to go find a bar and have a few beers and just leave the car in the river. It was probably all full of water anyway, cause all the windows were open. Anyway, that's what I did on my summer vacation.

"What do you mean, Get it yourself?"

BANK ROBBERY ATTEMPT FAILS!
Two Yellow Snow Men in Custody

Two Yellow Snow residents are in custody today after a failed bank robbery attempt at the Fourth National Bank of Yellow Snow. According to bank sources, the two men, identified as Sulo and Otto Salminen, brothers who live in an abandoned chicken coop on the outskirts of town, entered the bank soon after it opened yesterday morning. Armed with a BB gun, they handed a paper sack to the teller, demanding that she fill it with money. The brothers might have been successful in their robbery attempt, but their plans went awry as they were attempting to make their getaway. According to a Yellow Snow Sheriff's Department official who interrogated the pair, the brains of the operation was the older brother, Sulo. Apparently he had seen a robbery on a television show where the robbers wore nylon stockings over their heads so they wouldn't be recognized. The brothers were unable to find nylon stockings, so they used a pair of pantyhose. Each brother put one leg of the pantyhose over his head. Sulo later said, "It worked out okay as long as we walked really close together." But problems arose as they left the bank and attempted to make their getaway. As they hit the street, each brother tried to run in a different direction. Sulo wanted to run north to escape across the cedar swamp, and Otto thought they should go south across Helsten's field. Seldom able to agree on anything, the brothers got into an argument over which way to go. When Sheriff's deputies arrived two hours later, the brothers were still engaged in a tug-of-war outside the bank. They were arrested without resistance, and the money, totaling $45.17 in small bills, was recovered.

The Salminen brothers were paroled last month from the state prison where they were serving time for the kidnapping of the son Yellow Snow Mayor Urho Ahola in 1979. The kidnapping made front page headlines all over the county. The Salminen brothers snatched Mayor Ahola's son as he walked to school on May 5, 1979. After composing a ransom note demanding $100.00 in unmarked bills, the brothers argued over who would deliver it. Finally it was agreed that they would send the kid home with the note. Mayor Ahola was outraged when he received the note, but, as he said later to reporters, the safety of his son was worth any price. He sent the kid back with the money. After receiving the ransom, the Salminen brothers released the boy. They might have gotten away with the kidnapping, but when law enforcement officials examined the ransom note, they noticed that the brothers had signed it. When confronted with this evidence, the Salminen brothers confessed. They were convicted of the crime and sentenced to twenty years for the kidnapping and an additional five years for stupidity. Mayor Ahola was subsequently re-elected, and he still serves as Mayor to this day. ■

The long winters, the rainy summers, the mosquitoes, the depressed economy—why would anyone want to live in a place like this?

Top 11 reasons why Yoopers stay in the U.P.

11. Year-round deer season.
10. You can let your lawn grow long enough to hide the rusted car bodies and nobody cares.
9. One of the few places in the country where you can buy a car that runs for a 12-pack and a flannel shirt.
8. The only place where you can find a wife experienced in small engine repair and snow removal.
7. Save a lot of money on sun screen.
6. No need to lock your doors—no one has ever stolen a door in the U.P.
5. Enjoy the challenge of growing garden-fresh veggies in a 12-day growing season.
4. You never have to worry about drive-by shootings— it's impossible to drink a beer, smoke a Camel, drive, and shoot at the same time.
3. It's easy to lose weight—just sit outside and let the mosquitoes eat.
2. Don't want to bother learning a foreign language.
1. The family car won't make it out of the U.P.

Werner Warpula

Yellow Snow Wire Service

Waino Kempinen:
The best of both worlds

When you compare the qualities of all the candidates, you find that Waino "Wedgie" Kempinen has all the bases covered. He possesses all the best qualities of both his opponents and more.

When the political pundits and analysts put the candidates under the microscope and really take a long, objective look, they will find that one stands out from the pack—Waino "Wedgie" Kempinen. The Tailgate Party, unlike the other two major political parties, is willing to admit that each of the other candidates have some good points. Kempinen campaign strategists have enough confidence in their man to measure his presidential qualities against those of his opponents. Even when Clinton and Dole are shown in the best light possible, Tailgate Party strategists think their man will still come out on top in a comparison.

For instance, Dole showed a lot of courage in leaping out of the security of his Senate job to spend all his time and energy on his presidential bid. It showed that he was not afraid to bet it all on a long shot, sort of like Kennedy did during the Bay of Pigs, or like Nixon did with Watergate. It is a presidential quality, this willingness to risk everything on a hunch, on a gut feeling that everything might turn out okay in the end. And of course, because of Dole's stature in the government and in the media, his move became front page news. But what about Kempinen? It goes unreported that Waino Kempinen, in order to devote more time and energy to his campaign, gave up his position of 39 years as captain of the Buck Snort Bar cribbage team. This is a position that has provided Kempinen with a sense of security, a feeling that he actually had friends, and also a few free beers when the team did well in cribbage tournaments. To give all this up in order to pursue his dream is a leap of faith that shows presidential

courage. Kempinen has the recklessness it takes to gamble everything he has on a hunch. It seems logical then, that as president, he would have the guts to risk the future of the nation on a whim. And for Kempinen there is no going back. If he blows the election, his cronies at the Buck Snort Bar will not be quick to forgive him for his abandonment. Dole has a much better chance of getting back into the Senate than Kempinen has of being welcomed back by his cronies at the Buck Snort Bar, should he come crawling back a loser.

On the other hand, Bill Clinton exhibits another kind of courage; the stoic endurance of years of attacks on his character, including everything from rumors of extramarital affairs to draft dodging to Whitewater. Through it all he manages to carry on the duties of his office, and even manages to look as if he doesn't have a care in the world. Maybe he finally learned to inhale. At any rate, his Kennedyesque image of young vitality is definitely a plus. And of course, because of his position, he gets a lot of media coverage. But what about Kempinen? It is never reported that, despite constant attacks on his character by

political enemies, Kempinen continues to maintain a confident and dignified public image. Enemies have accused Kempinen of everything from draft dodging to income tax evasion. Responding to charges that he spent the entire Vietnam War in Canada, Kempinen explained that it was just a fishing trip, and he would have come back sooner, but his truck wouldn't start. Kempinen, like Clinton, has also had to contend with legal problems. In the famed Whizwater case, Kempinen was charged with indecent exposure while making a bush call on the way home from the Buck Snort Bar. Kempinen maintains that it was a case of mistaken identity. In the gloom of night, he had simply mistaken the mayor's wife for a lilac bush. Kempinen endures attempts to defame his character with a smile, although Mrs. Kempinen has been involved in several fist fights with his accusers. And as for Hillary Clinton being a strong and aggressive first lady, Kempinen contends that his old lady Helga could whip Hillary's butt without breaking a sweat.

So, in comparison to the other candidates, Kempinen measures up pretty well. Although he no longer has the impressive head of hair that Clinton wears like a crown, and he doesn't have Dole's advantage of a physical handicap (I hope that's the current politically correct name for it) he does have an Elvis wig in his closet and he has bad back that flares up when the snow flies. These physical endearments, along with the strength of his character and his stand on the issues, make him a force to be reckoned with in the battle for votes in November. ☺

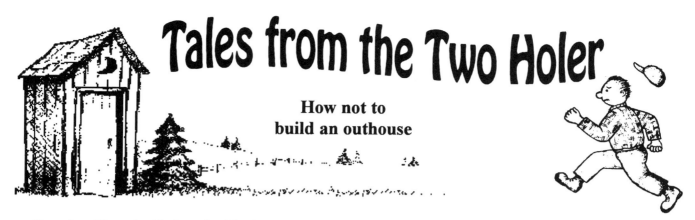

Tales from the Two Holer

How not to
build an outhouse

One day Eino decided to build himself a new outhouse. The old one was falling apart. The wood was beginning to rot and the tarpaper was worn and faded and full of holes. But building an outhouse was a pretty big job for one man, so he called his good friend and neighbor Toivo to come and help. Eino looked over the stack of lumber left over from building his sauna. He had a stack of pine boards for the walls and the roof. There was a big roll of tarpaper. He had plenty of nails. But he needed two by fours for the framework.

"I'll start digging the hole," he said to Toivo. " You go to the lumber yard and get two dozen two by fours." So while Eino sat with a cup of coffee and a Pall Mall, planning the digging of the hole, Toivo took the truck over to the lumber yard. He told Pirto at the lumber yard, "Me and Eino are gonna build an outhouse. I need two dozen two by fours."

"Okay," Pirto said. "How long do you need those two by fours?"

Toivo scratched his head. Eino didn't say anything about how long he wanted the two by fours. He thought about it for a while and then he made a decision. "We're gonna need 'em for a long time," he said.

Meanwhile, Eino sat with his Pall Mall and his coffee, thinking about what would be the best way to go about digging the outhouse hole. After quite a bit of thinking and planning, he decided the best way to go about it was to have Toivo dig it.

Just then Toivo came rattling up the driveway with the two by fours in the back of the truck. He stuck his head out the window and hollered to Eino, "I got the two by fours! Pirto says we can keep 'em as long as we want!"

Eino didn't quite know what he meant by that, but he didn't ask. He was sure to end up confused if he did.

"Okay," Eino said "You start digging this hole while I figure out how we're going to build the outhouse." Then he went in the house to get another cup of coffee to help him think. He sat at the kitchen table, drinking coffee and smoking Pall Malls, thinking about how he was going to build the outhouse.

A few hours later, Toivo called from outside. "The hole is done! What do we do next?"

Eino went outside and showed Toivo how to nail the two by fours together for the frame of the outhouse. Then he went back in to get another cup of coffee and a Pall Mall and think about how to put the pine boards on the walls and the roof. A few hours later Toivo called from outside. "I'm done with the frame," he said. "We're ready to nail the boards on!"

Eino went out an measured and marked the boards himself. Then he told Toivo to nail the boards onto the frame. He went back in the house for another cup of coffee and another Pall Mall. After a while he went back out to see how Toivo was doing. He watched Toivo work for a while. Toivo was hammering away on the outhouse wall. But as Eino watched, he noticed that every once in a while, Toivo would take a nail out of the bag, hold it up to the wall, shake his head, and toss the nail away.

"Why are you throwing those nails away?" Eino asked.

"Well," said Toivo. "Some of these nails are pointing the wrong way."

"You're so dumb," Eino replied. "Those nails are for the other side!"

"Oh," Toivo said, scratching his head. "Why didn't I think of that?"

"Because you're not as smart as I am," Eino answered.

"I am too as smart you are!" Toivo argued.

"No, you're not, and I'll prove it," Eino said. He held his hand up against the outhouse wall. "Punch my hand as hard as you can," he said.

"Okay," Toivo said. He wound up and swung at Eino's hand. Eino pulled his hand out of the way, and Toivo's fist smashed into the wall.

"Ouch! That hurts!" he said.

"See what I mean?" Eino said.

"Ya, but you gotta give me a chance to get even," Toivo said. He held his hand up in front of his face. "Punch my hand as hard as you can."

1	2	3	4
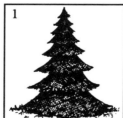		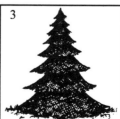	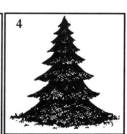

How observant are you?   Take this simple test and find out.
Three of the trees above are identical.   One is different from the other three.
Can you find the one that is different?   Answer on page 72

The life and times of Toivo Maki known by evil-doers and bad guys as...

YOOPERMAN

In our last episode... *Yooperman and his faithful companion Benny have survived starvation in the cave, and now they trudge through the wilderness in search of civilization, where Yooperman plans to blend into normal human society in his secret identity of Toivo Maki, where he will remain ever vigilant for evil, littering, and bad grammar. Little do they know that an evil plot is already afoot, and that Yooperman will soon face the greatest challenge of his young superhero career.*

Karl Kamper was born in a motor home at a rest stop on the outskirts of Detroit on the same day that Toivo Maki, also known as Yooperman, was born to ma and pa Maki in Yooperland. No one, except someone really, really smart, would have ever guessed that one of these little farts would grow up to become the world's greatest superhero, and the other would become the most evil villain to ever cross the Mackinac Bridge. Karl Kamper was born to Klarence and Karol Kamper, a couple of professional tourists who made their living by traveling around the country and dropping in on unsuspecting relatives for extended visits.

Although they were born on the same day, Karl Kamper and Toivo Maki could not have been more different. Toivo Maki always had a place to call home, first with ma and pa Maki and the dozens of little Makis, and later with the family of muskrats that had taken him in and raised him. Karl Kamper had been born on the road and had moved constantly, traveling with his parents to the homes of various relatives around the country. Toivo was a blonde haired Finn with the build of a long distance runner. Karl was of unknown ancestry. He sported thick black hair that not only grew out of his head, but also out of his nose and ears. He was short and squat and rather twisted, almost to the point of deformity. In short, Karl Kamper was a Troll. But even worse than that, Karl Kamper always disfigured words that started with "C", replacing the first letter with "K". He had learned this from his father who, before becoming a professional tourist, worked for an advertising agency in Detroit. His father had taught Karl that using "K" instead of "C" made words Kute and Katchy. Karl had acquired the habit at a young age, and carried it to such an extreme that he even *spoke* such words with a "K" instead of a "C". Needless to say, he flunked spelling in grade school, and this made Karl bitter. It may have been what caused him to go wrong in the first place. But bad spelling was not the worst of Karl Kamper's crimes. Since he never had a real home of his own, Karl Kamper never learned to respect other people's homes. He grew up to be the worst kind of tourist. He traveled around in his coal black motor home, leaving

a trail of empty beer cans, oil slicks, and graffiti everywhere he went. Karl Kamper had made it his mission in life to litter every mile of highway in the country. Along the way he had acquired a gang of misfits who were only too willing to join him in his evil plan. On the side of his coal black motor home he had painted "Karl Kamper and the Goodtime Gang." They traveled the highways of the land, littering as they went, lumbering along at 30 miles per hour on busy two-lane highways, and generally making life miserable for normal people. Now as Toivo Maki and his sidekick Benny tromped through the woods of Yooperland toward the town of Yellow Snow, Karl Kamper sat behind the wheel of his coal black motor home, studying his road map. He traced the red line that represented I-75 with his finger, up toward the Mackinac Bridge and beyond. "That's where we'll go next!" he said, tapping the map with his forefinger. "Up above the bridge! There's a lot of untouched natural beauty to litter up there!" His eyes glittered with evil anticipation. "And there are a lot of two lane highways up there, too!" he crowed. "We'll just poke along, holding up traffic and driving people nuts! It'll be kool!" There was a cheer and a few burps from the Goodtime Gang as Karl Kamper shoved the motor home into drive and stomped the gas.

Yooperman, disguised in his Toivo Maki clothes, sloshed along through a low, swampy valley. A few steps behind him, Benny struggled along, taking a few steps, falling, getting up, stumbling, and falling again with a splash into the mud and water.

"Glrzgh frrbllp!" Benny cursed in his native language as he tripped on a grass hump and fell for the fifteenth time. He struggled to his feet, mumbling under his breath. His blue face was even bluer with exertion and frustration.

"Did you say something?" Toivo asked. He had been walking along with his eyes closed, watching Gilligan's Island. Despite the high pine covered hills on both sides, he was getting good reception through the salad bowl in his head.

"Never mind," Benny grumbled. "You wouldn't understand it even if I translated it."

"Well, if you're not saying anything important, try not to say anything at all," Toivo said. It sounded like something his mother might have said, sort of. "I'm trying to watch Gilligan's Island," he continued. "This is the episode where

Gilligan gets really strong." He closed his eyes and trudged on. "I don't know why he doesn't jump at the chance to beat the crap out of the skipper," he mumbled under his breath.

"Slzrgh Zhbvrt!" Benny said as he hit the swamp for the sixteenth time.

Yooperman sloshed along with his eyes closed. Benny was preoccupied with falling down, cursing, and getting up again. Neither of them noticed the yellow sign that read: *DANGER! Quicksand Area!* They trudged onward, unaware that they were now traveling across a sludge pond, where iron ore tailings from a nearby iron mine were pumped, forming a wide and deep pond of muck that could easily suck them down to certain death. After they had walked in silence for a short while, Benny asked, "Hey! weren't you taller just a minute ago?"

Toivo stopped and looked down. To his alarm, he saw that he was thigh deep in muck and sinking. "I'm sinking!" he cried.

Benny perched on a nearby grass hump looking puzzled. "Why would you want to do that?" he asked. "Is it fun?" There was no such thing as quicksand on his world, and he didn't quite grasp the danger.

"You moron!" Yooperman snapped. "If you think it's so much fun, why don't you just jump in here with me?"

"Okay," Benny said, and he hopped off the grass hump into the muck beside Toivo.

"No!" Yooperman cried, but it was too late. "I was being sarcastic!"

"I know," Benny said meekly. " It dawned on me while I was in the air."

Toivo tried to stretch and grab the hump of grass that Benny had just vacated, but it was just out of reach. He had now sunk to the waist and was still sinking.

"I'm tired of this sinking business already," Benny said. "How do we get out of here?"

Toivo resisted the urge to give Benny a good slap. "Well, if one of us was sitting on that grass hump right there," he growled, "he could pull the other one out."

Benny thought about that for a minute, then he lowered his head. "Oh." he said.

"We have to figure a way to get out of here," Toivo said. He was now chest deep in the slimy muck, and Benny had sunk past where his belly button would have been.

They looked around. There was nothing within their grasp that they could use to pull themselves free. The situation looked hopeless. Toivo turned to Benny.

"Well," he said, "it looks like this is it, partner."

"This is *what?*" Benny asked.

This time Toivo did give him a slap. "This is *IT*, you moron! The end! The grand finale! We're gonna die!"

"Oh, *that* it," he said. Then it hit home. "OH! We're gonna die!" he screamed.

While Benny screamed bloody murder, Toivo closed his eyes. He figured if he was going to die anyway, he might as well catch the end of the Gilligan's Island episode on the salad bowl in his head before he went under. While he watched Gilligan and Benny screamed prayers and curses in his strange alien tongue, they sank deeper and deeper...

Is this the end of our heroes? Will Yooperman get to see

the end of Gilligan's Island before he meets his death in the slimy ooze of the pond? If Yooperman dies, who will save Yooperland from the evil Karl Kamper and the Goodtime Gang? Does anyone really care? Have you seen my watch? Do insects ever fart? What is the capital of Armenia?

For the answers to some of these stupid questions, consult your encyclopedia or watch the Discovery Channel. For the rest, *turn to page 77 for the next barely believable episode of* **YOOPERMAN!**

Chicken Escapes from Local Barnyard

Ray Maki, a local farmer, reported one of his 500 chickens missing yesterday. Local authorities, having nothing better to do, formed a search party to search the woods surrounding Maki's farm. The Yellow Snow Gazette editor, having nothing better to do, sent this reporter out to cover the story on his first day on the job. This reporter, having better things to do than to go around chasing a missing chicken, hereby resigns, effective immediately.

Arnold Einolinen, Former Gazette Reporter

Learn to talk good with the help of the Yooperland Dictionary

Butts: Cigarettes

Da ol' lady: The wife, when she's out of earshot.

Give 'er Tarpaper: To work feverishly, something Yoopers are famous for.

My better half: The wife, when she's standing next to you.

Night Club: Club used by Yoopers to beat off mosquitoes at night.

NMU: National Mine University.

Palmer Low Rider: Car with broken or missing springs and having a road clearance of less than six inches.

Pus: A public transit vehicle.

Raha: Money or other medium of exchange.

Retarded: No longer working. "I been retarded from da mine since last year."

Roadkill: Free lunch.

Sweetheart: The wife, just before she goes out to shovel the driveway.

Tot: Past tense of tink. "I tot it was your turn to buy."

Tinking: Yooper mental process, usually done with the aid of a Pall Mall and a cup of coffee (or a beer).

Trung: Threw. "I trung 'em all back in da river."

Turd: More than second and less than fourth.

Wurt: The value of something.

Ya but no: Phrase meaning, "I respect your opinion but I disagree.

Yellow Snow: Inedible snow, also the name of a mythical town in Yooperland.

#^~&*?!!!: A cuss word that is unprintable in any language.

FUND RAISER ENDS IN RIOT

Temperance League President Jailed

A beer and brats picnic held at the Yellow Snow City Park yesterday erupted into violence when members of the Yellow Snow Temperance League, led by Mrs. Edna Wattabitch, attempted to break up the event by pouring thirty kegs of beer into the Yellow Creek, which runs through the park. The picnic was organized by the Tailgate Party Presidential candidate, Waino "Wedgie" Kempinen. All proceeds from the event were to be used to buy beer for underprivileged deer hunters this deer season. According to Kempinen, many local deer camps are in danger of going dry this year because of a lack of funds. "Most of the hunters I know are unemployed, and it's hard for them to afford even basic necessities, such as beer for the deer camp." says Kempinen. "I'm just trying to do my part to help the less fortunate, and maybe get a vote or two."

Mrs. Wattabitch, a long time advocate of total abstinence from alcohol and a harsh critic of fun of any kind, has pledged that she will not rest until the town and its inhabitants are alcohol free. After the beer was dumped into the creek,

pushing and shoving evolved into an all out free-for-all in which Kempinen allegedly picked up Mrs. Wattabitch and threw her into the water. When she was finally fished out a mile downstream, she staggered back to the picnic site, swearing like a drunken lumberjack, and cold-cocked Mr. Kempinen with a left hook to the temple. She then climbed up on a picnic table and sang dirty songs while doing a strip-tease. It took five sheriff's deputies to subdue her and haul her off to jail. She was charged with public intoxication, assault, disorderly conduct, indecent exposure, resisting arrest, and singing off-key. Kempinen, who woke up in time to catch the end of her performance, is reported to have said, "You know, for a minute there, I almost liked her."

For the remainder of the afternoon most of those attending the picnic went swimming. Public Works officials warn that the town's water, which is supplied by the Yellow Creek, may taste a little funny for a few days. Public officials suggest boiling all drinking water until the creek clears up. ■

Deer Hunting Classes Offered at NMU

Because of the steady rise in the number of deer hunters coming from downstate and out of state to hunt in the local area, National Mine University is offering classes in hunter safety this year. Topics covered in the class include target identification and the proper handling of firearms. A course will also be offered on some of the defensive aspects of hunting. Students will be taught how to hit the ground at the sound of gunfire, how to low-crawl at high speed, how to cower in the underbrush, and the latest techniques in DNR evasion. Another class will teach hunters how to calculate the amount of beer and beans needed for a two-week stay at the deer camp to avoid having to leave the camp during the stay. Included in this course will be instruction on how to tell dirty jokes, the importance of not bathing or shaving, and some review of cribbage and poker.

Twisted TRIVIA
How twisted are you?
Take this simple test and find out.
Answers & psychiatric profile on page 72

Twisted Trivia Questions
(Hint: Think *really* stupid!)

1. What is the name for someone who lives below the Mackinac bridge?
2. Who invented the brassiere?
3. What can you do to a 1972 Nova to save on gas?
4. Who is buried in the Tomb of the Unknown Yooper?
5. Besides "Fire!" what is the most dangerous thing to yell in a crowded Yooperland theater?
6. If a Yooper had six beers and drank five, how many would he have left?
7. Who is the most famous Yooper in history?
8. How do Yooper girls catch husbands?
9. What is the prize in the Yooperland jackpot lottery?
10. What problem do Yooper wives have that their husbands don't?

"Hey mom, remember that puppy I wanted? Never mind!"

"What a stupid question!
Of course you can keep what you catch!"

News Briefs

NMU Enrollment Drive Underway

Because of a drastic drop in enrollment at National Mine University, the Board of Directors has approved a new two-for-one sale on classes for the fall and winter semesters. Any student enrolling in a class will receive another class of equal or lesser value for free. If the campaign fails to bolster sagging enrollment, the school may consider opening a student beer hall next year.

Top 10 smooth pick-up lines
used by Yooper men
(in order of their effectiveness)

1. "I got a six pack in my truck."
2. "My friend over there wants to know if you're easy."
3. "I'm clean, smell me!"
4. "How drunk are you?"
5. "I'll bet I can lift your car."
6. "I've had my eye on you all night, and you're better looking than I thought."
7. "I think warts can be really attractive."
8. "I just got neutered."
9. "The drunker you get, the better I look."
10. "I think I gotta go puke. Wanna come?"

Madame Brewsky's Horoscope

My readers have been constantly bothering me to do a horoscope reading. Well, you asked for it, so here it is.

ARIES (March 21-April 19)
Be careful today. Do not try to kiss a rabid dog. If you do, be sure to wipe your mouth afterward.

TAURUS (April 20-May 20)
Be alert for accidents. If you fall off a high bluff, be careful of the sudden stop at the bottom.

GEMINI (May 20-June 21)
Today is a good day to make some unexpected money. Come to think of it, so is any other day. Too bad you won't.

CANCER (June 22-July 22)
Today could be your lucky day. You could also be flattened by a beer truck. Flip a coin.

LEO (July 23-August 22)
Stay inside today. Try not to irritate the guards or the other inmates.

VIRGO (August 23-Sept. 22)
There is a chance that you'll win big in the lottery today. There is an equal chance that Helsten's cows will sprout wings and fly to Vegas for the weekend.

LIBRA (Sept. 23-October 23)
You will have cause to celebrate tonight. Don't puke on the new carpet.

SCORPIO (Oct. 24-Nov. 21)
Don't swat that fly. Everyone will think you're harmless.

SAGITTARIUS (Nov. 22-Dec. 21)
You may be taking a long trip soon. Or maybe a short one. Or maybe you'll stay home. Whatever.

CAPRICORN (Dec. 22-Jan. 19)
You'll face a big decision today. Wear the blue one. No, wait—the red one. What does it matter? You look fat in everything. Maybe you should just forget it and go back to bed.

AQUARIUS (Jan. 20-Feb. 18)
Try not to worry. Being horribly mutilated by a pack of wild dogs isn't the worst thing that could happen.

PISCES (Feb.19-March 20)
Today everything will come together. Finances look great. Romance couldn't be better. Happiness is assured. Oops! Sorry, that's not you. Your life is crap. Better luck next time.

Martha's Summer Kitchen

Ensio and I attended FinnFest '96 and had a wonderful time. We met some wonderful people, too. Our family gathered and we shared our heritage together with the young and old. The County Fair was open at the same time. I entered my tomatoes and blueberry pie and won blue ribbons again. My brother-in-law won a blue ribbon for his pumpkin. My sister is not too happy with him. He told her not to get too close to his pumpkin because she is bad luck. I think he was kidding. My sister's pickles didn't win anything as usual. We were very busy that week. I guess most people weren't happy with the weather this summer. It did seem a little on the rainy and cold side. There I go again, rambling on. I think it's my age, but Ensio says I have always rambled. But he's used to it now and that's good because I'm too old to change. Anyway, the recipe I have chosen for this issue is *Piimäjuusto*, a freshly made cheese dessert. When served with berries it is very delicious.

Piimäjuusto
(Buttermilk Cheese)

Ingredients:

2 eggs
1 quart cultured buttermilk

3 quarts skim milk
Salt and Sugar

Beat the eggs and the buttermilk together with a whisk. Put milk into a pot and heat to 175°F to 190°F. Gradually pour the mixture of buttermilk and eggs into the hot milk, stirring well the whole time. Keep the temperature of the milk at 180°F until the mixture curdles. When whey has separated, strain the whole mixture through a fine sieve or cheesecloth into a bowl. Add salt and a pinch of sugar to the cheese curd. Line a cheese mold with dampened cheesecloth or muslin and ladle in the curd. Fold over the corners of the cloth and press the cheese gently. Chill under a weight for 4 hours to overnight.

Home Sweet Hole

Words of Whizdom: Man who lives in glass house needs lots of Windex.

Answer to tree puzzle from page 67

Tree number 2 is different.

There is a rabbit hiding behind it.

Answers to Twisted Trivia

1. Lopers, appleknockers, or trolls. (Any or all of these is correct).
2. Otto Titsling. (is you don't believe us, look it up).
3. Park it.
4. Okay, you caught us. There's no such thing.
5. Free Beer!
6. Not enough.
7. You know—the one in the flannel shirt.
8. Have them followed by private detectives.
9. A dollar a year for a million years.
10. Husbands (My wife made me do this one).

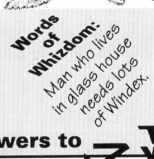

See below your score and evaluation

0-3 Correct
You're pretty smart.

4-6 Correct
You're getting dumber.

7-9 Correct
Don't be an idiot!

ALL 10 CORRECT

Congratulations, you're a total moron!

Wedgie Wins!

Unfortunately, the above headline was printed before the following late-breaking story was reported to our news desk. Rather than waste a lot of paper, we thought it would be easier and cheaper to just print the retraction right here. The above headline should read **"Wedgie Quits!"**

In a surprise move yesterday, just two days before election day, Waino "Wedgie" Kempinen announced his withdrawal from the presidential race. During a press conference at the Buck Snort Bar, Mr. Kempinen voiced reservations about spending the next four years in the White House. "You can't go anywhere or do anything," he said, "without the press hounding you and watching every move. You gotta shave and wear a tie every day. People are always bothering you, 'what're you gonna do about the federal deficit, and when are you gonna do something about taxes, and blah, blah, blah—' Who needs it? I didn't cause all those problems. Why should I put myself on the hot seat? What was I thinking? Nobody in their right mind would wanna take that job, not even if it paid in free beer. Nope. Count me out. I quit!"

Another reason for Kempinen's withdrawal from the presidential race and from politics in general is his disgust with the dirty political tactics of the opposition. He cited a speech in which one of his opponents referred to Kempinen's wife as "a fat, ugly, beer-swilling hog." "There should be a law against that kind of exaggeration," says Kempinen. "Helga never drinks before noon, except on weekends and holidays."

Supporters and campaign volunteers were at first shocked and angered by the unexpected last minute bail-out by their man, but after Kempinen bought a few rounds for the house and scattered some campaign fund money around, the crowd settled down, except for Mrs. Kempinen, who had already made plans for redecorating the White House. As the evening wore on Kempinen attempted to soothe her with a few beers. Unfortunately, she managed to get hold of a few shots of Wild Turkey, and by the time the police arrived, she had cleared out the whole bar. Tailgate Party officials will be meeting today to discuss whether they should use surplus campaign funds for Mrs. Kempinen's bail. She is being held on one count of public intoxication and fifteen counts of assault with intent to do great bodily harm. ∎

Great Moments In History!

Albert Einstein was actually a Finlander from Champion, Michigan. After failing math in grade school, he was so ashamed that he changed his name from Albert Einolinen to Albert Einstein. He later distinguished himself with his theory of relativity, which states that the number of relatives you have is directly related to how much you won in the lottery.

Women's Group Vows To Clean Up Deer Camp

The Yellow Snow Temperance League, under the leadership of Mrs. Edna Wattabitch, staged a demonstration in front of the Yellow Snow City Hall yesterday. The purpose of the demonstration was to address concerns over the behavior of local hunters during the two weeks of deer season. The Temperance League has been putting pressure on local government to pass ordinances banning such practices as beer drinking and poker playing in deer camps during deer season. The group charges that the practice of drinking beer at the deer camp leads to loud and crude behavior and a deterioration of morals and personal hygiene. According to Mrs. Wattabitch, the consumption of large amounts of beer promotes excessive gambling, the telling of off-color jokes, and crude and lewd behavior in general. She says that her 32-year-old son will be going hunting for the first time this year, and she is concerned that he may be corrupted by the uncivilized environment of the deer camp. The Mayor and other city officials were unavailable for comment, as they were all gone to camp.

Werner Warpula

Yellow Snow Wire Service

Wedgie Wimps Out

Whatever in the world made this backwoods bumpkin think he would stand a chance against real humans in the race for the presidency?

Well, as I sit down to write my column for the November issue, Waino "Wedgie" Kempinen is doing what he does best—quitting. Giving up. Letting down everybody who worked day and night for months to put him in the White House. Of course, I knew it all along. I just didn't want to be a party pooper. From the beginning I knew that this bozo was nowhere near presidential quality. And now he has proved it. Oh, sure, he has some of the qualities of a politician. Like making promises and then forgetting them. Like, for instance, the promise he made to a certain journalist that, when elected, he would appoint him press secretary. But now, on the eve of the election, he loses his nerve and bails out. I don't know what kind of lame excuse he has come up with to explain away this move, but I know the real reason. He lacks guts, conviction, intelligence, education, integrity, and any other qualities that make a man worth anything. As far as I know, the bum possesses only one positive quality—he'll buy beers for the bar when he's half in the bag. But a lot of good that does me. I'm on the wagon. So what about my cabinet post? I already had some T-shirts and a jacket made up with my name and new title on them. I knew on the day he married my sister that he was no good. And I now publicly and officially retract any good things I ever said about him. The only reason I wrote those things was because of pressure from my editor and the promise of a cabinet post in the Kempinen administration. Oh, and there was also quite a bit of cash involved. I would gladly return every penny if I hadn't already spent it. And then, of course, my sister was bothering me quite a bit about it. She really believed that no good husband of hers had a shot at the big time, and she can be a real pain when she wants something.

As I said, I don't know what reason Kempinen gave for withdrawing from the race. I suspect that he probably just didn't want to suffer the humiliation of a defeat at the polls. And if by some miracle he had won, there's the matter of his unemployment checks. It would have been pretty hard to keep his job as President of the United States a secret. His unemployment checks would have been cut off for sure. It's not that there's a lot of money at stake there. It's the principle of the thing. Kempinen considers it his mission in life to screw the government out of unemployment and tax money. For instance, they don't know that he makes quite a bit of money every year selling illegal deer meat to needy families, and at quite a hefty profit for himself, I might add. Then there was the VFW Widows and Orphans Christmas Fund affair, which Kempinen explained away by laughing and saying, "Oops! I must have misplaced it!" Soon after

that he bought the Last Gasp Nursing Home for back taxes, throwing the old gummers out into the street and converting the place into a beer hall, which turned a tidy profit for a year, after which he sold the building to an Iraqi biological warfare research corporation for an obscene amount of unreported cash.

Am I bitter? I'll admit I was a little perturbed when my dream of a lifetime was dashed to the ground by this two-faced, shiftless, no-account crook, but I have regained my composure now. It no longer bothers me that I could have been press secretary for the President of the United States, but now because of this spineless, conniving, back-stabbing weasel, I'm doomed to a life of writing this lousy editorial column for this cheesy backwoods rag whose hick readers have to ask their children what the big words are.

Not that I mind, really. My editor is such a wonderful person and such a great boss that I couldn't imagine working for anyone else. Actually, I'm very happy here. I'm so happy with my job that I'll probably never even ask for a raise. I might even be willing to take a modest cut in pay, if necessary. I feel very fortunate to have the opportunity to write for those wonderful readers who, though they may not be the cream of society, are actually the greatest people in the world. We must not lose sight of who the real enemy is. We must unite, dear readers, in an effort to rid our beloved community of this con artist who has violated our trust and slick-talked us into believing in his twisted dream. For Waino "Wedgie" Kempinen, I think a fitting exodus from our town should involve some tar and feathers, which I will gladly supply. ■

Top 10 stupid things people say after too many beers.

10. "Gimme a shot of tequila!"
9. "Thass too eashy, ossifer, I'll walk dat line on my hands!"
8. "Would you like to step outside and say that again?"
7. "I kin drive bether afther a couple drnkth!"
6. "Argh grft brddr erf nllwn!"
5. "Don't worry, my wife never comes to this bar."
4. "I don't usually play pool for money, but okay."
3. "Give everybody one on me!"
2. "I'll bet you $20 the Cubs will come back and win it in the ninth inning."
1. *"RRRRALPH!"*

Science Department

Professor Eino Aho, head of just about everything at National Mine University, takes a scientific look at a hunting tradition that dates back to the dawn of the human race—the Deer Camp.

Every year at this time in this part of the country, responsible and respectable men from all walks of life abandon their jobs, their families, and all other responsibilities, throwing off the thin mantle of civilization to answer a primitive call of nature—the call of the deer camp. What primal force drives these men? What biological and psychological changes take place at this time of year to drive decent, responsible men away from civilization and out to camp, where they consume vast quantities of strong drink, gamble away their paychecks, and generally engage in bizarre activities that resemble the antics of disorderly schoolboys? I have spent many years researching and studying the phenomenon of the deer camp, and here I present my findings.

To truly understand the phenomenon of the deer camp, we must understand its origin. In the beginning, the hunt was everything. Hunting was man's primary occupation, his way of providing food for his family. As with any occupation, where one goes to work day in and day out, doing the same thing all over again, eventually hunting came to be seen as drudgery, as a tedious task that needed to be done. In short, it was work. Every morning, cave women everywhere would arise at dawn and poke their sleeping husbands in the ribs, saying, "Ooh eegh ah wuff goog," which, translated into modern day English, means, "Get up, you lazy bum, it's time to go hunting!" The sleepy cave man would roll out of his bed of grass mumbling, "Ehh gug wuh bobo ergha kaka," which translates as "I hate this job. I wish I could get a job foraging for roots and leaves!" But of course the cave man had failed the foraging exam again so he was stuck with hunting. So he would go out and stalk wild game all day in the hot sun, or in driving rain, or freezing drizzle, and when he would come home at the end of the day with his catch slung over his shoulder, his cave wife would say, "Wuff, nana iki gog mukka poopoo," or "What? Lizard again? Can't you do better than that? Mumu's husband brings home ground hog and tree sloth, yak, yak, etc..."

Eventually it began to dawn on early man that the drudgery of the work-a-day world was miserable indeed, and he didn't feel he got the moral support he needed at home, where his cave wife constantly nagged him about his habits, like whizzing on the cave walls instead of going outside, or leaving lizard entrails all over the floor, or scratching his itchy butt with her kitchen utensils. You see, the cave wife spent the day in the cave taking care of the cave kids, and to relieve the boredom, she came up with the idea of cave cleaning. The cave man, on the other hand, spent all his time in the woods, where he could take a whiz anywhere he wanted, or make big smellies any time he

wanted, and he got used to the freedom. So the cave became the woman's domain, and she didn't let the cave man forget it. She ruled the cave with absolute supremacy, and life became more miserable for the cave man. So one day, in a fit of depression, he decided to end it all. While hunting in the woods, he came across a bush full of strange looking berries that he had never dared to eat because he was sure they were poisonous. In a desperate attempt to end his life of misery, the cave man ate berries until he could eat no more. Then he sat down and waited to die. But he didn't die. Instead he began to sing a song about a bow-legged cave woman named Oogah. He had accidentally discovered that, when berries were sufficiently fermented, they made you feel really good! The cave man was eager to share his discovery with other cave men who were as miserable as he was. So all the cave men from the cave village got together and ate berries and sang songs until they puked their guts out. It was the most fun they'd ever had. Then when they all staggered home that night, they were surprised to discover that their cave wives actually looked pretty good. After that the cave people population began to boom.

The cave men found that they enjoyed being together, eating berries in the woods, singing dirty songs, and whizzing anywhere they pleased. So they decided to find a cave far out in the woods where they would gather and hunt together. They found that when they hunted in packs they were able to bring down larger game. They especially liked deer. This preference may have had something to do with what I call "Antler Envy." At any rate, the cave men enjoyed hunting deer together, and at the end of the day they would go back to the "deer cave" to eat fermented berries, make big smellies, and whiz on the cave walls. When they had bagged enough meat, eaten enough berries, and run out of bow-legged cave women to sing about, they would go home to their cave wives to rest and recover. They all made a pact signed in blood to never ☞

reveal the location of the deer cave to their wives, and to never tell the truth about what they did there. And they set aside a certain time each year to leave their homes and go to the deer cave to hunt, eat berries, and whiz on the cave walls.

Eventually, cave society developed to the point where hunting was no longer the main occupation. Cave men found jobs farming, or working in the quarries, or shoveling mammoth manure. Some became philosophers, politicians, writers, or advertising executives. But they found all these occupations to be just as tedious and demanding as hunting had once been. And the cave wives still ruled the caves at home, and would tolerate no misbehavior. So the cave men kept the tradition of the deer cave alive down through the centuries, to give them some relief from the tedium and drudgery of work and family responsibilities. As we near the end of the 20th century, the tradition of the deer camp shows no signs of dying out. I suspect that, even far in the future, when every aspect of human life will most likely be dependent upon the computer, men will still be escaping the tedium of everyday life by spending time in the virtual deer camp, shooting holographic deer, whizzing on computer generated camp walls, and singing songs about bow-legged computer system design consultants named Oogah.

Rintala's
Believe it or Shut Up!

Deer Season

One deer season, Sulo Saari of Palmer, Michigan painted the word "cow" on all his cows so they wouldn't be mistaken for deer by downstate hunters. Mr. Saari lost no cows that deer season, but he did lose two pigs and fourteen chickens.

How to keep 'em Whipped!

Gravel Gertie's
Husband Training Tips

Dear Gertie,
I don't have a husband yet, but I soon will. I am planning to get married next month. I thought it might be a good idea to write to you first to help get my marriage off to a good start. Do you have a word of advice for a woman who is about to get married?
Tying the Knot

Dear Knothead,
DON'T!
Gertie

Dear Gertie,
My husband is driving me nuts. He is a perfectionist. He fusses over the smallest details. If he finds a speck of dust on the car, he washes and waxes the whole thing. He checks the furniture for dust with a white glove. He even makes me iron his socks! His nit-picking is driving me crazy. Can you help me?
Mrs. Perfect

Dear Perfect,
Send me your street address and a picture of your old man. I'll send Eugene and a couple of his cronies over. They'll kidnap your husband and take him out to camp for a week or two of reprogramming. By the time they return him to you, he'll be a burping, farting, beer-drinking no-account bum just like the rest of them. Then you'll really have something to complain about.
Gertie

Dear Gertie,
My husband is a typical Yooper husband. But there's a woman where he works that seems to think he's something special. She is obviously flirting with him. I think she is trying to take him away from me. He is no prize, but I've sort of gotten used to him, and I'd like to keep him. What do you suggest?
Fearful in Felch

Dear Fearful,
What a coincidence! I had the very same problem with my Eugene. Don't worry. Let her have him. If he's the typical Yooper man that you say he is, she'll be offering you money to take him back within two weeks. Meanwhile, enjoy the time off.
Gertie

Dear Gertie,
Every Saturday afternoon my husband sits on his lazy butt, drinking beer and watching sports on TV. After about three beers he starts yelling at the players and the officials as if they could really hear him. And no matter what I'm doing, I'm expected to drop everything to bring him another beer. I'd like some peace and quiet on the weekends. What can I do?
Mrs. Beer Bum

Dear Beer,
My Eugene used to think my main job on weekends was to run a beer shuttle service between the refrigerator and the couch. I must have put on 50 miles every weekend. So I bought a fifth of grain alcohol, and every time he hollered for another beer, I'd pour out half the beer and refill the can with the alcohol. After the third or fourth beer, it got nice and quiet. He usually stays out until the next morning.
Gertie

Dear Gertie,
My husband doesn't smoke or drink or chase women. In fact, he doesn't have any bad habits, except one. He's a violator. Instead of going fishing or golfing in the summertime, he goes out hunting deer. I think he's addicted to it. I don't know what to do. Do you have any ideas?
Mrs. Deerslayer

Dear Deer,
Buy a bigger freezer.
Gertie

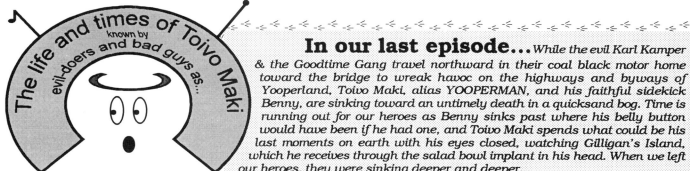

In our last episode... *While the evil Karl Kamper & the Goodtime Gang travel northward in their coal black motor home toward the bridge to wreak havoc on the highways and byways of Yooperland, Toivo Maki, alias YOOPERMAN, and his faithful sidekick Benny, are sinking toward an untimely death in a quicksand bog. Time is running out for our heroes as Benny sinks past where his belly button would have been if he had one, and Toivo Maki spends what could be his last moments on earth with his eyes closed, watching Gilligan's Island, which he receives through the salad bowl implant in his head. When we left our heroes, they were sinking deeper and deeper...*

Yooperman

As Gilligan ripped a big tree out of the ground by the roots, Toivo Maki, alias Yooperman, could feel the quicksand creeping up toward his neck. At first he had been concerned about dying. Now it was even worse. He might die before he saw the end of Gilligan's Island. He had seen this episode a few times before, and he knew that Gilligan didn't take advantage of the opportunity to kick the crap out of the Skipper, but Toivo always hoped for a miracle. Maybe someday they would show some out takes in which Gilligan actually did kick the Skipper's ample butt all over the island. But, judging from how fast he was sinking in the quicksand, Toivo knew he wouldn't live to see it. How inconsiderate death is, he thought. It always shows up when you've got something to live for.

Suddenly the picture went all funny. The vertical hold went out of control and then the screen was filled with snow. After a few moments the sound went out and a message came on the screen: We are experiencing technical difficulties. Please Stand By.

"Oh, great!" Toivo grumbled.

"What's the matter now?" Benny asked.

Toivo opened his eyes and looked at Benny, who had sunk nearly up to his chin.

"I'm getting some kind of interference on the salad bowl implant in my head," Toivo said.

Just then a shadow loomed over them. There was a high-pitched whine from above. They looked up. Hovering about thirty feet above their heads was the spaceship that had saved Toivo's life, the same one that had brought Benny to him. They could tell by the bumper sticker that read, *THIS IS NOT A UFO, IT'S AN INTERGALACTIC RECREATIONAL VEHICLE.* As they watched, a hole opened in the bottom of the spaceship and a little blue head poked out.

"Slrvb ghrrlz," the little blue guy said.

"Hooray! We're saved!" Benny cheered. Then he began a conversation with the little blue guy in the ship. They conversed in their alien tongue and Toivo Maki couldn't make out a word. (For the benefit of our linguistically challenged readers, I will translate the conversation into English.)

"Glizzl brfhp zrgl duh?" (*What are you guys doing here?*) Benny asked.

"Shlrzz bllghrt grp hbhb drvvle vbrrt rr xpkffldp," (*We came back for the keys to the spaceport*) the little blue guy in the ship said. "Shlrzz hrr bnbn ooo dxzglk." (*We were halfway home when we realized you still had them*)

How observant are you? Take this simple test and find out. Two of the above deer are the same. One is different. Can you find the one that is different? Answer on page 82.

"Nhi ll bgbr," (*No I don't*) Benny said. "Ll jvbr hrrb vzyy p znf %rnnxq duh?" (*I gave them to you, remember?*)

The little blue guy in the spaceship patted his pockets and suddenly a sheepish grin crossed his face. He pulled out a key ring with a mess of keys on it.

"Zzxnr uu wyl yszbt ~nhr grrbhll xhrzbrp!" (*Oops*) he said. "Bvd." (*I forgot I had them—sorry to bother you. Bye*)

His head disappeared and the hole in the space ship closed up. There was a high whining sound and the ship zoomed away toward the horizon.

"Hey, wait a minute!" Benny cried in English, but it was too late. The ship was out of sight.

Although Toivo Maki didn't follow the gist of the conversation, he could see the end result.

"You blew it, didn't you?" he said. "You had a chance to save us and you blew it!" He reached out toward Benny. "I had just about given up," Toivo said. "But now I have something to live for." There was an evil, murderous gleam in his eye.

Benny's little blue face broke in a sweat. "One little mistake," he said sheepishly. "It could happen to anybody."

He began to do a frantic backstroke to keep out of Toivo's reach. The desperate need to get his hands around Benny's little blue neck gave Toivo a burst of strength that he never knew he had. He began to dog paddle after Benny, whose desire to escape gave him a burst of super-human strength. He swam like an Olympic champion, with Toivo close behind. In just a few moments, Benny had reached solid ground and was up and running. Toivo was close behind, gaining on him, when Benny suddenly stopped.

"Wait a minute!" he cried.

Toivo was surprised by Benny's sudden stop. He screeched to a halt. "What?"

"Look!" Benny said. "We're out! We're saved!"

Toivo looked down at his feet. They were indeed standing on solid ground. "Hm," he said. "So we are." He advanced toward Benny with his hands outstretched. "Now hold still while I break your little blue alien neck," he said.

"Wait!" Benny cried. "Don't you understand what I did?"

Toivo stopped. He looked confused. "What do you mean?"

"Well," Benny explained. "I—ah—I knew that you had it in you to save yourself." He thought fast and hard. "I mean—uh— what if the ship hadn't come at all? What if you had to survive on your own?" He had a good grasp on the idea now. "You see, I know that in our business, we're going to get into deadly situations, and we can't count on some miracle happening to save us. I had to show you that you can find the strength within yourself to survive. I did you a big favor, and what thanks do I get?" There was now an indignant tone in his voice. "Well, if that's the way I'm going to be treated, maybe I don't need to be here." He turned and began to walk away.

"Wait!" Toivo said. "I'm sorry.

Maybe I was a little rough on you. Come on back." He held out his hand. "Put 'er there, pal."

Benny looked at Toivo's outstretched hand. He hesitated for a moment.

"Come on, buddy," Toivo said. "We're a team."

"Well, okay." Benny reached out and grasped Toivo's hand.

WHACK! Toivo's other hand shot out like a striking snake and caught Benny alongside the head. "There!" Toivo said. "Now don't ever do that again!" He looked around to get his bearings. "Now," he said. "Shall we go?" He started off through the trees.

"Gzbrhh!," Benny grumbled, rubbing his little blue head. "That really smarts!" Then he followed Toivo.

Meanwhile, Karl Kamper & the Goodtime Gang were crossing the Mackinac Bridge in their coal black motor home. Behind them a trail of empty beer cans and candy wrappers littered the highway. As the motor home neared the toll booth on the Yooperland side of the bridge, Karl Kamper, instead of slowing down, stomped on the gas and crashed through the barrier, scattering splinters all over the highway. A cloud of black smoke from the motor home's tailpipe enveloped the toll booths, rendering all the attendants unconscious. When they regained consciousness some time later, they had no recollection of a coal black motor home ever coming across the bridge. "This is kool!" exclaimed Karl Kamper as he lumbered down the highway at twenty miles an

hour. He looked in the rear view mirror at the trail of litter and the ugly black smoke he left in his wake. "I think I'm going to really like it here," he said. "By the time I get through with this place it'll look like Detroit having a bad hair day." He threw back his head and burst into a fit of maniacal laughter...

Will the evil Karl Kamper run amok through the pristine wilderness of Yooperland? Will there be no roadside left unlittered? Will his ugly black smoke soil the pure, pine-scented air? Will Yooperman and his faithful sidekick Benny be able to prevail against this powerful villain? Did you remember to feed the dog? Who forgot to flush the toilet? Has anyone seen the remote? What's this spot on my shirt?

For the answers to some of these questions, take a wild guess. For the rest, *turn to page 88 for the next incredibly mediocre episode of* **YOOPERMAN!**

TWISTED TRIVIA

How twisted are you?
Take this simple test and find out.
Answers & psychiatric profile on page 82

Twisted Trivia Questions

(Hint: Think *really* stupid!)

1. What kind of wood do Yoopers usually burn in their wood stoves?
2. How do you spell *Tahquamenon*?
3. Did you remember to floss?
4. Why does a six pack have only six beers?
5. What do tree farts smell like?
6. What irritates a Yooper most when he's deer hunting?
7. Whose picture is on a Yooper dollar bill?
8. What is the deer hunter's national anthem?
9. What do you call a 21 year old Yooper in the fifth grade?
10. What was the last question?

Hairold

"Judging by all the screaming and hollering, you musta got one."

Elvis Returns!

Early this morning I sat with my crystal ball at a table in the Buck Snort Bar, and a very interesting vision came to me. The reason I was in the bar is that sometimes the cosmic and psychic vibrations fluctuate. At times they are stronger or weaker in a certain part of the universe. Since my crystal ball is an older model, it gets better reception where the vibrations are strongest. This morning the vibrations just happened to be strongest in the Buck Snort Bar. Anyway, as I looked into my crystal ball I saw a vision of the future. It was a little cloudy, so I had a jumbo to help clear my vision. After a while the clouds parted and a bright light shone through. Gradually I began to make out the figure of a man, a fairly large man, and I could see that he was standing before a large crowd of people. He appeared to be speaking or singing to them, I couldn't tell for sure which. Although the figure of the man was hazy, he began to look very familiar to me. I could see the crowd cheering and applauding, and I could see the adoration in their faces. I could see that their faces were filled with hope, and that they believed their salvation was at hand. After a few swigs from my jumbo it came to me—this must be Elvis! He must be returning to earth to lead his followers to the promised land! Just then Bruno, behind the bar, switched off the TV, and everything went blank. Now that I think about it, I have my doubts about the vision. It may have been a vision of the second coming of Elvis. Or, possibly, it was a reflection in my crystal ball from the TV behind the bar showing reruns of the Democratic National Convention. Seeing the future is not an exact science. Sometimes there are several different ways to interpret a vision. Just to be sure, I took my crystal ball in to Bernie's Small Appliance Repair to have it checked over. As for the meaning of the vision, you'll have to decide for yourself.

Hi from Arizona

Dear Rudy,

I'm writing this letter to tell you about how it is in Arizona. At first I didn't know if I'd like being retarded because I been working since I was a young lad and I kind of got used to it. But I guess I can get used to doing nothing especially since I'm living in such a nice place to do it. First of all, I get up in the morning and I don't have to go out and shovel the driveway. Not that I ever did, but now the wife don't have to either. What do you think? They don't have snow here! This morning when I got up it was 87 degrees in the shade. And another thing. I been here three months now, and in all that time I ain't seen no new rust holes in the Chevy. I was thinking about getting rid of that old piece of junk and getting a new one, but if it ain't gonna rust away I might keep it cause it still runs. I don't see any other cars with rust holes out here, and none of them smoke at all, but I'm kind of attached to the old clunker so I might keep it. The same goes for the old lady. (ha ha)

And another thing. I sit outside in the evening and have a cold beer and guess what? No bugs! I ain't seen a mosquito since I left the U.P. I still put on my Cutter's though, cause the wife likes the smell. And sometimes when I get homesick I turn the air conditioning real cold and go and put on my longies. Then me and Elsie cuddle up and pretend we're out that camp on the Escanaba river.

All in all it's pretty nice here in Arizona, but there are a couple things I miss pretty bad. Of course I miss shooting the breeze with you and all the guys at the Buck Snort Bar. And another thing. You can't get a half decent pasty out here. They put that taco sauce in everything. And if you do manage to choke one down, they don't have no outhouse to go and relax in after. We got them inside outhouses, but they just don't have the same atmosphere. And if you wanna take a sauna, well you're just out of luck. Oh, they got these places called "spas" where they have some new-fangled electric saunas, but there ain't none where you can get a rip-roaring fire going and throw cold water on the rocks. And if you try to whiz on them electric elements they toss you out on your ear. And you can't run out of the sauna buck naked and jump into and ice cold lake, because all they have out here is them heated pools. And if you run out in the raw and jump into one of them the cops come and haul you away.

Well, I guess I gotta go now. Elsie has been after me to clean the garage. I figured out an easier way to do it. I'll just take everything I wanna keep into the house for the night and leave the garage door open. When I get up in the morning everything I left out there will be gone. Some folks around here will steal anything that ain't too hot or too heavy. You gotta lock everything up around here. Sometimes that don't even do no good. The neighbor kid chained his bike to the fence the other night and when he went outside the next morning, the bike was still there but the chain and the padlock were gone. Another guy had his lawn stolen while he was on vacation in Las Vegas. I don't know how they managed that one.

Well, Elsie's getting her bloomers in a bundle about the mess in the garage, so I gotta go and start moving the junk I wanna keep. Say hi to everybody at the bar for me. I'd like to come back for a visit, but I don't think the Chevy will make it that far. Write if you get time.

Your friend,

Ernie

DEER CAMP BULLETIN BOARD

Hi there big boy

I think this bug is dead. →
It hasn't moved all week.

It must have tried to drink the camp coffee!

Whoever left the 6-pack in my truck— I love you, man!

HOOST INKS!

Who doern't?

Whoever fishe...
...ever at our...

MISS DEER CAMP 1996

I've seen her without the bag— you don't wanna know!

She can't be that ugly.

OH YEAH? SHE MAKES YOUR WIFE LOOK GOOD!

Selma "Spooky" Salmi

Miss Salmi is a young swimsuit model who started out as a model for a halloween mask manufacturer. She hopes someday to become a cover girl for a fashion magazine.

Ya, as soon as she can save enough money for a face transplant!

She mo...

Personal Statistics

Bust: 36
Waist: 25
Hips: 35
Eyes: Two
Hair: Yes
Height: 5'6"
Weight: 118 lbs

Hobbies: Husband hunting, party crashing, power shopping, looking ...h the mirror.

The next guy who goes to town pick me up a case of Jumbos. Wake me up when you get back. Droopy

OF AMERICA
G 78937102 F
WASHINGTON, D.C.
DOLLARS

Martha's
Summer Kitchen

Well, I can't believe that it's already deer season again. The days just seem to go by so fast. All the hunters in our family seem to have camp fever now. Ensio says the deer are getting smarter and quicker every year. I think he goes to camp mostly to tell stories about the old days, when the deer were not so smart and not so quick. My brother-in-law was elected Head Cook at camp this year and my sister giving him all her best recipes for camp. Ensio is taking some spare food along just in case. Oh well, Ensio could lose a pound or two. Oh my, I nearly forgot to give you my recipe for this issue. Sometimes my mind wanders. I decided to give you a recipe from one of my Finnish cookbooks. The last time I cooked this recipe Ensio said I got a little tipsy but I think he was just teasing.

Happy cooking!

Wild Game (Saddle of Deer)

1 deer loin	2 tbs freshly ground
1 cup port wine	black pepper
1 cup red wine	Bacon
2 tablespoons Dijon mustard	Cornstarch
1 cup cognac	Parsley, finely chopped
2 tablespoons salt	

Combine port wine, red wine, Dijon mustard, cognac, salt and pepper. Marinate deer loin in mixture for 24 hours, turning loin a few times. Remove loin from marinade and wipe dry, saving marinade. Wrap loin in bacon, place in oven and brown at 400°F for 15 minutes. Pour marinade over meat and reduce temperature to 300°F. Bake until meat is medium (pink center). Remove meat from oven, saving liquid.

To make a sauce, thicken cooking liquid with 2 tablespoons cornstarch per quart of liquid. Slowly bring sauce to a boil and simmer for 10 minutes. Add finely chopped parsley and season to taste.

Words of Whizac
He who fights, then runs away, probably lost.

Answer to deer puzzle from page 77

Deer no. 2 is different. It is a stupid deer. It is running the wrong way. It is going to be killed in a head on collision with deer no. 1. The problem is, the innocent deer no. 1 will also be killed.

Wait—maybe deer no. 3 is the different one because the other two will soon be dead. It's all so confusing...

Answers to Twisted Trivia

1. Firewood.
2. T-a-h-q-u-a-m-e-n-o-n. If you can say it after six beers, give yourself a bonus point.
3. Just a Yes or No answer will be fine. No need to go into a long-winded explanation of how you floss or why you forgot to floss or the value of flossing—just answer the question already!
4. Because if it had more, we couldn't call it a six-pack, could we?
5. Trees don't fart.
6. Those noisy Fourth of July fireworks.
7. Washington.
8. The Second Week of Deer Camp.
9. Gifted. (An old joke, but we couldn't resist)
10. What was the last question?

See below your score and evaluation

0-3 Correct
You have nothing to worry about.

4-6 Correct
You're slightly schizophrenic.

7-9 Correct
So are you.

All 10 Correct
Does your jacket buckle up the back?

Elf Unrest Threatens Christmas

As the Christmas season approaches, there come rumblings of discontent from the North Pole that threaten to derail the season of good will and good cheer before it gets started. Our news desk has received reports of discord between the elf work force responsible for the making of millions of toys and the North Pole management, namely, Santa Claus. The story was first reported to us by a Yellow Snow resident whose cousin works for a company that delivers reindeer chow to the North Pole. A Gazette reporter was immediately dispatched to the North Pole by dogsled to cover the story. According to recent reports, the elves have delivered a list of demands to Santa's desk, and are threatening to bring operations to a halt if their demands are not give serious consideration. Among the concerns addressed are salary, benefits, and working conditions. An elf spokesman is quoted as saying, "Sweatshops like this place went out at the turn of the century. The man's a slave driver. Do you think he only uses that whip on the reindeer?" It is common knowledge that Santa's elves traditionally do not receive monetary compensation, but work for room and board. Management contends that the prestige that comes with being a North Pole workshop elf is more than enough compensation. Said Santa, "There are millions of elves around the world who would jump at the chance to work for me." Evidently, Santa's elves disagree, and plan to initiate a work stoppage on December 15 if Santa refuses to negotiate.

One of the demands on the list is that management provide elves with their own outhouses. Apparently the elves are forced to use outhouses that were built for normal size humans. They say that the large outhouse holes are dangerous to the elves, who are much smaller, and that three elves have been lost in the past year. According to management, the cost of building new outhouses is prohibitive, and the elves could take precautions, such as tying two-by-fours across their backs when they have to go. Another complaint concerns the quality of the food. Says an elf spokesman of Mrs. Claus, "Sure, she looks like a sweet old lady, but she just can't cook!" Mr. Claus admitted that his wife's cooking leaves something to be desired, but he was quick to add that she possesses other talents that more than make up for it. He declined to elaborate on the subject.

In summing up the situation, the head elf released this statement to the press:

We're sick of having to do all the work while he gets all the glory. We're stuck here, slaving away in this sweatshop, making toys to make him look good. He gets to go all around the world, and everywhere he goes they treat him like a hero. They leave him milk and cookies and all sorts of other goodies while we're stuck here with the old lady's leftover gruel. And that ho, ho, ho crap is really getting on our nerves. He has everything in the world to be jolly about, but what about us? All we really want is a little recognition for our sacrifices. If we don't start getting a little respect around here, we're walking out. Let him make the damn toys himself!

A U.S. Labor Relations official, when asked if their office would get involved in the dispute, said with a sigh of relief, "Thank God! This one's completely out of our jurisdiction!"

We here at the Yellow Snow Gazette hope that, for the sake of the millions of children around the world who are anxiously anticipating the Christmas Eve toy delivery by Santa, this dispute will be settled in time to avert a disaster.

Seven Dwarves Support Elves

The Seven Dwarves, in a show of solidarity with Santa's elves, are refusing to whistle while they work until the dispute is settled. Said Grumpy, one of the senior Dwarves, "Us little guys have to stick together." Snow White, in response to Grumpy's statement, replied, "I'll let it go this time, but those little runts had better be careful. They're really beginning to piss me off!" She later apologized for the statement, saying that they had just caught her at a bad time of the month. ■

Science Department

Does Santa Claus exist? Professor Eino Aho, head of just about everything at National Mine University thinks so. Here he presents what he believes to be conclusive evidence that the jolly old elf is as real as the Easter Bunny.

The holiday season has arrived again, and as I sit by the fireplace sipping homemade brandy which I concocted in my laboratory, I contemplate a controversy that has plagued mankind for generations. It is the age-old question—is Santa Claus real? There is no doubt in the minds of many. But others dismiss the old elf as a myth. There are many who remain undecided. No government agency has ever looked into the matter, and no scientific study has ever been made. As a result, there is no official, conclusive proof either way, so everyone is left to form his or her own opinion on the subject. In order to put this question to rest once and for all I will, with my customary scientific objectivity, show beyond a doubt that Santa Claus can and indeed does exist.

What evidence do the skeptics offer in their attempts to disprove the existence of this great man? Invariably, they will point to what they believe are the most obvious impossibilities, the foremost of which is that Santa rides in a sled pulled by eight flying reindeer. They state that it is physically impossible for reindeer to fly. I point out, however, that modern science has yet to determine how a bumblebee is able to fly. It should be physically impossible, yet bumblebees do fly. Is it such a stretch of the imagination, then, to suppose that eight reindeer and a sled might be hoisted into the air by thousands of bumblebees? A man living at the north pole, having nothing to do with his time for most of the year, might conceivably be able to train bumblebees, and all those elves could manufacture tiny harnesses for them in no time. No one has actually ever gotten a close look at Santa's sleigh in flight, but if they did, they might be surprised to discover that it is pulled by eight tiny reindeer and eighty thousand tinier bumblebees! Of course it is common knowledge that bumblebees don't normally survive the winters, but considering recent advances in genetic engineering, it seems likely that a new, genetically altered species could be produced which would thrive in cold weather. Another possibility is that all those elves, in their free time, could fashion tiny fur coats for them. At any rate, from a distance the bumblebees would be too small to be seen, so it would appear that the reindeer were actually pulling the sled through the sky.

Another feat performed by Santa that skeptics deem impossible is his ability to fit his chubby body down chimneys that are clearly too small. In answer to this, I suggest that those skeptics go back to their grade school science classes and review the experiment with the hard-boiled egg and the milk bottle. When you place the egg on the mouth of the bottle, it is clear that the opening is too small to allow the egg to drop into the bottle. However, if you set a piece of paper on fire, drop it into the bottle, and place the egg on top, it will soon be sucked down through the opening and into the bottle. This is caused by the vacuum created in the bottle when all the oxygen is consumed by the fire. The same principle applies to Santa. He merely plops his fat body over the opening at the top of the chimney and waits for the embers in the fireplace to consume enough oxygen to create sufficient suction. In short order he is sucked down the chimney in the same manner as the egg is sucked into the milk bottle. Of course it is imperative that he keep his mouth closed and exhibit superb sphincter muscle control in order to maintain a tight seal and prevent air leakage.

Perhaps the most mystifying ability attributed to Santa Claus concerns the amazing number of household visits he makes in the short time span of one night. To climb down a chimney, place gifts under a tree, gobble down a plate of cookies and slurp down a glass of milk, climb back up the chimney, and move on to the next house, should take at least fifteen minutes. At that rate, one would only be able to visit about 32 houses in an eight-hour period. Yet it is believed by many that Santa manages to make stops at millions of houses on Christmas Eve. Skeptics point to this impossibility as evidence that the whole idea of Santa Claus is nothing more than a fairy tale. So how does Santa accomplish this amazing feat? Time travel. Anyone possessing the superior intellect required to train eighty thousand bumblebees to carry a sled and eight reindeer around the world would probably have the ability to perfect a time warp device of some kind. (I would remind skeptics that Superman achieved time travel as early as the late 1930s, and the starship Enterprise bounces back and forth through time whenever the situation calls for it.) With such a device, all Santa would have to do when dawn drew near is to leap back a few hours in time to the beginning of

This illustration demonstrates the lesson we can learn from the egg and milk bottle experiment.

| Hard boiled egg will not fit into milk bottle. | Place burning piece of paper in milk bottle. | Never store extra gas in milk bottles. |

the night. He could perform this leap back in time as many times a necessary during the night, until all his visits were completed. Thus, a trip that to Santa took a period of months or years, would to us appear to have been accomplished in one night. Such a concept can be difficult for the rational mind to grasp, but it is perfectly clear to me. After becoming convinced of the bumblebee thing, it is only a small leap of logic to the time warp idea. Add to that a little homemade brandy to relax the mind, and many heretofore implausible concepts begin to make more sense.

So I have explained how Santa could accomplish some of the seemingly impossible feats attributed to him. Since these impossibilities, shown in the light of scientific examination, now seem possible, the claim that Santa Claus is real also exists in the realm of possibility. I have shown that Santa could exist. But have I proven that he in fact *does* exist?

To those who will not believe, no preponderance of evidence will convince. But I have physical evidence that proves, at least to me, that Santa is real. In the corner of my garage, untouched for many years, rusted, worn, and all but fallen apart, there sits a flexible flyer sled, left under the Christmas tree for me when I was aged seven. I still recall how its metal runners gleamed in the glow of the Christmas tree lights that morning. In all the rest of my life, I have seen many sleds, but none ever exhibited that unearthly glow, or exuded that aura, calling to me in a voice only I could hear, saying, "Eino, I'm for you." And on the tag it said, "From Santa."

Great Moments In History!

Henry David Thoreau was the pen name of Heikki "Dirty Shirt" Turunen, a Finlander from Bruce Crossing. He wrote his famous essay *Civil Disobedience* while hiding out from the Negaunee cops in a tarpaper shack at Waltanen's pond after a bar fight at Ed's Iron Inn.

How to keep 'em Whipped!

Gravel Gertie's
Husband Training Tips

Dear Gertie,
It's time again for the annual Christmas party at the sewage treatment plant where my husband works. I know he's going to drink too much and become obnoxious, as usual. He's going to chase all the secretaries around with that stupid mistletoe and try to kiss them and generally make a big fool of himself. It's so embarrassing. I talk to him about it every year, and he always promises to behave, but as soon as he gets a few drinks in him, he forgets and turns into a party animal. What can I do to cure him of this disgusting behavior once and for all?
Helpless in Humboldt

Dear Helpless,
I used to have the same problem with my Eugene at our Christmas party here at the YSG office. As soon as he had a few drinks, his hormones would go crazy and he'd start chasing all the girls around the office. I couldn't cure him, so I just outdid him. For every drink he had, I would have two. By the time the party got warmed up, I was dancing around wearing nothing but a G-string and a mistletoe in my hair. I can't get Eugene to come to the office party anymore, but I have a wonderful time!
Gertie

Dear Gertie,
We've been married for two years now, and my husband has changed. He used to want to be with me all the time. He was always bringing me flowers and surprising me with little gifts. Then we moved to Yooperland. Now, more and more, he stays out late at night and comes home smelling like beer. He goes fishing all the time with those new friends of his and has even started (Yech!)

chewing snuff. He hardly ever bathes or shaves anymore, and I can't seem to get him to help around the house. I'm worried. What should I do?
Newberry Newlywed

Dear Newberry,
So what's new? Write to me again if he starts to act abnormal.
Gertie

Dear Gertie,
My husband always lets the dog in the house at night. There's a perfectly good doghouse outside, but my husband says the dog gets lonely out there. My carpet smells like the dog and I'm constantly vacuuming up dog hair. Help!
Mrs. Doggy Daddy

Dear Doggy,
Scrub a spot on the kitchen floor so that it's clean enough to eat from. Then open a can of refried beans and roll them into a couple of good-sized loaves. Place the fake doggy logs on the clean spot on the floor and then call your husband to come and see what his precious dog did. Then start to nag and complain about the dog and say that it's driving you crazy. To prove to him that you're really around the bend, grab a spoon and start gobbling up the fake doggy do. Even if it doesn't cure the problem, it'll be worth it to see the look on his face.
Gertie

Dear Gertie,
My husband invited his mother to spend the holidays with us. What can I do?
Bummed Out

Dear Bummed,
Invite your mother. They will cancel each other out!
Gertie

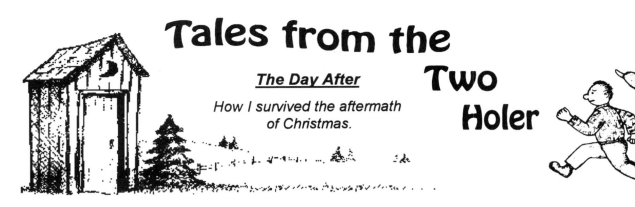

Tales from the Two Holer

The Day After

How I survived the aftermath of Christmas.

It's the day after Christmas and I'm laid out on the sofa, resting, recovering from yesterday's madness. I filled up on ham and fruitcake yesterday, and I overindulged in leftovers already this morning. My head is pounding from the Kessler's and beer of last night. All the wife's relatives descended upon my house three days ago, including her sister and her obnoxious husband, their three rug rats from hell, her mother, a fat old aunt that I don't remember ever seeing before, two brothers who are apparently in training to become professional free-loaders, their wives, and their screaming demons, which number either three or four. They never sit still long enough for me to get an accurate count on them. There could be an extra neighbor kid in there somewhere. I don't know for sure, and right now I don't care. I'd just as soon sell the whole bunch to slave traders and forget about them.

Since the invasion of the demon relatives from the netherworld began, I've had to sleep on the army cot in the basement. I haven't been able to get into the bathroom more than once in two days, and that opportunity only arose because the toilet was plugged and I'm the only one in the house skilled in the use of a plunger. I managed to remove the blockage, which turned out to be a ball of wet fur of some kind. I'm not sure what kind it is, but I don't remember seeing the cat around lately. And every time I mention the missing cat, those kids start giggling uncotrollably. I think there may be a connection. The monsters had become bored with their toys by yesterday afternoon. Since then they have been fighting over the boxes that the over-priced junk came in, and they have by now pretty well demolished them, along with the rest of the house. It hurts to think about all the money my wife spent on that junk, and how much I laid out for food and beer and Kessler's and vodka and mix. And most of it consumed by the relatives from hell. I'm broke now, and I'll be living on the remains of Christmas dinner for two weeks. I'll have to run a tab at the bar until payday and borrow cigarette and gas money from anyone who has it to lend.

Suddenly a pain shoots through my head as a kid screeches right next to my ear. I open one eye and take a peek. The monsters have got hold of the beagle who was lying on his back under the tree, bloated with table scraps, emitting foul-smelling gases. He looks like an over-inflated dog-shaped balloon. The kids are rolling him around the room, but the poor old dog seems too far gone to care. The only evidence that he's alive is a wheezing grunt when they roll him over the sharp corner of a demolished cardboard box. I think about rescuing him, but then I think, *naw. Better you than me.*

I look around the room from beneath the lid of the open eye, keeping the other one closed, mostly because it seems to be glued shut by some sticky substance. (I had nodded off earlier, and there was no telling what the kids had done to me while I was asleep) The room looks like a trailer park after a tornado. Broken toys, cardboard, and wrapping paper are everywhere. Something stirs under the wreckage near the tree. Uncle Heikki pokes his head out from under a pile of cardboard and paper, rolls his eyes, turns over on his side, and goes back to dreamland. I don't remember Uncle Heikki being here last night. He must have arrived late. At least twenty bucks worth of booze down the drain right there. I hate to think of how much he and the wife's beer-swilling brothers put away last night. I close my eye and try to shut out all the noise. Christmas carols are playing somewhere and I try to concentrate on that, but it's hard to sort the music out from the screaming and hollering of the demon-kids. I try to count sheep, but I can't concentrate enough to remember what a sheep looks like, so I give up on that and just count the throbs of pain in my head. After a while it begins to dawn on me that it is quieter than it was. In fact, it's too quiet. I'm almost afraid to open my eye to look. The kids might have remembered that I'm lying here on the sofa, and they might at this very moment be plotting some foul deed, like shaving my head, or gluing my finger up my nose with super glue. A wave of panic washes over me as I realize that I have fallen asleep, and I struggle to wake up before the kids get the jump on me. I finally manage to open my eye again. That was close! For a while there I was defenseless. With the eye that isn't stuck shut I look around the room. It is with great relief that I discover I am not the object of their evil design. Over by the fireplace my mother-in-law is

Help!

sleeping in my favorite chair. She's snoring like a chain saw and there's a big stream of drool running down her chin. The kids have found a ragged old string of Christmas lights and are busily stringing them on the old witch. They've already covered her with a good layer of tinsel and have taken two balls from the tree and hung one on each ear. I wonder if I should say something. But if I do that I'll draw attention to myself. No, it's better to let nature take its course. The kids are tip-toeing around, snickering and giggling, and I have to suppress a giggle myself as I anticipate the lighting of the Christmas hag. The kids have finished the decorations, and now there's a brief whispered argument about who should do the honors. Finally a chief electrician is chosen and the rest of the little monsters find hiding places around the room. Little Jeffery is the one chosen to do the plug-in. I would guess that they chose him because he's the youngest and cutest of the lot, and is less likely to receive a severe beating. So Jeffery looks around the room to locate a hiding place to scamper to as soon as the deed is done. Finally satisfied that he has a suitable escape route and hiding place, little Jeffery, with a final sinister giggle, plugs the lights into the wall and dives for cover under a nearby pile of wrapping paper. There is a sizzle, a loud hum, a shower of blue sparks and a puff of white smoke, and the old hag explodes out of the chair with an ear-splitting screech. Suddenly the room is full of frantic activity, with the Christmas hag dancing around in circles, slapping at her smoking hair, kids exploding from their hiding places in panic and scurrying out of the room like spooked cock-roaches, and adults charging in from every other room in the house, including the fat old aunt that I don't recall ever seeing before, dragging a long string of toilet paper behind her. My wife, always the practical and level-headed one, kicks the plug out of the wall with her foot and douses the old witch's smoking hair with a mug of egg nog. I try to put on a convincing sleeping act, but it's so hard to keep my belly from shaking. I peek over at the pile of rubble near the tree and I see that Uncle Heikki is having the same trouble. The pile of wrapping paper and cardboard under which he is hibernating is trembling and I think I can hear snorts and gasps emanating from it. Amid all the activity, no one notices me on the sofa. I have learned over the years the art of blending into the furniture and I can become almost invisible if necessary. As I listen to the excited babble of the crowd, I gather that there is no permanent damage done, and the new hair-do might even be an improvement. So all the women head for the bedroom to experiment with new hair styles while my wife's two beer-swilling brothers go back to burping at the TV in the other room, leaving me in peace. The kids have all been sentenced to confinement in various rooms around the house, and probably won't be heard from for the rest of the afternoon. All is quiet, and I can hear that Christmas music coming from somewhere. I notice that the pain in my head is gone, so with a deep contented sigh, I melt into the sofa, heading for a nice long winter's nap. Life is good. I just love Christmas!

Letters to Santa

Dear Santa,
I am 10 years old and I live in Eben Junction. Last year on Christmas day I found a turd in our yard. Did it come from one of your reindeer? My brother says it is from a dog.
Your friend, Jeffery

P.S. I almost forgot. This year I want the same stuff you brought last year, only make it so it won't break.

Dear Santa,
I am 9 and I am a good boy. My uncle comes to visit at Christmas. Last year he quit drinking. He used to be really funny but he's not anymore. Can you bring him some beer?
Your friend, Max

Dear Santa,
I am only five, so my dad is writing this for me. Please bring me a few small toys that don't have to be put together and don't cost very much.
Your friend, Derek

Dear Santa,
I know you are a phony. My big brother told me all about it. I am 7 years old and he says it's about time I knew the truth. He is in junior high and he knows a lot, so I don't believe in you anymore. But just in case, bring me a sled and a puppy.
Your friend, Chuck

Dear Santa,
I have been a good girl again this year. I am 10 years old and I want a divorced Barbie doll. It's the one that comes with all of Ken's stuff. Thank you very much.
Your friend, Melissa

Dear Santa,
I have been a bad boy all year. I am mean to kids who are smaller than me and I tease them all the time. Don't bring me anything for Christmas.
My brother Butch

Dear Santa,
Bring me all the toys in the toy book and on TV. My mommy is broke.
Your friend, Tyler

Dear Santa,
Please bring me something big and expensive. I've been a good girl this year. I don't know how my little brother started on fire. Nobody got hurt when the car blew up. The cat doesn't look that bad without hair. And grandma wasn't going to live much longer anyway. If anyone writes you a letter about me, it's a bunch of lies.
Your friend, Lisa Lynn

In our last episode... *When we left our heroes last time they had escaped from the quicksand and were continuing on their way toward civilization, where Yooperman would take his place in society, remaining ever vigilant for evil, injustice, and other bad stuff. Little did Yooperman know that the evil Karl Kamper and the Goodtime Gang were at that very moment crossing the bridge into Yooperland. Little did he suspect that soon he would be called upon to face the evil Karl Kamper and the Goodtime Gang.*

Slug Syria sat with his chair tipped back against the wall of Slug's Bar & Gas. It was a lazy, unusually warm autumn day, and Slug dozed in the sun. He was roused occasionally by the sound of a passing car, but for the most part, he managed to maintain a semi-conscious state. Above his head on the wall was a hand-painted sign that read, "Get Gas & Get Gassed." Slug was one of the few humans left alive who openly advocated the practice of driving while puking drunk. He had done it for forty years now, and never once had he had an accident or gotten a ticket. He always drove slowly, and always in the "drunk lane," that gravel part along the side of the road. And of course, he always drove the back roads, even resorting to the two-rut routes when he was especially snockered.

Slug had opened the Bar & Gas years ago, when it was standard practice to buy a case of beer and a pint of Kessler's and go cruising. It seemed that the first thing a guy wanted to do after a few drinks was jump in the car or truck and cruise, and of course, he needed some refreshment for the ride, so Slug came up with the idea of the Bar & Gas. It had made him a fairly decent living over the years, with not too much work involved. In fact, Slug was able to stay half in the bag most all the time and get all the rest he needed, while still managing to maintain his business. It was a pretty sweet setup. So he sat, dozing, trying to decide what he should drink for dinner, when the sound of a decelerating motor told him that he would soon have a customer. He didn't move until the sound of tires coming off the pavement onto the gravel of his parking lot told him that the motorist was indeed stopping. Slug

opened his eyes as a coal-black motor home skidded to a halt next to the gas pump. The long line of cars that had been trapped behind the motor home accelerated past Slug's place, most of the drivers honking their horns and making some sort of hand gestures as they passed. A banana peel came flying out the driver's side window of the

The life and times of Toivo Maki known by evil-doers and bad guys as.....

YOOPER MAN

motor home, then the door opened and a troll hopped out. Slug had never seen a real troll, but he knew this was one, mainly because it didn't look like anything else.

"What'll it be?" Slug asked.

"Fill 'er up," said the troll. "And I'll have three kases of beer to go, too."

Slug stuck the gas nozzle in the motor home and went in to get the three cases of beer. He brought them out and the troll set them in the motor home within easy reach of the driver's seat.

"That'll be twenty-five bucks," Slug as he finished pumping the gas.

The troll patted his pockets. "Whoops!" he said. "I left my wallet in my jacket pocket. I'll be right

back." He jumped back into the driver's seat and pretended to be looking for something. Then suddenly he started the motor, threw it into gear, and stomped the gas. Slug was about to shout and run after the coal black motor home when a cloud of black smoke from the tailpipe enveloped him. It took a few moments for the toxic materials in the smoke to swim upstream against the alcohol to his brain. When it finally took effect, Slug's eyes popped wide open.

"Wow!" He exclaimed. "What a buzz!" He inhaled deeply a few times. "Why have I been wasting my time with booze all these years?"

Then he remembered that Karl Kamper was driving off without paying. He took of at a dead run after the motor home. Just then Toivo Maki, alias Yooperman, and his faithful sidekick Benny stepped out of the woods onto the road. Slug saw them and yelled, "Stop him! He didn't pay! He owes me twenty-five bucks!"

Toivo saw an opportunity to do a good deed. "Wait a minute!" he yelled back. "Do you have an outhouse?"

Slug stopped dead in his tracks. "Well—ya, over there behind the store!"

"I'll be right back!" Toivo yelled, and took off running for the little shack.

Slug looked at Benny, who anticipated the question.

"Uh—he has a touchy stomach," Benny explained. "When he gets excited he has to go."

"Oh." Slug nodded as if he understood. "My mother is the same way," he said.

A few moments later Toivo came stumbling out of the outhouse in his Yooperman costume.

Slug looked Yooperman over.

"Now who da heck are you?" he asked. Slug's brain didn't work too well under the burden of the alcohol and the carbon monoxide, and he wasn't that smart to begin with. "And what happened to that other guy?"

"No time to explain now!" Yooperman yelled. "Besides, it's kinda complicated."

"Oh," Slug replied. "Never mind, then." He didn't feel much like trying to think right now. He was enjoying his carbon monoxide buzz.

"You wait here," Yooperman said. "This is a job for—" He turned and leaned over to Benny. "What was my name again?

"Yooperman!" Benny hissed.

"Uh—right," Yooperman said. "Stand back!" He ordered. Using his ability to run faster than anybody except guys who can run really fast, he took off down the road, with Benny following close behind.

Karl Kamper looked in his rear view mirror and saw Yooperman gaining on him. "Hey," he yelled to his henchmen. "There's some moron in the long johns following us! And a smurf!"

The goodtime gang stuck their heads out the windows and looked back, then they fell upon the floor and rolled around in hysterical laughter. Karl Kamper stomped the gas and began to pick up speed. To his amazement, their pursuers continued to gain on them.

"He's gaining on us!" Karl Kamper cried. "He must have the ability to run faster than anybody except guys who kan run really fast!" He began to realize that he was not dealing with an ordinary man. No one in their right mind would dress like that in public. He hit upon an idea.

"Grab those empty beer kans!" he ordered. "Toss them out!"

The goodtime gang began to gather up the empties that littered the motor home and toss them out the window. Yooperman, having to dodge the beer cans, was slowed down a bit. He still managed to keep pace with the motor home, but was unable to gain any more ground.. Benny, who had fallen behind somewhat, was beginning to realize that they probably would not be able to catch up with Karl Kamper, but he had an idea. He pulled a pad and pencil out of his pocket and began to make notes as he ran. After a few miles, he put the pad and pencil back in his pocket.

"Yooperman! Stop!" he yelled.

Yooperman paid no heed. He was determined to do a good deed if it killed him. He was getting his second wind and was actually beginning to gain on the motor home again, but as he drew to within ten feet of the vehicle, Karl Kamper flipped the black smoke switch, and a cloud of black smoke billowed from the tailpipe. Yooperman, enveloped in the smoke,

Hairold

kept up his pace for a few hundred feet, then he began to gradually slow down. Finally he stopped and just stood there, staring blankly down the road as the coal black motor home chugged around a bend and out of sight. Benny came huffing and puffing behind him.

"We don't have to chase them anymore," he wheezed. "I kept count on the beer cans they threw at us." He took out his pad and flipped through the pages. "250 cans at ten cents apiece—that's twenty five dollars, the exact amount that they owed."

Yooperman just stared down the road. "Duh?" he said.

"What's the matter with you?" Benny asked. He waved a hand in front of Yooperman's face. Yooperman just stared straight ahead. Benny snapped his fingers. "Hey!" he barked. "Are you there?"

"Duh?" Yooperman said.

Whack! Benny gave him a good slap alongside the head. Yooperman looked at him blankly.

"Duh?" he said.

"Oh, no!" Benny said. There must have been something in that smoke." He took Yooperman by the shoulders and shook him. "Must be some kind of brain damage. We'd better get you to a doctor." He took Yooperman by the hand and led him back down the road.

When they got back to Slug's place, Benny told Slug about the twenty-five dollars in returnables, and he helped to gather the empties in garbage bags. Then he led Yooperman back to the outhouse where he helped him change back into his Toivo Maki clothes. While they were there he made Toivo sit on the hole for a while, just in case he had to go and didn't know it. Then Benny took Toivo by the hand and led him down the road in search of a doctor. According to Slug Syria, there was one in the town of Yellow Snow, about ten miles down the road.

As they walked, Toivo stared, zombie-like, straight ahead, and responded to Benny's chatter only with an occasional "Duh?" Something was seriously wrong in his brain. Something more wrong than usual, that is. Even the salad bowl implant in his head was malfunctioning. He still received Gilligan's Island on it, but it was only one still frame, like when a videotape is on pause. Toivo stared at Gilligan, who was frozen in the act of getting slapped in the head by the Skipper's hat. Just as the picture was still, so was the activity in Toivo's brain. He was, for all intents and purposes, a zombie. No thoughts went through his mind, and he could utter no words except for an occasional "Duh?" Benny hoped that the doctor in the town of Yellow Snow would be able to help. But he also had to face the possibility that the damage to Toivo's brain was permanent. If that was the case, he thought he might be able to work up a half decent ventriloquist act, with Toivo as his dummy. So Benny practiced talking without moving his lips as he led Toivo down the road...

What will become of our hero? Will the doctor be able to fix Yooperman's brain? Will he be able to find Yooperman's brain? Is Yooperman doomed to spend the rest of his life as mindless zombie? Will the Packers win another Super Bowl? Is ear wax really necessary? Is Elvis really dead or just having a really long nap? Will Jay Johnson ever become president? Do mosquitoes have lips? Who cares anyway?

For the answers to some of these ridiculous questions, call the psychic hotline. For the rest, turn to page 97 for the next incoherent episode of **YOOPERMAN!**

How twisted are you?
Take this simple test and find out.
Answers & psychiatric profile on page 92

Twisted Trivia Questions
(Hint: Think *really* stupid!)

1. Who was the town of Ralph named after?
2. What is the first important event in a Yooper's life?
3. Name a word that starts with "D".
4. When navigating by the stars, why did Columbus use the Big Dipper?
5. Why was Charles Dickens not buried in Westminster Abbey in 1869?
6. What is the most popular Yooper magic trick?
7. How long does it take to get to Munising?
8. How was your day?
    a. Fine
    b. It sucked.
    c. Don't remember.
9. What's the difference between a boy elf and a girl elf?
10. Name three guys named Bob.

Hi from the U.P.

Dear Ernie,

I know you can't read too fast so I'm writing this real slow. How are things in Arizona? Have you seen any of them hula dancers yet? So how do you like your life of leisure? Did you buy one of them leisure suits yet? Things are pretty good here. My back went out again so I'm on comp for a while. I can't shovel, but the wife is able, so I ain't worried. Besides, I'm gonna get her a brand new used snowblower for Christmas.

Well, as you know, the annual Buck Snort Bar Christmas party is next Saturday. We're gonna miss you, but we'll be sure to have a couple drinks in your honor. Speaking of a couple drinks, I got a good joke for you. Stop me if you've already heard it. This Finlander walks into a bar and says, "Give me a shot and a beer." So the bartender gives him a shot and a beer. He throws down the shot and chases it with the beer. Then he says, "Give me another shot and a beer." Then the bartender says, "We don't serve Finlanders in here." I forget how the rest of it goes, but I know it was real funny.

Well, we had 38 inches of snow last week, but it's been pretty nice since then. The temperature has been staying up around fifteen below, so I guess we can't complain. It wouldn't do no good anyway. I've been complaining about the weather for 40 years and nobody ever did anything about it. I guess if I don't like it I could just move to Arizona like you did. Trouble is, I'd feel bad about leaving all my friends behind. Some people can just pick up and move and leave all their friends behind and never give it a thought. Some guys can lounge around in Arizona in the warm sunshine with no bugs and no snow, just taking life easy, when all the time they know their best friend is stuck up here in the U.P. working his life away at the mine, battling the snow and the cold and the bugs. What kind of a guy could do that to a friend? I know I couldn't. Now that I think about it, I never really did think you were much of a friend anyway. Always borrowing my tools and bumming beers off me at the bar and smoking my camels. I don't even know why I'm bothering to write to you. I hope you get a bad sunburn or get bit by a rattlesnake or sit on some cactus or something. I got better things to do than waste my time writing to you. I think I'll go down to the Buck Snort Bar and have a few beers with the guys. None of them ever liked you much either. That's all I got to say.

Your Friend,
Rudy

P.S. You still owe me that twelve bucks you borrowed last year.

SANTA: Saint or Scam Artist?

Well, it's that time of year again. Actually, it was that time of year around Halloween. I was shopping for a Halloween costume for the YSG Halloween party, and I noticed that I had to wade through aisles and aisles of Christmas junk already in the stores. So I went home to relax and watch TV and what did I get? Long, boring commercials advertising the same worn out Christmas tapes and CD's by the same has-been recording artists that I've heard for the past twenty years. What really burns me is that I end up placing an order to replace the Christmas albums that got thrown out with the old wrapping paper and empty boxes last year.

I recall a time when there was not a single Christmas ad to be seen anywhere until the day after Thanksgiving. Not that I blame any of the advertisers for the frenzy of commercialism that has grown in recent years to overshadow the true meaning of Christmas. Let's place the blame squarely where it belongs. Santa Claus. He is the one responsible for the blatant display of greed and gift-mongering that goes on from late October until December 25. I think the FBI should conduct an investigation of this overweight, unshaven cat-burglar who unlawfully enters millions of homes every year. Sure, he puts on a good act as a benevolent giver of gifts and good cheer—but how many gifts do you get that actually come from Santa himself? In all the Christmases I recall, I don't remember ever getting more than one gift a year with a tag that read "from Santa". And the one from Santa usually turned out to be a cheap, ugly tie that I wouldn't wear to my own funeral, or a hideous sweater with five-foot-long arms, or a stupid gift certificate from the lo-

cal IGA store. All the good and expensive gifts were given to me by my wife and kids, and we all know where they got the money—from my meager paycheck.

And what about our kids? As soon as the holiday season comes around, they are urged to make a list of all the extravagant and expensive toys they desire, and who do they mail it off to? Santa! And what does he get out of it? Do you think he goes through all that trouble every year out of kindness and generosity? Not a chance! The old crook is probably getting kickbacks from all the toy manufacturers.

But that's not the worst of it. What does this old slickster do every year? He comes stealing like the thief in the night that he is, entering our homes while we sleep, eating our milk and cookies, scattering soot all over our living room carpets, scaring the crap out of our cats and dogs, and what does he leave in return? Some cheap little trinket that he can't even give away. And we're supposed to get all misty and choked up when we open the "special" gift that came from Santa himself. How does he get away with it? Well, for one thing, we're all brain-washed early in life to think of him as a jolly old elf. He's chubby and wears a cute red suit. If he was a skinny old buzzard in a flannel shirt and blue jeans, do you think he'd get away with it? Not a chance. He'd go flying back up that chimney with a backside full of buckshot. That's the beautiful part of his scam. We're programmed early in life to let this crafty old fart have free run of the house while we sleep. Do you ever notice that after Christmas, things seem to have disappeared from the house? It's never anything big, like a TV set or a microwave oven. It's little things like my 35-year pin from the mine, or my genuine simulated gold cuff links, or the twelve dollars of beer money in the bottom of my sock drawer. It doesn't seem like much, I know, but when you think of the millions of homes this sneaky old burglar hits every year, well, it adds up to quite a haul. Jolly old elf, my

aching bunions! Ho, ho, ho, indeed! I'd be laughing too, if I was making out the way he is.

But he's not going to get away with it much longer. Ever since I came to realize what is really going on I've made it my mission to stop this scam artist in his tracks. For the past three Christmas Eves, I've sat up with my shotgun, waiting for the old crook to make an appearance. Unfortunately, I've been unable to stay awake long enough to catch him in the act. He's a sneaky bugger, and he always waits until I've nodded off before he comes down the chimney to ransack my house. So I urge all concerned citizens to join me in my crusade to rid the world of this menace. Keep a silent vigil this year, and when this outlaw comes bouncing out of the fireplace, blow him all the way back to the North Pole, or wherever he really comes from. Or maybe you prefer to be more sporting and try to shoot him down on the fly. Either, way, I am personally offering a $25.00 reward to anyone who brings him down and recovers my genuine simulated gold cuff links, my 30 year pin from the mine, and my twelve bucks in beer money. Remember, he is unlawfully trespassing. That's what they let us have guns for. Merry Christmas.

Rintala's Believe it or Shut Up!

Amazing Party

On December 18, 1982, the Aho clan of Deer Lick, Michigan held a Christmas party in the town hall. Over 300 Ahos gathered for the three day celebration. Amazingly, when the party finally broke up they actually had beer left over!

Martha's Summer Kitchen

Well, Christmastime will soon be here again, and Ensio is tromping through the woods behind our house, searching for the perfect Christmas tree. The one he brought home last year was a little scrawny, but with a little love and attention it turned out fine. This year I'll share my recipe for Christmas Piggy Cookies. Children in Finland know that Christmas is coming when they begin to see these piggy-shaped cookies in the bakeries! Crispy and spicy, the cookies can be made out of piparkakku dough as well as this one. However, this dough retains its shape beautifully, without spreading so much as it bakes. Nissu nassu are the Finnish children's pet names for pigs. You may pipe a name across the back of each cookie just as it is done in Finnish bakeries. My sister also bakes these cookies every Christmas, but hers always turn out looking more like sheep. Ensio and I wish you all a happy holiday season.

Christmas Piggy Cookies
Nissu Nassu

3/4 cup softened butter
3/4 cup brown sugar
1 tablespoon cinnamon
2 teaspoons ground ginger

1 teaspoon ground cloves
1 1/2 teaspoons baking soda
2 1/2 cups all-purpose flour
1/4 cup water

Cream the butter and sugar together until blended. Mix the cinnamon, ginger, cloves, soda and flour. Add to the butter-sugar mixture. Blend well. Stir in the water until dough is smooth and pliable (depending on conditions, you may need to add a teaspoon more water to the dough). Chill if necessary before rolling out. Roll out and cut into pig shapes with a pig-shaped cookie cutter. Place on lightly greased cookie sheet and bake at 375° F for 7 to 10 minutes until very lightly browned and crisp. Decorate, if desired with frosting made of powdered sugar and egg white. Makes 5 to 6 dozen cookies.

Profound and Inspiring Poetry Section

Ode To Mother

Who takes me from my nice warm cot
And sits me on an ice cold pot
And makes me go when I cannot...
Me Mudder!

Words of Whizdom:
A journey of a thousand miles begins with an argument over which route to take.

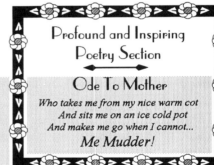

Answers to Twisted Trivia

1. Ralph.
2. Birth.
3. Duh, if you can't get this one, give up!.
4. Because he was really thirsty.
5. He wasn't dead.
6. Turning into a bar.
7. About a six pack and a half.
8. A, B, or C. We don't really care!
9. The boy elf has an itsy bitsy teenie weenie.
10. Bob, Bob, and Bob.

See below your score and evaluation

0-3 Correct
You're as smart as Einstein.

4-6 Correct
You're as smart as Frankenstein.

7-9 Correct
You're as smart as a beer stein.

ALL 10 CORRECT
Can you say "Duh?"

Killer Storm Hits Yooperland!

Old man winter was on a rampage over the last few weeks, bringing extreme blizzard conditions to the much of the midwest. Winds of up to 50 miles per hour, coupled with snowfall accumulations in some areas reaching 36 inches made traveling difficult and dangerous. Temperatures in some areas dropped to 35 below zero, with wind chills as low as 92 below. This is the same blizzard that wreaked havoc across most of the lower midwest, causing many of the areas hit by the storm to be declared disaster areas. Numerous deaths were reported across the lower midwest, and the National Guard was called out to help evacuate many who were left without heat due to power outages.

As the storm raged across the Upper Peninsula, however, reaction of residents is mixed. "This is a pretty good storm," says Rudy Heikkenen, a resident of the town of Yellow Snow. "My snowblower's been on the blink, so I had to shovel out by hand. Took an hour and a half. It was an emergency, too. I was outa beer and I had to get to the store quick!" Neighbor Noogie Nault disagrees. "Dis ain't no storm," he says. "You remember dat one back in '56? Now dat was a storm!"

Most U.P. residents, when interviewed by our news reporters about the killer blizzard that raged across Yooperland, seemed unconcerned. Except for a few residents who moved here from warmer climates, all seemed to agree that the storm was nothing out of the ordinary for this part of the country.

U.P. Town Lost In Storm

Baraga County Search and Rescue teams are out in force tonight in an attempt to locate the town of Toivola, which was reported lost in the storm last night. According to residents returning from a night of revelry in nearby Baraga, the town was still where it was supposed to be when they left. Upon returning from a snowmobile convention late last night, they were unable to locate the town. Search and Rescue units began their search in the area of the town's last known location. "Towns don't just get up and move in the middle of the night," says one sheriff's deputy. "We have to assume at this point that the town is still there somewhere under the snow." Pictures of the town are being circulated in the surrounding area in hopes that someone might recognize it and come forward with information. According to local authorities, there is no immediate cause for alarm. Said one searcher, "We get at least one case like this every winter. If we don't find them, the towns usually show up on their own by spring." Search and Rescue officials request that anyone who remembers seeing the town of Toivola after 11:00 p.m. last night please contact your local police department.

Bitter Cold Assaults Area

The winter storm that raged across the area over the last few days has brought with it extremely cold temperatures. Reports of record low temps have flooded into our news desk from the surrounding area. Many areas were unable to report exact temperatures because the mercury has frozen solid in their thermometers. Residents of the town of Ralph report being bombarded by chickadees frozen solid in flight and falling to the ground. One farmer near Pelkie reported that his cows broke into the house to escape the bitter cold. A Negaunee man suffered a concussion at his camp yesterday when his brother threw a pan of dishwater out the window. The man was standing outside the window and was struck in the head by the water, which had instantly turned to a block of ice when it hit the cold air. A National Mine resident was treated for cuts received when he

"I guess it's been a long winter for everybody!"

stepped outside and was injured by the jagged edges of the frozen air, which had cracked from the cold. Emergency rooms across Yooperland are being flooded with people needing snotsicles removed from their upper lips. Emil Juntila, a 96-year-old resident of Yellow Snow, called in with his usual commentary on the weather, saying, "You call dis cold? Why, I remember back in da winter of turdy eight, *yak, yak, blah, blah, blah..*" ✱ ✱ ✱ ✱ ✱

Kempinen Jailed!

Last Saturday night Waino "Wedgie" Kempinen, a prominent Yellow Snow citizen and former presidential candidate, was arrested for purse-snatching. The complaint was filed by Mille "Moose" Millimaki, an exotic dancer who gained local fame in 1995 as winner of the Yellow Snow Gazette Miss Deer Camp pageant. Kempinen, who plans to act as his own defense counsel in the case, admits that he did take Miss Millimaki's purse, but maintains that the act was justified. According to eyewitness accounts, Kempinen and Millimaki were throwing back shots and beers in the Buck Snort Bar when they got into a heated argument on politics. The argument escalated into a scuffle, and then into a fist fight. "I was doing pretty good," said Kempinen, "until we got into a clinch and she bit off a piece of my nose. I had to do something, so I took her purse. What's the big deal? Nobody complained when they took Tyson's purse, and he had a lot more in it. I only got three bucks, a bunch of make-up, and a butt-ugly picture of Millie in her bloomers and bra." No charges will be filed against Millimaki for the incident, since nose-biting is allowed in fights at the Buck Snort Bar. However, a judge may rule that she must pay for the surgical re-attachment of Kempinen's nose, which was performed by a local taxidermist who happened to be in the bar that night.

 How to keep 'em Whipped!

Gravel Gertie's
Husband Training Tips

Dear Gertie,
My husband and I fight over the thermostat. I set it at 68 degrees, then he comes along and kicks it up to 80. I tell him to put on a sweater if he's cold, but it does no good. He just turns up the heat. I'm sweating all the time and our heating bill is awful. What can I do?
Hot in Houghton

Dear Hot,
My Eugene and I used to battle over the thermostat all the time. He wasn't happy unless it was set at 85 degrees and I was sweating like a pig. Meanwhile, all our money was going up the chimney. Finally one day I told him that I gave up and he could have it as hot as he wanted. Then I started stripping. I told him it was just too hot and I couldn't stand it. I walked around the house in my bra and bloomers. It scared him so bad that he turned the thermostat down to 45 degrees and went and put on a snowmobile suit.
Gertie

Dear Gertie,
My husband and I have been married for 23 years, and in that time he has never once remembered our anniversary. He has absolutely no idea when it is. I remind him every year after it's gone by, and he runs out and buys me something out of guilt. How can I get him to remember?
Forgotten

Dear Fool,
You don't know when you've got it good. I'm also one of the lucky ones whose old man has no idea when our anniversary is. So about five or six times a year I give Eugene hell because he forgot that our anniversary was yesterday. I make the poor slob feel so guilty that he runs out and buys me a nice gift or takes me out to dinner. I feel sorry for those wives who are stuck with just one anniversary a year.
Gertie

Dear Gertie,
My old man never helps me with snow shoveling or other yard work. In fact, every time there's a chore to be done that's the least bit strenuous, he complains of a bad back. I always end up doing it myself. What can I do?
Tired in Toivola

Dear Tired,
My Eugene had back problems that came and went. They came when chores needed to be done, and they went when it was time for hunting or fishing. So I went out in the garden one day, and after a while I came hobbling in and plopped down on the couch. I told him I threw my back out while tilling the garden. I stayed on the couch for two weeks. No cooking, cleaning, or laundry was done. When he finally asked how long I thought it might take for my back to get better, I told him, "Mine will get better when yours does." It was a miracle! His back was better the next day.
Gertie

Dear Gertie,
My husband argues with me about everything. No matter what we talk about, he always disagrees, and before long we're in a heated argument. The only way I can end an argument with him is to give in and agree with him. How do you win an argument with a husband who just won't listen to reason?
Wanna Win One

Dear Wanna,
What a coincidence! I used to have that same problem with my Eugene. He used to argue with me about everything, and there was no way to get him to listen to reason. I don't even bother to argue with him anymore. I just go right to the knuckle sandwich.
Gertie

Science Department

When the winter blues set in and we tend to settle into that lethargic state of near-hibernation, it can be difficult to motivate ourselves to begin even the simplest chores. Thanks to modern science, the technology now exists with which to jar ourselves out of our sedentary doldrums and get moving!

Professor Eino Aho

The Eino Aho Self-Motivator

As we approach mid-winter in this part of the country, we begin to experience a phenomenon that is unique to the northern climates—the winter blues. The holidays are over and we have nothing to look forward to except a drab eternity of heating bills and snow shoveling. Our driveways get narrower as we run out of room for the excess snow. The snowbanks close in on us, and in our drab black and white world, it sometimes seems that we shall never see the sun again. Except for the few winter fanatics among us, who pretend to enjoy freezing to death on a snowmobile, or huddling in an ice fishing shanty on a frozen lake, we tend to react to these conditions by withdrawing into the confines of our homes and merely existing, idly awaiting the first signs of spring. This period of depression and inactivity is commonly known as the "Winter Blues." During this time, daily activity slows to a near halt. We tend to find it difficult to motivate ourselves to perform even the most necessary tasks. We watch the snow build up in our driveways, and we hope against hope that there might come a miraculous mid-winter thaw to save us from the drudgery of shoveling out one more time. We tend to give up on trying to get our frozen automobiles to start in the morning, electing to call a co-worker who is blessed with a heated garage for a ride to work. Even inside chores are neglected as we attempt the escape the winter depression by sitting in front of the television and stuffing fattening snacks into our faces. How do we combat this debilitating mental disease that plagues us for so many months out of the year? Fortunately for the thousands of people afflicted with this malady, I have devoted my scientific energy and intellect to finding a solution, and after days of diligent experimentation in my work-shop, I have arrived at what I believe may be the answer—the Eino Aho Self-Motivator.

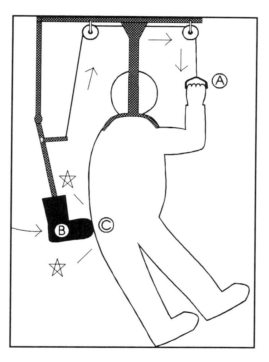

After much study of the phenomenon of the winter doldrums, I concluded that the answer to the problem would not be a psychological one. Since winter blues sufferers regress to a time in human evolution that is more akin to animal than human behavior, I deduced that psychology would be useless, and that the initial motivational tool must be a physical one. Further, it must be an extreme physical stimulus, one that cannot be ignored. I recalled from my teenage days times when my father wished to motivate me to mow the lawn or wash the car, or some such boring and menial task that I believed was beneath my level of talent and ability. I remembered how quickly he was able to motivate me with the sudden impact of his size 12 boot against my lazy posterior. I found his method to be extremely effective. That motivational stimulus is the basis for my Self-Motivator.

The design of the Prof. Aho Self-Motivator (see illustration) is basically a simple one. The Self-Motivator is activated by a sudden pull on the motivational impact device initiator (A) which, through a rope and pulley system, brings the impact device (B) into contact with the wearer's lazy posterior, (C) thereby producing basically the same result as the size 12 of an angry father.

The Self-Motivator can also serve as a self-punishment device, for those times when one has inadvertently committed some regrettable act which one deems worthy of punishment. We all have committed such foolish errors from time to time. (Such as being invited to the Dean's home during the holidays, drinking too many screwdrivers, and vomiting profusely into his kitchen sink. Such a mistake deserves repeated pulls on the motivational impact device initiator)

I have been experimenting with the prototype of the Prof. Aho Self-Motivator, and it has performed mechanically beyond my expectations. There are, however, still a few flaws which need to attention. Most of these flaws can be corrected with minor adjustments. There is only one major problem which needs to be solved before the Prof. Aho Self-Motivator is ready to go into mass production. Although the machine very effectively supplies motivation once the motivational impact device initiator is pulled, I have not yet found a way to motivate the user to pull the rope.

* * * * * * * * * * * * * * * * * *

 **Mail Call**

Dear Professor Aho:

I am 23 years old, a sophomore in high school, and fair complected. That is not the problem. The problem is that we have been studying geometry and ever since we started I have been grappling with the concept of πr^2 For all of my entire life it has been my observation that πr round and cake r^2. Do you have any hints or advice as to how to get this straight in my melon?

Duane

Dear Duane,

You are correct in your observation that πr round. I hasten to point out, however, that some cakes r round and some r^2, depending on what kind of pan you use. To avoid confusion I would suggest that you use only ^{2} cake pans when baking cake.

Prof. Aho

TRIVIA

How twisted are you?
Take this simple test and find out.
Answers & psychiatric profile on page 104

Twisted Trivia Questions
(Hint: Think *really* stupid!)

1. What is the main ingredient in ice?
2. What is the main export of Yooperland?
3. What does every Yooper need for snow shoveling?
4. What happens every Christmas Eve?
5. Think of two things. Which one is bigger?
6. Which of these beer cans has more beer in it?

7. In Yooper folklore, Heikki Lunta is the God of _____.
   A. Beer   B. Snow   C. Rust
8. How do you get a Yooper fighting mad?
   A. Insult his mother.
   B. Insult his sister.
   C. Spill his beer.
9. Pick a number.
10. What is the main occupation of Yoopers?

Madame Brewsky's
News that ain't happened yet

The Gazette's resident Certifiable Professional Psycho brings you the news before it happens.

The other night as I sat in the Buck Snort Bar trying to get some news from the future on my crystal ball, I happened to pick up a signal from the television station just down the road. It was a commercial for one of those psychic hot lines or some such silly thing. I figured I might as well watch for a while to see what the competition was up to, so I ordered a jumbo and sat back to watch. The first thing this idiot says is "you won't see any high-priced celebrities on our commercials." So I watched, and sure enough, I didn't see any well-known actors. What I did see was a bunch of unknown starving actors who are desperate and will work really cheap. So what does she say next? "These are real people." If I was a high-priced celebrity I think I'd be a little insulted at that one. Last time I checked, high-priced celebrities were just as real as those cheaper nobodies who are desperate enough to show their faces on a psychic commercial. Maybe it's the beer that's making me crabby, but I'm getting fed up with those commercials that try to pass unknown actors off as ordinary people off the street. So I watched for a little while until I was about to blow my lunch, then I switched the channel. It's a good thing I had a channel changing knob installed on my crystal ball when it was in the shop for repairs. I had to flip through three more psychic commercials, four lawyer interviews about things they botched in the O.J. trial, and half a dozen exercise machine ads before I found a clear channel. The blank channel was the most interesting and intelligent programming of the lot. I ordered another jumbo to help me get into the trance-like state that I need for seeing into the future. My crystal ball looked a little murky at first, but after a while, as I began to slip into my trance, I began to see things. I didn't get anything really clear, but I did get bits and pieces of things that are going to happen in the next year or so. Unlike those phonies on TV, I have the guts to put my predictions in writing, so you can save this article and check off these predictions as they happen. Here's my list of amazing predictions for the future:

Madame Brewsky's Predictions...

1. A politicain is going to be connected to a scandal involving one of the following:
   a. A prostitute
   b. Tax evasion
   c. A farm animal named "Bessie"
   d. All of the above
2. A supermarket tabloid will predict that the world will end in 1997.
3. The news media will constantly bother us with details of the O.J. Simpson civil trial.
4. Someone connected to the O.J. Simpson trial is going to write a book.
5. You're going to come into some money, probably sometime around next payday.
6. Death.
7. Taxes.
8. I'm going to have another jumbo.
9. My crystal ball is going to get too fuzzy to see pretty soon.
10. I'm going to be really sick in the morning.

The Life and times of Toivo Maki
Known by evil-doers and bad guys as ...
Yooperman

In our last episode... *Toivo Maki, alias Yooperman, and his faithful sidekick Benny, step out of the woods just in time to see Karl Kamper speed away from Slug Syria's gas pump without paying. They give chase, and although they are unable to catch Karl Kamper's motor home, they do recover the amount due in returnable cans. But during the chase, Yooperman is overcome by the mysterious black smoke from Karl Kamper's tailpipe, and he becomes a mindless zombie. As we join our heroes, they are headed down the road toward the town of Yellow Snow, where they hope to find a doctor who can restore Yooperman's mind.*

Toivo Maki's brain sat like a lump of cold mashed potatoes inside his skull. There seemed to be no activity there to speak of, other than the impulses that drove his motor skills and what was left of his vocabulary memory banks, consisting of one word, which Toivo repeated constantly. "Duh?" he inquired, as he inspected something he had just picked out of his nose.

"Stop that!" Benny scolded. He led Toivo over to a yellow birch tree on the side of the road and pulled off a strip of bark with which to wipe the obscene object from Toivo's finger. "Listen to me!" Benny shook Toivo until the salad bowl implant in his head rattled. "Don't do anything! Don't stick fingers in any holes you find, and don't play with any body parts!" He grabbed Toivo's hands and shoved them down into the pockets of his blue jeans. "Keep your hands in your pockets!" He grabbed Toivo's head and looked him straight in the eye. "Do you under- stand me?"

"Duh!" Toivo said.

Benny couldn't really tell if there was a spark of comprehension in Toivo's eyes. Of course that wasn't unusual. Maybe Toivo was nearly brain dead, but he always appeared to be that way to Benny, so it was actually hard to tell any difference. But since his encounter with the black smoke from Karl Kamper's exhaust pipe, Benny figured it could be said of Toivo Maki now, that he really was as stupid as he looked.

"Come on," Benny said, grabbing Toivo by the front of his shirt. "We've got to find a brain surgeon, or at least a small engine repairman." He led Toivo down the road.

As Toivo walked along in his state of brain-freeze, he kept his eyes closed most of the time, watching the still-frame of Gilligan getting slapped by the Skipper's hat. The black smoke that had frozen his brain had not interfered with the clarity of the reception through the salad bowl implant in his head. Though the picture was frozen, it was still clear. The part of him somewhere deep inside his mind, or maybe deeper than that, the part of him where an appreciation for fine art resided, that part of him watched, and was dimly aware. It was that part of him that felt a vague anticipation, as if something was supposed to happen, but hadn't yet. It was also that part of him that suddenly had to pee. He could feel the pressure, but in his brain- damaged state he had no idea how to go about relieving it.

"Duh?" he said. He continued to walk down the road with his legs crossed. Benny, leading him by the front of the shirt, looked back and immediately got the hint. He led Toivo over the the side of the road, into the woods, and behind a bushy spruce tree. He helped Toivo get unzipped and ready to go, then he went back out on the road to wait and watch for traffic.

"Hurry up," he called. "Let me know as soon as you're finished. And don't be playing with things."

As Benny waited, it occurred to him that he had been feeling the urge to go number three, so he dashed across the road and into the trees. He figured he'd only be a moment, since to go number three always took 7.3 seconds, no matter how bad you had to go, or how long it was since you last went. For Benny it had been 17 years since he had last gone number three, so he had to go pretty bad. He didn't know about on earth, but on his world 17 years was a pretty long time to go without—well, going. Benny took care of his business in short order and then he walked back across the road to see how Toivo was doing.

"How's it going in there?" he called. "Are you finished yet?" He listened, expecting to hear the usual

Hairold

"Duh?" from his confused companion. But there was only silence. Benny headed into the trees to check on Toivo. He found the spot where he had left Toivo, but his friend was nowhere in sight. Benny ran frantically around in a small circle, thinking that maybe he had come to the wrong tree. But a close inspection of the ground showed the wet spot that Toivo had left on the ground. This was the place, but where was Toivo? Benny began to search the immediate area, but he could find no clue as to which way Toivo might have wandered. So Benny began to search the woods. For hours he wandered, calling Toivo's name, but to no avail. As dusk fell, he finally gave up. He decided to make camp in the woods for the night, and tomorrow he would go on into town and get help from the local authorities. He built a fire and settled down for the night. He hoped that, in spite of his brain-dead condition, and because of his muskrat upbringing, Toivo would instinctively know how to survive the night in the woods. He leaned back against a stump, munching on a rubber bathtub stopper as he stared up at the stars.

As Benny settled down for the night in the woods, Toivo dozed off in his warm bed at the Marquette County Brain Farm, a local hospital for folks with all sorts of brain problems. After wandering off into the woods, he had circled back to the highway where he had been picked up by the local sheriff's deputy. Since all the deputy could get out of Toivo was an occasional "Duh", and since he was wandering down the middle of the highway with his fly down and everything hanging out, the deputy didn't even bother to bring him back to the Sheriff's office. He figured he'd save time and paperwork by just delivering Toivo directly to the Brain Farm, where he obviously belonged. The doctors were delighted to see Toivo. They had never seen such an extreme case of whatever it was that Toivo had such an extreme case of. They were looking forward to getting inside Toivo's head to see what was what. They argued about what could have caused his condition. Some said it was a life of too much booze. Others said it was the war.

One said it was probably too much booze during the war. But they all agreed that the rattling sound that came from Toivo's head when they shook him was very interesting. And they all agreed that Toivo needed some intense therapy, and if that didn't work, they'd probably have to operate. So they put Toivo in a room with soft walls and floors and looked at him through a one-way window until quitting time. Then they all went down to the the Buck Snort bar to have a few beers and to plan his treatment.

So as Benny shivered by the fire in the woods, Toivo dropped off to sleep watching the still-frame of Gilligan getting slapped by the Skipper's hat. As he slept, no dreams flickered through his still mind, no spark of awareness smoldered in the darkness, and the part of Toivo Maki that was Yooperman, the guardian of truth, justice, and good grammar, faded toward oblivion...

Will Benny be eaten in his sleep by smurfeating bears? Will Toivo ever get his mind back? Did you remember to shut the garage door? Who stinks? Did you know there was a little green bug in your salad? Where am I?

For the answers to these and other burning questions, follow the continuing adventures of Yooperman in the pages of The Yellow Snow Gazette. For subscription information write to Shields Publishing Company or call (906) 485-5998.

News Briefs

Local Man Arrested for Assault

Oscar Olsen, 52, was arrested for assaulting a store mannequin. Olsen, who had spent the better part of the day in the Buck Snort Bar, wandered into Ruthie's Rag Shop and tried to pick a fight with one of the store's mannequins. During the scuffle, the mannequin fell on Olsen, breaking his nose. As he was led away in handcuffs, Olsen reportedly yelled, ***It was a sucker punch! Next time I'll be sober!"***

Packer Products Hot Items

With the triumphant return of the Green Bay Packers to the god-like status as Super Bowl XXXI heroes comes a frantic retail feeding frenzy that we haven't seen around these parts since the Cabbage Patch Doll insanity a few years ago and the more recent Tickle-Me-Elmo madness. Nowhere was the Packer memorabilia madness more evident than at the Packer Backer auction held at the Yellow Snow American Legion Hall yesterday. Official Green Bay Packer souvenirs of all kinds went on the auction block, including such items as bags of Lambeau Field turf, T-shirts, hats, and mugs. But besides the usual souvenir items, a few more unusual and rare items were auctioned off. Half-ounce vials of Packer Sweat went for anywhere from $80.00 to $400.00, depending upon the player. As expected, Brett Favre sweat went for top dollar. Each vial of sweat underwent extensive DNA testing before the auction to verify authenticity. The original authentic pair of Reggie White undershorts (with skid marks intact) worn during the Super Bowl game, went for $250.00. Two moustache hairs from Mike Holmgren's lip went for $75.00 each. But as hot as today's Packer items were, the top bid went to a piece of the past. A boot that once belonged to a Lambeau Field groundkeeper whose cousin's uncle went to school with a guy whose wife's ex-husband once shook Vince Lombardi's hand went for a whopping $2500.00! ■

Packer Hit By Truck

While crossing Lombardi Avenue yesterday, Green Bay Packer defensive tackle Gilbert Brown was reportedly hit by a beer truck. Brown sustained no injuries, but the truck was totalled.

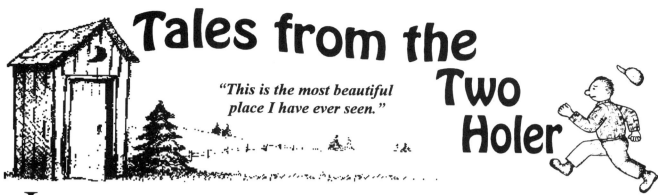

Tales from the Two Holer

"This is the most beautiful place I have ever seen."

John Trollman came to Yooperland in the fall of '89. Born and raised in Mt. Clemens, he had never been north of the Mackinac Bridge before. But he had heard about the land up north, where the measure of a man was the size of his woodpile, where no one ever locked their car doors, where the sound of a gunshot in the night was someone bagging a little extra meat for the freezer, and not someone getting shot over the color of his underwear. John had finally had enough of life down in troll valley, and he decided to move up to Negaunee to live the life nature had intended, away from cellular phones, drive-by shootings and freeway traffic jams. It was the middle of October when he arrived. The colors were awesome. There was just a bit of a nip in the air beneath the warmth of the October sun. A hint of wood smoke drifted on the breeze, and as he smelled it, he knew that he had found heaven. November was beautiful. Deer Season was a blast. He could hardly wait to experience a real Yooperland winter. Christmas was absolutely wonderful. Then came January. John has since moved back down to Mt. Clemens. The following is an excerpt from his journal, in which he recorded his stay in Yooperland.

Jan. 2— Today it snowed. It was beautiful.

Jan. 4— It snowed again today. It's a winter wonderland. I spent the afternoon shoveling.

Jan. 6—Snowed again. It was pretty. I shoveled out where I shoveled yesterday.

Jan. 8—Snow. It looks kinda nice. I finally wised up and bought a snowblower. It was a lot easier clearing the driveway.

Jan. 10—Damn snow again. Good thing I bought that snowblower. Too bad the CENSORED thing broke down. Had to finish shoveling by hand.

Jan. 2— CENSORED snow! If this CENSORED snowblower would work it wouldn't be so bad.

Jan. 14—More CENSORED snow! Just finished the CENSORED driveway and the CENSORED snowplow came by and left a twelve foot bank. Took two CENSORED hours to shovel through it.

Jan. 16—Guess what? Yup. Three CENSORED feet of CENSORED snow! Just finished shoveling out and my CENSORED neighbor came along with his CENSORED snowblower and threw snow on my nice clean CENSORED driveway. If he does it again I'm going to blow his CENSORED head off!

Jan. 17—- CENSORED Snow! Shoveled my CENSORED driveway by hand because my CENSORED snowblower wouldn't start. Just spent $79.00 to fix that piece of junk.

Jan. 18—Didn't snow today. It was too CENSORED cold. My CENSORED water pipes froze and split. On top of that I was late for CENSORED work because my CENSORED car wouldn't start. I was a CENSORED idiot to come to this CENSORED place!

Jan. 19—Big CENSORED news! It Snowed! The CENSORED snowplow driver took out my CENSORED mailbox! I'll be waiting with my CENSORED deer rifle next time.

Jan. 20—Thought I saw the CENSORED sun today. Will we finally get a break?

Jan. 21—Must have been a CENSORED UFO! Got two CENSORED feet of CENSORED snow and then the mercury went out of sight. It's so CENSORED cold I can't get my CENSORED snowblower to run. The CENSORED car wouldn't start either. I don't give a CENSORED anymore! You CENSORED people have to be total idiots to live in this place!

Jan. 22— CENSORED CENSORED This CENSORED place! I'm on the next CENSORED bus outa here!

Global Warming: Yeah, right

Is global warming a fact? And if so, is it a bad thing?

It seems that every time I pick up a newspaper or a magazine these days, somebody is griping and moaning about global warming. Well, I've got just one question. Where? When I get up in the morning, put on my longies, thermal socks, my boots, my parka, my hat and scarf, my gloves, and I head outside to build a fire under that old junker of mine—well, I guess I just don't get it. Where is this "global warming" when I'm freezing my buns off trying to fix the water pipes that froze and split, turning my basement into an ice rink? When I'm out there breaking my back, shoveling my driveway at five in the morning so I can get to work by eight, I'd be glad to see a little global warming. The truth is, I just don't see it. Greenhouse Effect? All I know is the Outhouse Effect. When I take my paper and head to the outhouse I don't even get through the funnies before I'm frozen to the bone and ready to put a torch to the old shack just to warm it up a little. I don't know who it is that's doing all the complaining about global warming. Probably some poor rich bum laid out on the beach in southern California or some old fart at a beach front retirement home in Florida. They get a little sunburn on their noses and all of a sudden they're yelling about global warming and the hole in the ozone and all that. They ought to come up here to Yooperland for a while. That'd get all the global warming nonsense out of their heads. As far as I can see from where I sit, they've got it all bass-ackwards. It's freezing that's the problem. And it's not some new-fangled idea like nuclear winter, either. It's just the same plain old-fashioned winter that we've always had. There has not been a day gone by this winter without some snow falling. My snowblower is working overtime and my driveway is getting narrower as I run out of places to put the snow. The banks are already eight feet high in the middle of January. And if the snow isn't bad enough, now the temperature is dropping out of sight, and will probably stay that way until the end of March. Oh sure, It will warm up occasionally, just long enough to dump more snow on us, and then the mercury will go into hiding again. So you can't win. When it's not snowing it'll be only because it's too damn cold to snow. Global warming, my aching bunions! And when my car won't start because of the ice chunks in the water pump, and I have to pull the whole thing apart in the dark in blowing snow at 38 below, where are these global warming freaks then? Are they here giving me a hand? No. They're sipping some exotic tropical drink on some topless beach, griping about how we have to cut back on our fossil fuel emissions. Well, I've got news for them. My Chevy ain't doing any emitting when it's sitting here in three feet of new snow with motor oil thicker than molasses and water hoses swelling and splitting from the ice. Sure, it's easy for those people who are born with nice new four-wheel drive Broncos and a nice warm heated garages to talk about global warming. But to those folks I say just come on down here in the snow and ice and wrestle with this worthless piece of junk for a while. Pretty soon you'll be sporting an attitude that will make disgruntled postal employees look like social workers in comparison. And you won't give a whit about global warming or the greenhouse effect. In fact, you'll be dreaming of the day when the polar ice caps melt and the global flooding washes the snow out of your driveway, rust-bucket Chevy and all. I know that it is the prevailing attitude among all my friends and neighbors, because whenever we get together, the main topic of conversation is how miserable it is to live in the toilet bowl of the universe. So, you might ask, with all the griping and moaning about the cold and the snow that we do around here, why don't we just move to a warmer climate? Why do we put up with it? Well, the answer to that one is simple—we love it here!

Rintala's

Believe It or Shut Up!

Winter Olympics

In the 1971 Winter Olympics, Toivo Toivonen of National Mine, Michigan won the 100 yard dash snowblowing competition with a time of 17.9 seconds. Mr. Toivonen commented later, **"I coulda done it quicker if dat bloody snowblower woulda started."**

DO COWS BITE?

While the boom box perched on the kitchen window sill twanged out some soulful country tune about being dead and gone and glad of it, Rudy grabbed a handful of wrenches from the toolbox and went under the hood of the truck. The old GMC pickup seemed always on the verge of falling apart. But with a little ingenuity, some skinned knuckles, and a little luck, he usually managed to keep it on the road. With his head aching slightly from a Kessler's hangover, Rudy hummed along with the music as he attacked an ailing water pump.

"H'lo." a little voice said.

Rudy pulled his head from under the hood of the truck and looked around. "Great--now I'm hearing voices," he muttered, and then dived back under the hood with a wrench in each hand.

"Whatcha doin'?" The little voice came again.

Rudy jumped this time, bumping his head on the hood. A word formed in his mind, but he managed to hold it in. He stepped back, feeling for a lump, looking for the source of the little voice. A large pair of blue eyes under the turned-up bill of a baseball cap peered over the fender of the car. One of the neighborhood yard apes.

"Oh," Rudy said. "I'm fixing my truck." Exchanging one of the wrenches for a pair of vise grips, he attacked the motor again.

"Is it broke?"

"Yup."

Two grimy hands appeared on the fender as the inquisitive little monkey strained to peek over it.

"Kin I watch?" He asked.

Rudy glanced over at him and stifled a snicker--Kilroy was here. "Okay," he said. "Just don't touch anything." A few moments of busy silence passed. A bumblebee droned lazily by.

"I'm five," Kilroy said.

"Huh?" Rudy's attention was divided between the water pump and the bumblebee.

"I'm five," Kilroy repeated, holding up four fingers.

"Oh," Rudy replied. "That's nice." A wrench clanged to the ground,

inevitably landing under the exact center of the engine.

"I'll get it!" Kilroy yelped, and scrambled under the car, appearing a moment later on the other side, triumphantly holding the wrench aloft. "Kin I help?" he asked.

"Nope." Rudy plucked the wrench from his hand and went back under the hood. A crow cawed twice nearby. Another answered in the distance.

"You have hair in yer nose," Kilroy observed.

Clink! A screwdriver followed the trail blazed by the wrench.

"Get that, willya?" Rudy grunted, applying pressure to the vise grips.

"Why do grownups have hair in their nose?"

Knuckles met iron. "Ahh!" Rudy's head connected with the hood again. "AAAHH!" he repeated, with more conviction this time.

"My dad bumped his head once and he said a bad word," Kilroy said.

"Never mind," Rudy hissed. "I'll get it myself." He went after the wrench, tearing his shirt and losing some skin from his back. The springs squeaked slightly and Kilroy's voice came from above.

"What's this thing do?"

"Don't touch it!" Rudy snapped. Kilroy was back on the ground before Rudy could scramble out from under the truck. Rudy grabbed a hammer and went back under the hood.

"I bet my dad could fix that easy." Kilroy said. A short silence. "Yer finger's bleedin'," he said.

"I know." Rudy grunted as he wrestled with the water pump.

"Does it hurt?"

"No." *[wiggle wiggle tap tap]*

"I bet it does."

"Okay it does." *[squeak squeak tink tink]*

"How much?"

"A little bit."

[tap tap squeak rattle rattle]

Kilroy jammed a finger up his nose and wiggled it around a bit.

"Do cows bite?"

"No." *[squeak jiggle tap tap]*

"Do alligators?"

"Yes." *[squeak]*

"Do they like people?"

"Which?" *[jiggle]*

"Which what?"

"Cows or alligators?" *[tap]*

"Cows or alligators what?"

"Like people." *[wiggle jiggle tap tap]*

"How should I know? I'm only five. Kin I help?"

"Yes--NO--AAAHH!" The hammer rattled its way to the ground. "I'll get it!" Two voices yelled in unison. The kid scrambled under the car while Rudy sucked his skinned knuckles. A moment later he crawled out with the hammer. He handed it up to Rudy, then he climbed up on the bumper.

"Listen!" Rudy cupped his hand to his ear. "Is that your mother calling?"

Kilroy jumped down and began to inspect the contents of Rudy's tool box. "Naw," he said. "She ain't home. What's this for?" He held up an allen wrench.

"It's a wrench," Rudy said.

"A wrench? It don't look like one."

"It's a wrench, honest it is. Put it back."

"How come it's bent?"

"It's supposed to be bent. Put it back."

"Why?"

"Because I said so."

"No, why's it s'posed to be bent?"

"I don't know," Rudy said, both hands fully occupied with a task that required three hands. *[tink, tink, rattle, squeak]* Finally, out of desperation he asked, "Do you wanna help?"

Kilroy inspected the allen wrench with a thoughtful frown.

"Naw."

[KLANGGG!] "AARGH!"

"Ya dropped yer wrench." Kilroy said.

Rudy clenched his teeth, wiped the sweat off his forehead with a torn, greasy sleeve, and inspected the fresh raw scrape on his wrist. "I don't suppose you wanna get that for me?" he asked.

"Naw, I'm busy," Kilroy said, now standing with his hands clasped behind his back, staring at the sky.

"Busy?" Rudy echoed. "Doing what?"

"Thinking."

Rudy followed his gaze, wondering what could have distracted him. In the distance a towering bank of cumuli-nimbus clouds blazed majestically in the summer sun. A soaring hawk circled slowly, a mere speck against the clouds. A slight, cooling breeze caressed his face. It was a beautiful day. Rudy had been too wrapped up in his troubles to notice.

"Thinking," he echoed again, this time in a softer tone. "About what?"

"Nothin'."

Rudy stood beside him, hands clasped behind his back, absently massaging aching knuckles, and together they stared off into the summer sky. Kilroy's mood had changed. He was very quiet and still. He seemed lost in deep thought, and Rudy could tell from the intensity of his gaze that he wasn't day-dreaming. He was thinking. Rudy could sense a question forming in Kilroy's little mind, and he sensed that it was an important one. He felt very humble and very wise, and very sure that he, with his vast store of knowledge and experience in life, could give the little guy the answers he sought. Rudy broke into the quiet moment. "You must be thinking something."

"Well..." The kid's little brow crinkled in deep thought. He looked down at the ground, seeming to search for the words to form his question.

"Yes?" Rudy whispered breathlessly.

Kilroy tilted his little freckled face up and looked at Rudy with one eye scrunched shut against the glare of the sun.

"Do duck turds float?

HISTORY OF TOWN IN DOUBT

National Mine University historians doing research on the origin and history of the town of Yellow Snow, Michigan have made a startling discovery. While analyzing soil samples taken from the spot where Rudy Rintala is said to have stopped to relieve himself while exploring the area in January of 1802, researchers concluded, after conducting DNA tests on urine traces in the soil, that the traces could not have come from Rintala. Legend has it that Rintala, after relieving his bladder in the snow, was so struck by the beauty of the yellow design that he had made that he decided to build a town around it. But scientists now have concluded that the urine traces were not those of Rintala, or of any other human. An NMU spokesman, in an exclusive interview with the YSG, said that the traces are possibly those of a wolf, or more likely, a dog. A storm of controversy surrounds the recent discovery. Some local residents accuse the researchers of sloppy evidence gathering and contamination of the samples in the laboratory. Some even accuse residents of the nearby village of Suomi of planting false evidence, the motive being jealousy over Suomi's humiliating defeat in last year's snowshoe races at the hands of the Yellow Snow team.

But most Yellow Snow residents believe that the NMU scientists have arrived at the truth. There is now an ongoing debate among residents as to whether the town should be renamed. Several suggestions have been offered. Suggested names range from the descriptive "Dog Whiz" to the more exotic and Indian sounding "Puppee." Some say that, even though the yellow spot was not that of Rudy Rintala, it was still a spot of yellow snow, and therefore no name change is necessary. But local politicians, having no other controversy upon which to build their careers, say that since the whole history of the town is based on a misconception, the town should be renamed in order to set history straight. Foremost in the campaign to keep the old name is Waino "Wedgie" Kempinen, a former presidential candidate who lost to Bill Clinton by a narrow margin in the last election. Says Kempinen, "We have nothing to be ashamed of. Much of American history has been re-written to make it look more noble in the history books. We should set an example for the rest of the country. Wolf, dog, or Finn whiz, it's still yellow snow. Whoever it was, let's just be glad he didn't have to go number two." ∎

News Briefs

Robbery Attempt Foiled

Elmo Salmi, 42, a Yellow Snow resident, entered the First National Bank of Yellow Snow last Thursday, handing the teller a paper sack and demanding that she empty the vault. Upon being informed that the vault was on a time lock and wouldn't be opened until Monday, Salmi wrote down his name and address, handing it to the teller and saying, "Mail it to me."

The Revised National Mine University Entrance Exam

Because of a recent drop in the number of new students enrolling at NMU, and because of the nationwide primary and secondary education crisis National Mine University has been forced to lower its entrance standards. This entrance exam replaces the earlier exam, which was criticized as being "just too darn hard." The following is a partial list of questions taken from the new entrance exam.

"Got change for a twenty?"

Math:

1. If Toivo has six beers and you take half of them away from him, what will you have?
    a. A broken arm.
    b. A black eye
    c. All of the above

2. Rudy is at his sister's house in Shingleton. Sulo is at a bar in Houghton. Rudy heads west in his Chevy at 45 m.p.h. Sulo drives east in his Pontiac at 55 m.p.h. Where will they meet?
    a. California
    b. Alpha Centauri
    c. They won't. Rudy's Chevy broke down and Sulo took the wrong road.

3. How many toes do you have? (*There may be more than one correct answer*)
    a. Ten.
    b. Five on each foot.
    c. Enough.

4. If Rudy has $3.15 and Eino gives him $2.50 more, how much will he have?
    a. More than he had before
    b. Less than he had before
    c. About the same as he had before

5. If you have a board eight feet long and you cut three feet off, which of the two resulting boards will be longer?
    a. Neither one. Both will be shorter.
    b. Throw the short one away. The one you have left will be the longer one.
    c. All of the above
    d. None of the above
    e. Some of the above
    f. a and b
    g. e and c or f
    h. a, b, c, d, e, f, and sometimes g

History:

1. Who was the first president of the United States?
    a. George Washington
    b. George Washington
    c. *George Washington*

2. Vince Lombardi was the coach of what famous football team from Green Bay?
    A. <u>Green Bay Packers</u>
    b. Koski Corners Muskrats
    c. New York Yankees

Rest Period

    Please put your pencil down and put your head on your desk for a 7 minute rest period before continuing on to the next question.

History:

3. Complete this famous phrase in which Patrick Henry made no reference to food or drink. "Give me liberty or give me_____."
(*hint: a or b might not be good choices*)
    a. A pasty
    b. A beer.
    C. None of the above.

4. Which of the following was never elected President of the United States? (*hint: He has a big red nose*)
    a. Ted Kennedy
    b. Tip O'Neil
    c. Ronald McDonald
    d. All of the above

English:

1. Which of the following sentences contains no errors?
    a. I found six **errors** on my spelling test.
    b. I can't believe he committed eight **errors** in one inning!
    c. This sentence is perfect.

2. Which of the following is not a sentence fragment?
    a. This is a.
    b. Sentence fragment.
    c. This is a complete sentence.

3. Which of the following is a question?
    a. This is the wrong answer.
    b. So is this.
    c. If a and b are incorrect, do you think c might be the right answer?

4. Which of the following contains the correct punctuation?
    a. Dont pick this one
    b. Nope not, this; one' either?
    c. How about this one?

5. Which of the following sentences makes the most sense?
    a. I for am why and yes.
    b. Hw dyn lnvy sywp nmqp.
    c. Horses are bigger than mosquitoes.

THE END

The correct answers to the questions on this exam can be obtained at no charge. Send $500.00 to cover shipping and handling costs to The Yellow Snow Gazette, Rt. 1, Yellow Snow, MI 49865.

TOP 10
things to look for
when buying a used car in Yooperland

10. Check the trunk for dried blood and tufts of deer fur. This car has probably spent a lot of time on rough roads.

9. Patches of silly putty. This car probably has shoddily patched rust holes.

8. Tailpipe connected with beer cans. Unless the cans are the old steel kind, this car's muffler system will not last long.

7. When the seller starts the car for you, watch his lips to make sure he's not going, "brrrrm, brrrrm!"

6. Try to stay alert if the seller gets you puking drunk during his sales pitch.

5. During your test drive, make sure the car also runs *uphill.*

4. Beware of a seller who says, "Once I show you how, you'll be the only one who can start this car."

3. Beware of a car that is up on blocks in a backyard, even if the seller offers to throw in a free set of tires.

2. Rust holes in the engine are not good.

1. If there are more wire coat hangers on the underside of the car than in your closet, don't buy the car.

Martha's Summer Kitchen

Well I can't believe it! My sister joined a cooking farm! They guaranteed that when she was through with the session she would be the best cook on the block. She left on January the 15th and won't be back until February the 29th. We wish her all the luck in the world and hope for the best. I think what really pushed her over the edge was when my brother-in-law refused to buy her any more kitchen utensils. You see my sister, bless her heart, can't seem to boil water without burning up a few pots and pans. It can get a little expensive after 35 years of marriage. So I'd just like to wish her the very best . Go get 'em Sis. Make us all proud of you. Well, I suppose I can stop rambling on long enough to tell you about my recipe for this issue. St. Urho's day is just around the corner, and in keeping with the season, I have chosen for this issue another Finnish recipe, and one of Ensio's favorites, St. Urho's Day Rye Bread. He enjoys it with a slice of summer sausage and a cup of coffee. I guess you can't tell that Ensio is a Finn.

St. Urho's Day Rye Bread
Pyhän Urhon ruisleip

This makes one big loaf of bread fragrant with anise, fennel and orange peel. This bread is firm and close textured, excellent sliced thinly and served with cheese.

1½ cups (12 oz. can) dark beer	½ cup milk
2½ cups dark or pumpernickel rye flour	1 cup cracked wheat
2 teaspoons salt	1 teaspoon crushed anise seed
2 teaspoons crushed fennel seed	tablespoon grated orange peel
2 packages active dry yeast	¼ cup warm water, 105° F to 115°F
1 tablespoon dark corn syrup	2 to 2½ cups bread flour

In saucepan, heat beer and milk to a boil (milk will curdle). Measure rye flour and cracked wheat into large bowl and add boiling mixture. Stir in salt, anise, fennel and orange peel. Let cool to 105° F to 115° F. In small bowl, dissolve yeast in the warm water and add the corn syrup, let stand until foamy, about 5 minutes; stir into cooled mixture. Add bread flour gradually to make a stiff dough. Let stand 15 minutes. Turn out onto lightly floured board and knead for 10 minutes until dough is smooth and springy. Wash bowl, grease it, and put dough into bowl. Turn over to grease top, cover and let rise until doubled, about 1½ to 2 hours. Punch down. Turn out onto lightly oiled surface and shape into a smooth round loaf. Cover baking sheet with parchment paper or lightly grease it. Place loaf on prepared baking pan with smooth side up. Let rise until almost doubled, about 45 minutes to 1 hour. Slash with sharp knife or razor blade in three parallel cuts going each way on the loaf, making 1-inch squares. Preheat oven to 375° F. Bake for 40 to 45 minutes or until loaf sounds hollow when tapped. Makes 1 large loaf.

Great Moments In History!

Patrick Henry was a Finlander from Eben Junction who, before changing his name from Pirto Heikkenen, addressed the Congress Bar in Ishpeming, ending his speech with the immortal words "Give me liberty or buy me a beer." He rewrote the speech in the Marquette County dry-out tank and later delivered it to the Continental Congress under the name of Patrick Henry.

Words of Whizdom:
Never slam your head in a car door because it might hurt.

Answers to 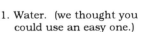 **Twisted Trivia**

See below your score and evaluation

1. Water. (we thought you could use an easy one.)
2. Unemployed Yoopers.
3. Snow.
4. My drunken uncle goes berserk and attack the christmas tree.
5. How would we know! You pick one.
6. Neither one. They're not really beer cans, they're only pictures on paper.
7. Snow. We knew you'd get this one.
8. A, B, and C. Spill his beer on his mother while insulting his sister.
9. Okay.
10. Unemployment.

0-3 Correct
Duh!

4-6 Correct
Duh!

7-9 Correct
Duh!

ALL 10 CORRECT

Duh!